MOTHER OF ALL MYTHS

AMINATTA FORNA

MOTHER
OF ALL MYTHS

How Society Moulds and
Constrains Mothers

HarperCollins*Publishers*
77–85 Fulham Palace Road,
Hammersmith, London W6 8JB

Published by HarperCollins*Publishers* 1998
1 3 5 7 9 8 6 4 2

A catalogue record for this book
is available from the British Library

ISBN 0 00 255696 0

Set in Meridien

Printed and bound in Great Britain by
Caledonian International Book Manufacturing Ltd, Glasgow

To Simon

Contents

Acknowledgements

The Harkness Fellowships and the Commonwealth Fund of New York provided me with the opportunity to develop my ideas and continue my research at the University of California at Berkeley. Without them this would not have been the same book at all. I am immensely grateful. Those at Berkeley who guided me along my way (particularly my work on cross-cultural comparisons of motherhood) include Professor Jewelle Taylor Gibbs, Professor Stephen Small and Professor Evelyn Nakano Glenn. I would like to thank them all, as well as Professor Dorothy Roberts at Rutgers University who provided direction with several sections of the book. The Institute for the Study of Social Change in Berkeley gave me an early and useful forum to test my work in progress.

My special thanks go to David Godwin, as gracious an agent as any author could wish for, who gave me his encouragement from the very earliest; and Lucinda McNeile, my editor at HarperCollins, for her mother's-eye perspective, clear editorial judgement and for her enthusiasm and respect for my work. My husband, Simon Westcott, has been my constant support, sometime researcher and main listener. Louisa Saunders at the *Independent on Sunday* has encouraged me to write articles based on some of the book's findings, and brought them to a wider audience.

Others who gave me time and made valuable suggestions include Judith Stacey, Carol Stack, Cynthia Daniels, Barrie Thorne, Diane Eyer and Nancy Chodorow. As well as all those writers and academics whose scholarship provided the critical foundation and some of the influences for this book, I would also like to thank all the many dozens of others who took my calls, answered questions, chased facts, faxed information and shared contacts, as journalists too rarely get the opportunity to formally acknowledge all those without whose efforts we could not do our jobs.

The many research organizations on whose work I relied for facts, statistics and analysis were numerous, but I would like to mention in particular: the National Council for One Parent Families, La Leche League, the Human Fertilization and Embryology Authority, Kidscape (Michelle Elliot), the Centre for Reproductive Law and Policy in New York and the Center for Women's Policy Studies in Washington, the Institute for Public Policy Research, Family Policy Studies Centre, Demos, Equal Opportunities Commission, Maternity Alliance, Daycare Trust, Policy Studies Institute, Henley Centre, the Office for National Statistics, ISSUE, the Institute for the Study of Drug Dependency and the Economic and Social Research Council.

Some sixty mothers agreed to be interviewed and help me find answers to the questions. Many are quoted in the text, but as many others helped me in less direct ways. To them all, and in particular to those whose testimonies appear, I am specially indebted.

Most of all thanks to both my mothers for their different styles, their aspirations and influences. In particular to Yabome who spent a week proof-reading my entire manuscript.

chapter 1

Introduction:
The Motherhood Myth

There have been a few key public moments during the research and writing of this book which serve as good illustrations of what it is all about. On a daytime chat show about teenage rebellion, a woman seeking desperately to explain the behaviour of her adoptive daughter apologized over and over again: 'I know I'm not her *real* mother, but . . .'[1] During the O. J. Simpson trial in 1995, prosecutor Marcia Clark fought simultaneous battles to win a conviction in the trial of the decade and to keep her children. Her ex-husband was trying to win custody on the grounds that she was working too hard to be a good mother. When the toddler Jamie Bulger was murdered, I recall reading that his mother had received hate-mail blaming her for looking away for an instant! After the second royal divorce, on what did the press blame the British royal family's misfortunes? Not their own constant intrusion but on the notion that the Queen was a cold and distant mother. Then there was the firestorm of criticism that greeted the announcement of Madonna's pregnancy. Comment on her unsuitability as a mother led to the dismissal of the child's father as a 'sperm donor', followed, naturally, by speculation after the birth that the state of motherhood would change the singer, a woman who is herself the mistress of image manipulation.

The most public humiliation any mother has ever been forced

to undergo was reserved for Deborah Eappen. She was the mother of Matthew Eappen, the small child whose death was at the centre of the murder trial of British au-pair Louise Woodward. For many people, from the very beginning, she was the person who was on trial and not Woodward, because she chose to work three days a week as an ophthalmologist instead of being a full-time mother, because she was married to a doctor and did not 'need' to work, because she left her children to be cared for by someone else. A woman grieving the loss of her child was being torn apart instead of comforted, derided instead of consoled. In the fervour of the lynch-mob mentality, little Matthew was all but forgotten as people carried placards in front of the court bearing the words 'Don't Blame the Nanny. Blame the Mother!' They called television and radio phone-ins to scream how she deserved to lose her baby, and vented their hatred of her in a specially-created Internet website. People ignored the fact that Deborah Eappen came home to breastfeed at lunchtime and that she had halved her workload. People ignored the fact that Matthew had another parent who was also a doctor. It was left to Sunil Eappen to defend his wife, because she could not defend herself and because he, merely the father, was not seen to be at fault. The baby died because *she* wasn't there.

A great deal has been said and written about motherhood. The only purpose of the bulk of what has already been published is to tell women how to do the job better. You could fill the Augean stables with past volumes of advice to mothers. This book purports to do none of that. I hope it will be many things to many people, mothers and non-mothers, but it is absolutely not a childcare manual.

The rhetoric of motherhood has remained unchallenged for so long that it has become woven into the fabric of our consciousness. For once let's turn the searchlight on those who presume to tell mothers what to do; to analyse *their* actions, unpick *their* motives and judge *their* handiwork, just as they have done not only to mothers but to all women because they have the potential to be mothers. Once held up to the light, the agendas behind many of our assumptions and beliefs about contemporary mothering are exposed, whether their roots are in popular culture, so-called scientific findings, historically accepted fact or the legacy of tradition. First you find the flaws in what are presented as crystal-clear truths and then you see how the flaws form patterns. Finally, you begin to realize that myths have been created about motherhood and see how those myths refract through the many prisms of our culture and through time itself.

The motherhood myth is the myth of the 'Perfect Mother'. She must be completely devoted not just to her children, but to her role. She must be the mother who understands her children, who is all-loving and, even more importantly, all-giving. She must be capable of enormous sacrifice. She must be fertile and possess maternal drives, unless she is unmarried and/or poor, in which case she will be vilified for precisely the same things. We believe that she alone is the best caretaker for her children and they require her continual and exclusive presence. She must embody all the qualities traditionally associated with femininity such as nurturing, intimacy and softness. That's how we want her to be. That's how we intend to make her.

The ideology which accompanies the myth of the perfect mother can only conceive of one way to mother, one style of exclusive, bonded, full-time mothering. Despite the changes in the working and family lives of millions of women, despite the talk of an age of 'post-feminism', attitudes towards mothers are stuck in the dark ages. Thirty years on from the start of the second wave of the feminist movement, we are still debating the effects of daycare on the children of working mothers and blaming never-married or divorced mothers for their children's problems. This vision of idealized motherhood still permeates every aspect of life from the division of labour at home, to our employment laws, policies and legal rulings, and it drips down continually through popular culture, books, television, films and newspapers.

The ideal mother is also the 'natural' mother, hence the stereotype of the wicked stepmother. The maternal ideal is based on a belief in what is natural, on notions of maternal instinct. Today there is a renewed reverence for ideas about maternal instinct, which has been prompted by the fear that motherhood, one of the two pillars upholding the institution of the family alongside marriage, is being threatened. It stands to reason, then, that if maternal qualities are natural, all women must have them. The growing number of women who choose to delay or avoid motherhood altogether fascinate and alarm the myth-makers because they defy the myth. For them, new mini-myths are invented to try to co-opt them into the maternal state.

There's a moment in the popular film *When Harry Met Sally* in which the main character, played by Meg Ryan, is discussing man problems with her best friend. 'You're thirty-one. The clock is ticking!' warns her chum. 'No it isn't,' she replies. 'I read it doesn't start until you're thirty-six.' The notion of the so-called 'biological clock' is a great example of contemporary myth-making. The clock has two hands. On the one hand there's the fact that a woman's fertility declines over time, which is true and which is being shamelessly exploited to make women anxious about the decision when to have a child. On the other hand, there's the notion, as expressed by the character Sally in the film, that the urge to have a child strikes all women at a particular time, without warning and independent of all intellectual thought processes, which is palpable rubbish and has no scientific basis whatsoever. Those women who say they have experienced a natural urge or need to have a child do so at different times of their lives and in different ways; plenty of women never do. Nevertheless, these two ideas are rolled into one and delivered as gospel in such a way as effectively to browbeat women (including those who may feel ambivalent about having children) into the institution of motherhood. Listen to your heart not your head, is the message.

Women's magazines and the women's pages of newspapers are full of it. 'The price of delaying pregnancy is high,'[2] warns a writer. 'The brood instinct is a biological time-bomb with a dicky fuse,'[3] postulates another. 'What time is it by your biological clock?'[4] asks a third. The logic goes like this: if you are over thirty you are running out of time to have a family; you may think you don't want one, but you are wrong; the feeling will strike but by then it may be too late! This unpleasant and exploitative mind-game is played out over and over. Meanwhile no one never hears the flip side of the coin, from the women who have children mainly because they don't quite dare not to, because they are afraid of losing out, and of 'missing the boat'. Or from the woman in her mid-forties who preferred to tell people she was infertile rather than explain her decision not to become a mother. Nor do you hear from women, like the television director I spoke to, who cherished her children but regretted her decision to become a mother. There's silence on that. In the language of the myth it is important to believe that all women come from one mould, with the same biologically programmed responses.

Beliefs about motherhood are passed off as 'traditional' and 'natural', as though the two words had the same meaning; and, as both traditional and natural, these beliefs have become unassailable. Yet, as any historian will tell you, the most enduring of these ideas is not more than a few hundred years old. There have been periods in history when women appeared not to care much for their children at all, routinely sending newborns away to wet-nurses and using infanticide as a means of family planning. There have been times, specifically the early years of colonial America, when fathers and not mothers were thought to be the best people to raise children. The current maternal ideal is simply the product of a particular time and place, and at its height lasted no more than a few years from the end of the Second World War until the early 1970s. It just happens to be the version that was in place when most of the people who are now running the country were born, and comes to us washed with the sentiment of nostalgia.

Today, caring for children is still virtually an exclusively female task. It is also harder than ever before. As the quantity of available information about childcare and child development has ballooned, so motherhood has become increasingly pro-active and interventionist. The job now starts at conception. The mother-to-be is expected to give up tea and coffee, alcohol, cigarettes, including passive smoking, soft cheeses and other unpasteurized foods; she must avoid stress and too much aerobic exercise and take folic acid and multivitamins – and that is the very minimum. If she consults any of the several dozen contemporary advice manuals available she will find an unending list of do's and don'ts, some doubtless valid but many irrelevant, perhaps even the product of the 'expert's' own imagination. Throughout her pregnancy the growth of her child and every aspect of her own behaviour will be closely monitored by her doctor and hospital.

Once a mother fed, clothed and comforted her offspring, and there, for better or for worse, lay the limits of her obligations. Today her responsibilities have doubled. She is also in charge of her children's emotional stability and psychological development. In the mid-twentieth century, Freud and the psychoanalysts who followed and developed his theories – John Bowlby and D. W. Winnicott in particular, who wrote in the 1940s and 1950s – emphasized the mother's role and her competence in a way that had never been considered before. They issued dire warnings about children who would turn into retards or psychopaths if women failed in their duties as mothers. Since those days, added to her responsibility for her child's mental well-being, mothers have also been given the third task of driving their offspring towards intellectual and academic achievement. Successful motherhood now means producing a high achiever as well as a well-balanced adult. Bookshops today sell volumes entitled *Discovering Your Child's True Genius* and toys come from the Early Learning Centre.

Mothers are besieged with information, more than they can possibly absorb. The advice is always presented as 'best for baby' but masks any number of other agendas – professional, political and social. Careers are not made by agreeing with the findings of the last researcher; newspapers need stories to sell; and authors must have something new to say. So modern mothers find themselves faced with a plethora of often conflicting advice. One doctor might warn her not to gain weight; another might tell her to eat for two. Childbirth choices go in and out of fashion, mirroring power struggles in the hierarchy of hospitals: natural versus interventionist; home versus hospital; midwife versus consultant. One month a mother may hear that she should bring her new baby into her bed; the next she will be chided and told she risks smothering her baby, either literally or emotionally. In an era when delinquency and the breakdown of discipline are at the forefront of social and political debate, the mother who strikes her child is condemned.

Nothing exemplifies the paradox of motherhood as a state which is both revered and reviled, natural and yet policed, more clearly than the issue of breastfeeding. Bottle-feeding is frowned upon and the pressure on mothers to breastfeed is immense, yet there are still very many people in the UK who regard the sight of a breastfeeding woman as obscene. In August 1997 a woman breastfeeding her child in a courtyard had water thrown over her by a disgusted shopkeeper. She turned out to be an *Express* newspaper journalist and the story, which was carried on the front page of the next day's newspaper, prompted a national discussion. Many people, including Anne Winterton MP, supported the shopkeeper's view that women should breastfeed out of sight, but in Britain there are extremely few public breast-feeding facilities and the combined effect of public disapproval and lack of facilities keeps breastfeeding mothers virtually homebound. In Britain the Campaign for Rights in Breastfeeding lobbies MPs to prevent women being thrown out of restaurants, shops and public places for breastfeeding their babies. In the USA harassment of women feeding their babies in public has required twelve states to pass laws clarifying a mother's right to do so.

This contradictory response to motherhood is evidenced in other ways, too. A woman announcing her pregnancy will be offered congratulations, will find herself treated as though she has done something very special, but the display of a pregnant body inspires a degree of repulsion which is not properly explained by the suggestion that such images are merely indecorous or inappropriate. When Demi Moore appeared on the front cover of *Vanity Fair* and exposed the painted curves of her pregnant body, some newsagents insisted the magazine be sold in an opaque wrapper. In 1997, when the new women's magazine *Frank* ran a fashion layout using pregnant models, the magazines's offices were deluged with complaints. Mothers should not be seen. Neither should they be heard.

One rarely hears mothers complain, and then never in public. Their compliance is bought or ensured in three ways: by glorifying aspects of motherhood; by making women who don't feel or do what is required feel guilty; and finally, and as a last resort, by punishing mothers considered actually deviant (for example, women who leave their children inspire a moral wrath not visited on the thousands of fathers who do the same; legal sanctions are being levied on pregnant women who refuse medical treatment or abuse their own bodies).

The best-known image of the ideal mother has been with us for centuries in the form of the Madonna and Child, the most compelling depiction of pale, calm, benevolent motherhood. Whether sculpted by Pisano in 1300 or painted by Dali in the mid-twentieth century, she is always portrayed cradling her child in her arms and gazing at him in a moment of private pleasure, or looking outwards contemplating the viewer with a smile of peace and fulfilment playing upon her lips. Although Christianity did not, on its own, invent the motherhood myth, the Church has been highly efficient at marketing the maternal ideal. Mary is held up to Catholic women everywhere as an inspirational figure. In parts of Catholic Central and South America there exists even today a kind of cult of motherhood named after her: Marianisma. Poor women sacrifice and deny themselves everything for the sake of their children, especially their sons, in the hope that they will one day repay their mother's love and loyalty when she is old. Motherhood in this instance is capable of delivering earthly salvation.

Baby Jesus is never painted with his head thrown back and bawling. His mother never looks testy or tired. No one paints her trying to prepare Baby Jesus's food with one hand while jiggling him on her hip with the other. Or ignoring him while he screams his lungs out in the next room. No one has ever painted Mary going about the mundane tasks of motherhood: giving Jesus a bath, feeding him or dressing him. The Madonna and Child are frozen in eternity in a moment many mothers experience with their babies relatively infrequently.

The image of the maternal idyll is presumably so appealing because it reminds both those who paint such images and those who look at them of a time when they were children and found comfort in a mother's embrace. It isn't really a comment on women's experience of motherhood, although it is often read as one. The power of the image is derived from what society wants from women.

The ideal mother is everywhere in art, poetry, fiction, film. She is the dream for whom Peter Pan searches, a beautiful memory to Cinderella and Snow White whose stepmothers are cruel to them. She is there on the cover of *Good Housekeeping* and *Family Circle*, in television programmes such as *Happy Days* and *Little House on the Prairie*. In more contemporary depictions like the *Cosby Show*, a nod to modernity has allowed her a job. She is such an archetype you sometimes don't even notice her, but there she is in Hollywood action movies standing behind Mel Gibson or Harrison Ford, vulnerable, warm yet wistful, part of the hero's home and family life that he must protect. And be sure she exists by design and not by accident. In 1997, when Disney again adapted Dodie Smith's *The Hundred and One Dalmatians* for the screen, writer-producer John Hughes changed Smith's original version in which Cruella DeVil is an old school chum of the dalmatians' owner Anita. Instead, he made her Anita's former boss and owner of a fashion design company, unmarried and childless, whose motive for wanting to kill the puppies is her fury at being deserted by Anita, who gives up her job when she becomes a mother. In the first version of the tale it was Snow White's natural mother who was her adversary.

Mothers are stereotyped and so are women who choose not to become mothers. In 1995, researchers ascertained the attitudes of a group of college students towards motherhood.[5] They showed that married mothers who stayed at home were seen in a positive even sentimental light, but stepmothers were held in poor regard, divorced mothers were viewed as failures, and single mothers as deviants and losers. Traditional mothers were even thought to be nicer people. Our beliefs about motherhood are pervasive and powerful. Whether Snow White and Cinderella helped to create the myth or simply perpetuated it, they illustrate its appeal. Marketing men use it to sell feel-good movies, baked goods and cold remedies. Today the same idealized image is even being used to sell motherhood itself, as a multi-million-pound market in reproductive technology flourishes using glossy brochures containing colour pictures of mothers and their babies to sell infertility treatment to childless couples.

In the 1960s feminists rejected an overly romantic vision of motherhood and identified its silken cords of oppression. Before the changes wrought in the 1960s only one line of promotion was available in the lives of most women: from perfect bride to perfect wife to perfect mother. An oversight on the part of the feminist movement as a whole has been to ignore motherhood from that point on, believing that if all the available political energy was devoted to increasing women's career choices and achieving economic independence, motherhood would somehow take care of itself. At the same time, another school of popular feminism actually bolstered myths about motherhood by arguing women's moral and social superiority in relation to men and laying claim on behalf of womanhood to qualities such as creativity and emotional sensitivity.

Even the so-called 'power feminists', such as Naomi Wolf, author of *Fire with Fire*, argue that there is nothing stopping women today except their own victim mentality. In her analysis Wolf overlooked motherhood, the one area of women's lives feminism has barely acknowledged. The dated, unchanged, narrow institution of motherhood which obliges women to mother in a certain way is the Achilles' heel of modern feminism. Despite Wolf's exhortations to think positively, no woman manager can compete with her male colleagues on fair terms if she is also a mother. Yet the word 'motherhood' does not even appear in the index to Wolf's book, and in the page and a half of text given to the subject the author merely repeats the old feminist adage that biology is not destiny. End of story. In fact, the story of how feminism must tackle the issues surrounding motherhood is only just beginning.

It is unrealistic to suppose that the majority of women will stop having children. Many women talk, in convincing terms, of a strong, biological impulse which produces the desire to have children; others simply love children and wish to raise them; others still value family and the links created through the generations by blood ties. This vital and valuable commitment to children nevertheless means that today, while the perfect bride is no more than a one-day fantasy and the perfect wife has been consigned to the waste disposal, the perfect mother as an instrument through which women's actions and choices can be controlled and manipulated has survived, because while men can be left to look after themselves, children cannot. And while a woman might rightly walk out on an aggressive, incompetent or uncaring man, few women would wish to forsake their children.

Working alongside the idealized depiction of motherhood is the second tool of enforcement: guilt. Guilt has become so strongly associated with motherhood that it is often considered to be a natural emotion. It is not. Guilt is *not* a biological, hormonally-driven response. Women feel guilty because they are made to. Mothers are told that every failure, every neglected task, every dereliction of their growing duties, every refusal to sacrifice will be seared upon their child's psyche, will mar his or her future, and damage not only the mother–child relationship but every subsequent relationship in the child's life. That is, if the mother who is found to be wanting doesn't create a juvenile delinquent or a fully-fledged criminal.

A culture of mother-blaming, by everyone including children, has become so deeply entrenched in our society that bad mothering is considered to be a contributory cause in an astonishing array of contemporary problems. In America, when the Unabomber was arrested, a leading news magazine hypothesized that the rage which had caused him to wage a twenty-year bombing campaign might have been provoked by an early episode when his mother left him. The desecration of inner-city communities is laid at the door of single mothers instead of economic policies or even absent fathers. A psychologist assessing a child's bed-wetting, or a teenager's use of recreational drugs, will often look first to the mother – does she work, how much time does she spend at home? Maternal guilt can be elicited directly in newspaper headlines ('What kind of mother are you?') or indirectly, as in the advert for a company selling home-office products: 'When I finally got home, John was waiting.[6] Half asleep he asked the question he'd been saving all day: Mom, can we play now?' In 1997 the BBC programme *Panorama* produced new 'evidence' showing how children fared badly when their mothers worked.[7] All this time, the responsibility of fathers has gone unquestioned.

In the 1990s the accumulated result of the hailstorm of advice and threats is a hyperconsciousness about mothering, particularly among middle-class women, many of whom work and have children in their thirties. The current pressures on mothers mean that such women embark on motherhood with guilt built in from the start, and they approach the role with an enormous degree of anxiety, determined to do it right, determined not to be criticized. A lack of support from the wider polity means they are like trapeze artists, flying without a safety net, unable to afford the luxury of a single mistake. They become control freaks. Everything is sublimated to the needs and wishes of the child. There is a rigidity about the running of the household, which has become totally child-centred: the telephone is switched off during afternoon naps; bedtimes, bathtimes and mealtimes take precedence even over the appearance of visitors, and certainly over entertainment and other social events; there's a baby intercom in every room and a planner on the kitchen wall with every activity from 'Water Babies' to music play carefully timetabled. Because the buck stops with her, the mother sees herself as absolutely indispensable and no one else, except perhaps a carefully-vetted nanny, is entirely trusted to take care of her child. To non-mothers she appears ridiculous, but she is driven by guilt and fear, and cannot see how excessive her own actions are. In this lie the makings of a tragedy.

On the flip side of the coin are those mothers society views as so wicked and unnatural that they have to be forced into taking responsibility. The rhyme about the little girl who had a little curl could just as well have been written for mothers, certainly in terms of the way they are seen by society. 'When she was good she was very, very good and when she was bad she was horrid.' In America women are being prosecuted and imprisoned for taking illegal drugs while they are pregnant; forced into having caesarean sections against their wishes; or hospitalized by court order for failing to follow a doctor's orders. The notion of 'foetal rights', which underlies many of these convictions, is burgeoning and is rapidly being exported to the UK. In contrast to the over-anxious mother who is generally white and middle-class, these 'unnatural' mothers are usually poor. In Britain women are being charged and imprisoned for leaving their children at home alone. For those women who deliberately harm their children, society reserves a strength of hatred unequalled for any male killer.

Women, because of their ability to bear children and also because society assigns them the task of raising children, have a set of uniquely different responsibilities and therefore liabilities. For some women, who might find themselves accidentally pregnant, these responsibilities are not even asked for. There is a complicated set of moral and legal issues to be answered over how far a woman can be held accountable for what she does to her own body which also affects an unborn child. These are questions which are presently being dealt with through the entirely inappropriate medium of the criminal courts.

Recent events amount to nothing less than a legally sanctioned witch-hunt against mothers, an extraordinary vilification of women as mothers unparalleled at any time in history. It is no coincidence that such events, representing the extreme tip of a general contemporary culture of victimizing mothers, are taking place at this time. Society has always turned its critical eye upon mothers at key moments: in the nineteenth century during the Industrial Revolution, when women's role as home-maker was born, and after the Second World War when women had to be encouraged back into domesticity to give men their factory jobs back. And so it is now. The prosecutions mentioned above come in an era of perceived instability and uncertainty, during which the placebo of family values has been placed at the top of the political and social agenda by politicians and law-makers under pressure to provide solutions. Mothers in general, and mothers who are actually or perceived to be deviant in particular, are taking the brunt of our fear and despair over a collective failure towards the next generation. All this mother-blaming is a displacement activity for all the problems we can do nothing about, from corporation downsizing, to urban decay, to the emergence of new world economic powers which disrupt domestic economies and employment patterns.

Women are criticized for abandoning their traditional duties, while the truth is that women today carry a greater part of the burden of caring for children than ever before, with no corresponding policy changes to support them. Our urban, post-industrial lifestyles have removed grandchildren from the prox-imity of their grandparents, nieces and nephews from their uncles and aunts and cousins from each other. Divorce – 40 per cent of marriages – has frighteningly eroded the role of fathers in the lives of their children. In England and Wales alone in 1994, 164,834 children saw their parents divorce.[8] The mother-centric philosophy of the motherhood myth has contributed to the growth in numbers of single mothers. Many children start off in life without any kind of paternal commitment at all.

What do women get instead of real solutions to coping with the dual role? Companies which market pagers so that children can reach their working mothers in an emergency, and surveil-lance specialists who offer to film the babysitter secretly to check whether she is abusing your child. 'A woman's place is in the house', asserts an advertisement for Knorr stock cubes, which depicts a female MP rushing home to cook for her children. Women continue to be responsible for the domestic sphere. The child has merely substituted the husband as the person for whom she must continue to carry out those tasks. The work is the same, but now women do that work as mothers not as wives.

Nothing provokes the fear that motherhood, as we know it, is under threat more than the new reproductive technologies that have made mothers of older women, lesbians, even virgins. Such births, because they appear neither 'natural' nor 'tra-ditional', are a blatant challenge to an accepted view of what motherhood should be. The policy-makers' answer, which is to try to limit these women's access to the science, says it all. Technology has dramatically challenged the most basic assumptions around mothering. Take the simple verbs 'to mother' and 'to father'. How they are defined reveals an abundance of meaning. 'To father' just means to beget, an act of procreation; but 'to mother' means to nurture, to rear, to feed, to soothe and to protect. Today, techniques enabling human egg retrieval and donation mean that women, just like men, can be the biological parents of children they never see and to whom they do not give birth.

At the same time, growing numbers of women are rejecting motherhood altogether. Women individually now have fewer children and fertility levels are at an all-time low; women leave starting a family until as late as possible, often into their thirties; and many have opted not to have children at all. A 1993 survey published in the *British Medical Journal* stated that 12 per cent of a group of women now in their forties had remained childless.[9] An OPCS survey put the figure of 20 per cent on women who are young now and will elect not to become mothers, compared to 1 per cent in 1976.[10]

Much has been read into such statistics by parties with a stake in the debate. Some feminists greet them with delight; other people are sceptical and smugly assert that young women who say they don't want children will almost certainly change their minds; still others argue that these women are not childless out of choice but because they can't find a suitable partner or have trouble conceiving. I say there's a modicum of truth in all these points. After many conversations with mothers and non-mothers, I have found that most women are not rejecting babies as such (although some certainly are), they are repudiating motherhood as an institution and much of what goes with it. I have spoken to many women who, in conversation, will state that they don't like children; but what they then go on to talk about in detail is in fact motherhood, the changes to their lives, the sacrifices, the compromises. They don't talk about children. Essentially, some of these women may want children but not that much, and that in itself contradicts many popularly-held assumptions about women and biology. 'In pain thou shalt bring forth children,' says the Bible. Motherhood is supposed to be its own reward. Our society has always imagined that it could ask any sacrifice, be as exacting, as demanding and as controlling of mothers as it wished because women's hormonal impetus would impel them towards motherhood despite themselves. Not so, it would seem.

Perhaps this very blatant threat to fundamental assumptions about women's character is what has fuelled the growing interest in socio-biology, and the opportunity it offers to reassert what are considered traditional mores, as well as removing the obligation to reform something once it has been deemed 'natural' and inevitable. In the 1990s, ideas based on Social Darwinism have found a ready audience among intellectuals and the general public alike as an explanation of why, for example, poor people are poor. It is because, so the theory of 'survival of the fittest' goes, the cream of society rises to the top leaving the less able at the bottom. The poor are not adaptive, talented or motivated, that is why they are poor. It is nobody's fault and no amount of welfare or educational programmes will help because this state of affairs is natural and unavoidable – *quod erat demonstrandum* the continued existence of the poor despite fifty years of welfare. The poor will be with us always.

Much the same ideas have frequently been applied to the debate around motherhood. Today, finally freed from the over-powering constraints of a decade or so of political correctness, or so advocates of the science would have us believe, notions that women's role and behaviour are biologically derived are now being discussed as the obvious truths they are. Observations on motherhood based on the behaviour of goats or rats, plus a burgeoning fashion in the new science of genetics, are re-affirming old ideas about the naturalness of motherhood.

Ideas about 'maternal instinct' have resurfaced with a new vigour. While most scientists will give a cautious nod to the notion that some form of instinct is at work within all of us, few would venture to try to describe precisely how instincts manifest themselves in behaviour in any predictable way. The real question is, why is it so important to label these feelings instinctual? A clue to the agenda that lies behind the enthusiasm for notions of 'instinct' is evidenced by the delight and satisfaction which greet the news that a woman previously considered a 'career woman' (particularly a high-profile woman) has given up her job to have children. The departure of Penny Hughes from a high-profile job at Coca-Cola, and the stories it sparked, is one example I deal with in a later chapter. Such a woman is perceived as having bowed to the inevitable, given way to nature and fulfilled her true destiny. In short, women are made to be mothers not managers and here is the proof.

The facts are that a great many policy decisions rest on our accepted views of motherhood. The new determinism offers a neat solution to complicated policy issues relating to the family and women's position within and outside of it and the flexibility of the workplace. If it is accepted that women are biologically programmed for motherhood, some would argue, many things follow. Social commentator and columnist Melanie Phillips, for example, has argued that the biological differences between men and women mean that men should have first call on jobs. In *The End of Order*, Professor Francis Fukuyama argues that women's entry into the workplace (and dereliction of the duties of good motherhood) is responsible for the breakdown of the social fabric. For both Phillips and Fukuyama, motherhood means stay-at-home motherhood.

Where the fundamentalists' view of maternal instinct as a single, compelling force really goes askew is in relation to mothering styles. What is 'natural' is almost always presumed to be a 1950s model of motherhood. To back up this scenario, which supporters trace back to a time when males went out to hunt while females nested, advocates turn to the natural world, picking and choosing from what nature has to offer in order to advance their arguments. They ignore lionesses, hunters for their entire pride, who skilfully combine work and motherhood while the lion babysits. They also ignore the matriarchal hyena who, as dominant female, banishes males from the pack and is succeeded by her daughter. Nor do they consider the many species of birds who parent together as male and female and whose mating and pairing rituals biologists often compare to those of humans. There is also an assumption that everything that comes from nature is necessarily good. Anyone who has ever witnessed the sight of a caged rabbit eating her newborn might beg to differ.

It can be argued much more convincingly that women, like the caged rabbit, are not supposed to rear their children alone in their homes; nothing could be more unnatural than the mother alone in the highrise block or the suburban home with her children. You could say that, like lions and cheetahs, it is a natural function of motherhood to go out into the world to provide for offspring. Or, if you take the view that in prehistoric times men were hunters and women were gatherers, you might think, in that respect, that women's skills are better suited to the modern world of work, with its emphasis on communication, information, negotiation and research, than are men who excel at mammoth-hunting or tribal fights.

There is another school of scholarship quietly growing, away from the spotlight. Psychologists such as Susie Orbach, Ann Dally and Diane Eyer argue that 'traditional' ideas about motherhood are neither natural nor helpful to children or women. Indeed, the narrow, exclusive mothering style can even be harmful. Eyer and Dally argue that the relationship between mothers and their children has palpably failed to thrive in the artificially claustrophobic world of the private, nuclear family. Nor are children or women helped that such an immensely important task as childrearing (which today requires almost superhuman capabilities) is placed principally on the shoulders of just one person. No one person can do it all; no one person was ever meant to.

Think about how obsessed we are with our mothers. They have the capacity to disappoint us, anger us, frustrate us and burden us in a way no one else does. The entire discipline of psychoanalysis was built on the back of the mother–child relationship. Today, people enter analysis, seek therapy and attend re-parenting classes because of their relationship with their mothers. In sitcoms, relationships with mothers are a source of humour. In *Mad About You* Jamie develops a facial tic every time her mother visits; Roseanne cannot abide her mother; the humour in *Absolutely Fabulous* wittily confounds mother stereotypes. There are innumerable books, films and plays con-taining the same theme: *Psycho*, *Postcards from the Edge*, the Debbie Reynolds satire *Mother* (which, despite a sympathetic portrayal of the mother figure, nevertheless confirms its own thesis that she is to blame for her son's problems). During the writing of this book I asked a group of friends gathered at my home one evening how many of them had problems with their mothers. Everyone raised a hand. Every single one! One claimed his mother was too domineering; another was angry at his mother spending so much time at work; a third felt her mother favoured her elder sister and the lack of encouragement she received was the reason why her career was stagnant; a fourth rejected the imposition of his mother's values; and a fifth felt that now she was an adult, her mother had forgotten her. For a group of normal, intelligent, functioning people to have so many grievances towards their mothers is not at all natural, nor is it desirable, however common it may have become.

Motherhood is in crisis because it has been set into conflict with itself. The legacy of past modes of thinking has been to emphasize the primacy of mothers to the exclusion of everyone else. Women are primarily responsible for children in 96 per cent of families.[11] Most of them also work, yet after three decades of female emancipation, work and motherhood have still not been reconciled. Women make up half the workforce and therefore half the taxpaying citizens of the country, but to date there are absolutely no serious political proposals on the table to provide universal, affordable childcare. In a straightforward cost/benefit analysis it is no surprise that women, whether or not they decide to become mothers, feel a growing ambivalence about entering an institution so full of evident hazards and somewhat vague rewards.

Fifteen years ago we imagined that new family structures and an acceptance of women's work meant that fathers would step into the light after years in the background. That has spectacularly failed to happen on any significant scale, though is it any surprise within a culture which mythologizes motherhood and condemns fathers to be eternally and irrevocably seen as second-best?

In every society there is a tendency to assume that there is only one way to look after children, and that is the way it is done in that culture. Anthropologists and sociologists, however, have demonstrated that motherhood is a social and cultural construct which decides how children are raised and who is responsible for raising them. There are places in this world where motherhood has been differently forged; where a mother is not alone in her responsibility to her child and no one would expect her to be so; where men are far more involved in the lives of their children; where there is no conflict for women between having children and going to work; and where mothers are not made to feel guilty for the personal choices they make.

So far, feminist attempts to deconstruct the myths around motherhood – from the historical perspective (Elizabeth Badinter, Shari Thurer); from the psychoanalytic perspective (Nancy Chodorow, Dorothy Dinnerstein); from the journalistic perspective (Jane Bartlett, *Will You be Mother?*, Melissa Benn, *Madonna and Child*) – have concentrated exclusively on Western women as mothers and the Western concept of motherhood.

They have omitted, or chosen not to look at, the experience of women who are mothers in other cultures where a different ideology may be in place or where there is no constraining ideology at all. They have largely ignored women who belong to 'minority' cultures in the West for whom the dominant ideology has little relevance.

In the West we often dismiss the experience of other cultures, particularly those seen as 'less developed' than our own. Or we tend to the romantic, ascribing to other people a simple wisdom which is in its way greater than our own because it is free from modern technological clutter. When it comes to motherhood, there are lessons to be learned from looking at others and the first and most vital is that there are many different ways to mother. Motherhood is fashioned by culture, it can be adaptive and it can be flexible. Not until we understand and accept that will we be able to liberate ourselves from a collective tunnel vision which prevents us from looking beyond the boundaries of our mythologized version of motherhood to realities and new solutions.

In the 1970s as a child I was raised in two different cultures by two women. The first, my own mother's culture, was British. My other home was in Sierra Leone in West Africa with my African father and his second wife, my other mother. I spent my childhood between two homes until I grew up, went to university in London and made that city my home.

In Sierra Leone as a child, growing up with my brother and sister, I was loved by many people, who also had the authority to guide me, discipline me or advise me. As children we had many 'mothers' and many 'fathers'. We also had many 'brothers' and 'sisters', as sharing the physical care of other people's children is common. Before taking on my siblings and myself, my African mother had already raised her young half-sister and to this day continues to share her home with the children of friends and relations. She has been mother to many. There, it mattered less whom we 'belonged to' biologically, because children belong to everyone. In contrast, within my Western family, everything, whether practical or emotional, rested on my mother. As an adult visiting West Africa, one is barely aware of the idealized image of motherhood so prevalent in the West.

So this book is written both from the perspective of an inquiring journalist and as the fortunate beneficiary of two kinds of mothering. In both these capacities and as a non-mother, throughout the process mothers have used me as a confessional, an objective sounding-board for their fears and perceived inadequacies. Indeed, while some people (mostly men) imagined it must be hard to write a book without being a mother myself, it would be a very hard book to write as a mother. The fear of criticism silences many women, as Adrienne Rich acknowledged when she wrote *Of Woman Born*. Certainly, this was the dread of the many mothers to whom I spoke. Entire social occasions could be given over to talking to a woman who thought she didn't feel enough for her baby; or someone struggling with the fact that she cared less for one child than another. Too numerous to count were the guilt-ridden women who left their children with hired help while they went out to work. They confessed to me details of their lives they did not even dare tell other mothers, for women can be among the harshest critics of their own sex. They were desperate to discuss their feelings with someone, but terrified of being judged to be falling short of the standards, of being a less than perfect mother.

The insistence that a certain style of motherhood is 'natural' leads women to question every aspect of what they do, think and feel and to measure their own experience against an impossible and rigid standard. Every one of us assesses our own mother's record, picking over her failures and all too easily forgetting her accomplishments. Collectively we judge the mothers around us personally and through our institutions. The myths around motherhood are seductive traps which set up women in the cruellest way. This book traces the origins of those myths and examines how they continue to control and manipulate women.

Perhaps by revealing the traps, and tracing how we have arrived at current ways of thinking about motherhood, we can blow the most destructive of these myths away altogether and move on to a new approach to raising children. One which is flexible and giving instead of rigid; one which is inclusive of other people, especially fathers, instead of exclusive; and one in which the model of motherhood embraces woman in all her roles instead of placing her needs and other interests in conflict with the function of parenting. By exposing the hidden agendas around motherhood we may place children where they really should be, at the very top of the agenda.

chapter 2

A Brief History of Motherhood

Motherhood was invented in 1762. That is to say, 'motherhood' as we now know it was formulated then. Jean-Jacques Rousseau came up with the idea and laid it down in his extraordinary book, *Émile*. Historians, as one might imagine, quibble over the date and the details. Some argue that Rousseau did not really succeed in changing ideas, that it was the Victorians who really refined and institutionalized motherhood, draping it in swathes of sentiment.

What most scholars of this period of European history agree on is that even if one can't draw a perfect timeline of events, motherhood was a very different matter prior to 1762 and in the hundred years which followed. Before *Émile*, mothers appeared by and large indifferent to their children; in fact, on the evidence it is clear they did not much like them at all. They sent them away from birth, spent as little time with them as possible and apparently hardly cared if they died. But somehow a revolution was wrought, and at the beginning of the next century a mother's love ruled and women were expected to be only too keen to sacrifice themselves in ways large and small for the well-being of their children. In between those two points there were changes in many aspects of human life: philosophy, discoveries in science, new family structures and ideas about marriage, a revolution in industry and the redefining of gender roles. And it is out of all this that the institution of motherhood was born.

Maternal instinct versus maternal reality

Childhood up until and including the eighteenth century was short and sharp. The mother–child relationship, so exalted in modern times, barely existed. In *Centuries of Childhood*, the historian Philippe Aries talks of the 'idea of childhood' as something which simply did not exist, as a concept alien to early society. A child was born and, if she survived (and that was a big 'if'), she received only as much sustenance as she was deemed to require, and very little attention. Once of a certain age she entered adult life, which meant for most people, being put to work. Childhood was not, as it is for us, a separate state of growth, vulnerability and innocence which requires special attention. Children were not merely 'little people', but worse. It was believed that man was born into sin, and the parents' only duty towards their offspring was to (usually literally) beat a moral sense into them. Without childhood, it stands to reason that the interdependent state of motherhood did not exist either.

Aries and Edward Shorter, among others who have used records and accounts from the time, describe a style and manner of mothering characterized, at best one might say, by sheer indifference to their children on the part of women. Infants came last in the household hierarchy. Their needs were surpassed by almost everything and everyone else, from the requirements of running a household, obligations to husband and other family members, work and other duties. Eventually a child's needs came to be put first as they are today, surpassing those of every other member of the family and providing the focus of the nuclear family. Matters were so very different in the past that many people find it difficult to accept what historians now know to be true, as Shorter himself observes: 'The little band of scholars who for some time now have been arguing that in traditional society mothers didn't love their children much has met with stark incredulity.'[1]

At the time Rousseau was writing, wet-nursing – that is, sending infants away to be breastfed by a woman paid to do the job – was common, in fact standard practice. Moments after the birth, the newborn was whisked away without even being fed once by its mother, and driven miles across the city, commonly to the outskirts or the countryside to the home of a woman of lower class. There the infant would stay for at least two but often three, four, five years before returning to his parents. It would be more accurate to call wet-nursing 'boarding out', for nannies rarely moved into the home to share the workload with the mother and provide an alternative source of comfort. To the child, she was it. Mothers very rarely even bothered to visit their infants. Elizabeth Badinter, the French historian who has chronicled maternal practice among the French between 1700 and 1900 (a period particularly rich in sources and from which much of our information comes) gives this account: 'once the baby was left in the nurse's hands the parents lost interest in his fate. The case of Mme de Talleyrand, who not once in four years asked after her son, was not unusual, except that she, unlike many others, had every possible means for doing so had she cared to: She knew how to write and her son lived with a nurse in Paris.'[2]

Newborns were often shipped out in their dozens in the charge of one woman. If the child survived the journey, and many did not, either because they were too weak, or because – and there are instances aplenty of this – they fell out of the cart or were crushed under the weight of others, a grim reception awaited them. Most wet-nurses were women who lived in extreme poverty, who had made the choice to care for and feed another woman's infant for a small fee, in the meantime depriving their own child. Frequently a woman took in several infants, more than she could possibly feed even if her milk supply was good. It was also clearly in her interests to wean each child as quickly as possible to make way for the next and there are innumerable accounts of nurses forcing babies on to solid foods well before their young digestive systems could take it.

Wet-nurses cared little for their charges, for this was hired labour not a labour of love. Conditions were generally poor, children were ignored for long periods of time, left bundled in swaddling clothes, silenced with alcohol or beaten out of frustration. Many wet-nurses were desperate women or down-right charlatans, whose own breasts had stopped producing milk but who borrowed babies they passed off as their own. Some of the accounts given by Shorter and others, of infants left to starve, lying side by side on urine-soaked straw mattresses, are too harrowing to bear. As one can imagine, the death rate of babies in these circumstances was phenomenal, generally around double the normal rate rising, in one area around Rouen, to 90 per cent in the eighteenth century.

Wet-nursing was practised widely throughout Europe as well as in America. In Paris in 1780, of 21,000 children born in the city that year all but 1,000 were sent away. Elizabeth Badinter observes that boarding-out began with the aristocracy in the sixteenth century, was taken up by the bourgeoisie in the seventeenth century, and a century later anyone who could afford to have someone else rear their child did so. Why? For some women, such as the wives of artisans, work had to take priority over childcare. Other women who could have looked after their own children chose not to. According to Badinter and Shorter, they simply didn't want to. Elizabeth Badinter's detailed account of the lives of upper-class women of the period shows them to have been interested and engaged in matters of state, the intrigues of court, and their own 'salons' devoted to the pursuit of intellectual and artistic matters. They failed what Shorter calls 'the sacrifice test', which is a golden requirement of contemporary parenting. People in those days found children irritating and time-consuming, and their mothers found they had better things to do than nurse a child. 'Do they know, these gentle mothers who, delivered from their children devote themselves gaily to the entertainments of the city, what kind of treatment the swaddled child is getting in the meantime in the village?' asks Rousseau.[3]

From the perspective of the late twentieth century, the behaviour of the women of this era towards their offspring seems extraordinary. Were these women as truly indifferent as their manner suggests? History tends to record actions and not sentiments, and the actions appear to speak for themselves. If parents had feelings for their children, they were not thought worthy of comment. There are historians who interpret the evidence more generously. Olwen Hufton, in her account of three centuries of women's lives in Western Europe,[4] maintains that a knowledge of the beliefs held about childrearing at the time is essential to understanding a custom like wet-nursing. The milk of aristocratic women was considered weak and lacking in nutrients, compared to the healthy fare which could be provided by a farmer's wife. And the city, quite rightly, was thought to be an unhealthy, disease-ridden environment for youngsters. Women believed that they were sending their babies away for their own good. Mothers, says Hufton, did care for their children.

But there is also a great deal of evidence of maternal practice that is immensely hard to justify as springing from real concern. Elizabeth Badinter uses her considerable findings to cast doubts on maternal instinct, particularly the idea that it includes automatic love for a child on the part of a mother. Maternal love, she argues, grows out of the mother–child relationship and is an expression of free will. The enormous love most women feel for their children is nurtured and supported by the environment and social values which exist today. The responses of the women of the eighteenth century were underscored by the mores and conditions of the time. The mother–child relationship did not only fail to flourish, it barely thrived at all. Numerous women may have felt immense regret at giving up their newborns, may have preferred to keep them close by, but they were part of a culture in which it was accepted and expected that a mother give up her child for the first few years. 'At the very least,' writes Badinter, 'the maternal instinct must be considered malleable, able to be shaped and molded and modified, and perhaps even subject to sudden disappearances, retreats into civilization's shadows.'[5]

In the context of the period, the behaviour of women was by no means out of keeping with the norm. What passed as standard childcare practice in those days would be classified as child abuse today. 'The history of childhood is a nightmare from which we have only recently begun to awaken,' writes Lloyd de Mause in the opening pages of *The History of Childhood*.[6] The book is subtitled 'The Untold Story of Child Abuse' and recounts many of the horrors to which infants have been subjected in the name of care. From birth babies were wrapped tightly in swaddling clothes and often hung up on a peg. The rationale was that it kept babies from harming themselves and made their limbs grow straight, but in reality de Mause argues it had far more to do with keeping them out of the way altogether. Red in the face from the pressure, overheated and steeped in their own urine and faeces, babies were left in this way for days. Then there was the popular method of getting babies to sleep by 'rocking' them, in actual fact shaking them literally insensible in the name of peace. It goes almost without saying that children ('the Devil's seed') were frequently beaten and bullied, when they weren't left alone to cry for hours or burn themselves in the open hearth while their peasant mothers worked in the fields.

The death of a child was a commonplace event and merited little in the way of mourning or even grief. Parents, including mothers, rarely bothered to attend the funeral if there was one. Infants were regarded as eminently replaceable. Michel de Montaigne, writing between 1580 and 1590, famously observed: 'I lost two or three children during their stay with the wet nurse

– not without regret, mind you, but without great vexation.'[7] Madame de Sévigné, a French noblewoman who left numerous letters and other records, remarks in passing of a friend's distress upon hearing the news of her daughter's death: 'She is very much upset and says that she will never again have one so pretty.'[8] An observation which neatly captures the pitiful extent of a child's worth in the eyes of even her own mother.

With the infant mortality rate much higher than it is today, it is perhaps not all that surprising that both mothers and fathers took such news in their stride. Edward Shorter, though, concludes that their behaviour had less to do with stoicism than with indifference. Women frequently were unable to remember their children's names and ages, referred to infants as 'it', and, most remarkably, could not even remember how many babies they had given birth to. Nor, as he indicates, did they have the excuse of ignorance in matters of hygiene and basic childcare:

> Now by the late 18th century, parents knew, at least in a sort of abstract way, that letting newborn children stew in their own excrement or feeding them pap from the second month onwards were harmful practices. For the network of medical personnel in Europe had by this time extended sufficiently to put interested mothers within earshot of sensible advice. The point is that these mothers did not care, that is why their children vanished in the ghastly slaughter of innocents that was traditional child-rearing.[9]

In addition, infanticide, often by exposure, was a common method of 'family planning'. It was the sight of dead and dying infants heaped in the gutters of London that led Thomas Coram to establish a foundlings hospital in the eighteenth century. (In *Macbeth*, one of a range of objects the three witches throw into their pot is the finger of a strangled infant.) Not all these children could have been the offspring of the poor; descriptions of their clothes indicate that some clearly came from wealthy families.

The attitude of women towards their offspring in the seventeenth and eighteenth centuries could not be more different from approaches to motherhood today, which view children with enormous sentiment and place immense value on them. Seen from a historical perspective, women's behaviour in the eighteenth century must cast doubt on current theories of biological motherhood such as Richard Dawkins's 'selfish gene' theory, which posits that women are more committed than men as parents because they have already invested much more in a child whom they have carried for nine months and then laboured to bring into the world. What we now know is that, for several centuries in Europe, mothers like everybody else frequently saw children as, at best, amusing but more likely as enervating and time-consuming and, at worst, unwanted. What is particularly hard to comprehend is that these attitudes, although generally held, were not fostered or forced on women by men. Among the very poor and those unwed mothers who left their children to die, perhaps the instinct to survive outweighed maternal instincts, but there is no such rationale for the attitudes of middle-class and upper-class women.

All this information is tremendously uncomfortable, and the ramifications of historical knowledge are not always clear. One thing is certain: motherhood has worn very different guises at different times. The politics of maternalism which later flourished in Britain and in America in the nineteenth and early twentieth centuries could never have taken seed, or indeed made any kind of sense at all, at a time when motherhood was linked with negative and not positive qualities. Fairytales told during the period, such as Snow White, indicate how mothers were generally seen, for in the original tale Snow White was persecuted by her natural mother. It was the Brothers Grimm in the nineteenth century (by which time the cult of motherhood was at its height) who later changed the character to a stepmother.

Much of the research on wet-nursing and childcare has been undertaken by French historians, but that does not mean that their findings do not apply to England, where Puritan dogma urged parents to eradicate sin from children by beating the devil out of them, and where an infant's cries were interpreted as expressions of anger rather than distress. Wet-nursing was endemic here as well, as was cruelty. In *The English*, Christopher Hibbert recounts this story of an upper-class mother: 'Lady Abergavenny whipped her daughter so savagely for so long that her husband was drawn into the room of punishment by the child's shrieks, whereupon the mother threw the girl to the ground with such force that she broke her skull and killed her.'[10] According to Hibbert, it is only towards the end of the eighteenth century, due to the eventual spread of the humanitarian ideas of John Locke, that children came to be treated a little better as evidenced by, for example, the appearance of toys for the first time and of books specially written for children.

Motherhood came with no special status, duties or assumptions. A woman gave birth and that was the fact of the matter. She was not presumed to love the child, unless she chose to. It wasn't even assumed that she would take care of the baby. Indeed, in instances of divorce in England, France and America it was usually the father who kept custody of the child, often at the mother's behest. In colonial America it was fathers, not mothers, who were in charge of the children, not just in matters relating to discipline and moral rectitude as one might imagine, but they were also the parent who got up in the night to comfort a crying child.[11] Women were considered too amoral, too inferior and too weak to be given such responsibilities. In this context, given the task of building a nation, children were valuable and regarded as too important to be entrusted to mothers. In Europe the opposite was true. Children had no value and therefore nobody, including women, could be persuaded to care for them. That view was set to undergo a radical change in the course of the next century.

The creation of maternal love

Europe in the eighteenth century underwent a massive shift in the way that people thought. It was the most significant change since Martin Luther jettisoned notions of Original Sin during the Reformation and the Italian Renaissance elevated art, music, poetry and the finer human sensibilities. These served as the background to another smaller, yet in its own way (certainly as regards the history of motherhood) equally important, change in values. This was a 'revolution in sentiment'[12] for which one catalyst was the Enlightenment movement, a school of philosophy which emphasized man's right to happiness, his true noble character, romantic love, freedom and nature. This change would eventually lead to love (rather than status or social obligation) becoming the principal reason for marriage and children being regarded as the fruit or gift of that love. Maternal love arose out of all of this.

Jean-Jacques Rousseau, a leading light in the world of philosophy and already a darling of French intellectual life, published *Émile* in 1762. It is a fictional account of the education of a young boy and it projected a new vision of childhood and of children themselves. To Rousseau, children were naturally good, not the sinful little monsters they were generally presumed to be. Many of his ideas echoed those of England's John Locke who, in the 1690s, spoke of children as *'tabulae rasae'*, blank slates upon whom parents and educators could write. Unlike Locke's, Rousseau's ideas spread like wildfire and attracted a popular following. He urged parents to give their children freedom – first and foremost from swaddling clothes – and education, as well as encouraging self-expression in which he anticipated Maria Montessori by two hundred or so years.

Most importantly, Rousseau took issue with mothers who sent their infants away. He told them to breastfeed and to care for their children, and he chastised them for preferring to pursue other interests. 'Not satisfied with having given up nursing their children, women give up wanting to have them,' he wrote.[13]

'The result is natural. As soon as the condition of motherhood becomes burdensome, the means to deliver oneself from it completely is found.' It was Rousseau who made, and elaborated upon, the vital link between motherhood and morality which has been a cornerstone of maternal ideology ever since: 'But let mothers deign to nurse their children, morals will reform themselves, nature's sentiments will be awakened in every heart, the state will be repeopled. This first point, this point alone, will bring everything back together. The attraction of domestic life is the best counterpoison for bad morals.'[14] His comment about the state being 'repeopled' is a reference to a nascent interest in demography and the view held during the Enlightenment that the European races were in danger of dying out. With the perspective of hindsight, Rousseau's words are prophetic, for, as we shall see, ideas about 'motherhood' are wheeled out every time there is a perceived social crisis, whether in eighteenth-century France or Thatcher's Britain in the 1980s.

Against a backdrop of such extraordinary cruelty towards and neglect of children, almost any kind of change would have been for the better. French women began to breastfeed and to find a renewed interest in their children and Rousseau's ideas became popular in England too, although it must be said that wet-nursing continued in France until the 1920s and breastfeeding continues to go in and out of fashion. The next man to make a career out of taking issue with women who did not breastfeed would be Truby King in the 1920s. Nevertheless and overall, attitudes towards children began to change from the beginning of the 1800s, according to Edward Shorter. It would still take some time for mothers to become totally responsible for childcare. Most early tracts were aimed at men. The 'good mother' as we know her, with her natural propensity for self-sacrifice, her universal and automatic love for her children and her total fulfilment in the tasks of mothering, had not yet been invented but she was well on her way.

From the Reformation onwards, Europe had been undergoing

almost continual political shifts. A new middle class began to emerge which no longer owed loyalty to the clan, but directly to the king. They spent their new-found wealth on the immediate family, the home and their lives. By the time of the Industrial Revolution in England, followed by France, Germany and the post-Civil War United States, the nuclear family comprising a man, his wife and their offspring had emerged as the central family unit. It is interesting to note that while the 'traditional' nuclear family is today seen as the basis and seed-bed of values such as sharing and community responsibility, there are historians who now regard its evolution as arising out of exactly the opposite disposition: the wish to lessen commitments and to restrict the benefit of new gains and profits to a small number of people.

The revolution in industry in the first half of the nineteenth century is commonly agreed to have set in motion massive social shifts, the aftershocks of which we are still feeling today. There are many excellent and detailed accounts of that period, but what concerns us here is what happened to home life and the family, and the effect of such changes upon women's lives. In a short space of time, a rural way of life which had persisted for centuries and in which the home was the centre of production with the entire family participating in yarn-spinning, cheese-making, the sowing and reaping, ribbon-weaving – or whatever occupation the family derived its income from – was wiped out. In its place came factories which fed on human labour – preferably adult, male labour but often child labour and that of women, too – and forced a reliance on wages determining the fate of entire communities. Home life could no longer be combined with working life, and this schism between public and private took its toll, mainly upon mothers. Elinor Accampo, a family historian, writes:

> It put women in a particularly difficult bind because they could not combine household responsibilities with wage-

earning activities in the same manner as they had in the past. Even if they continued to perform productive labour in the home, this labour brought such meager compensation that they had to work long hours. Men's absence from the home, furthermore, meant that fathers had a much reduced role in the socialization of their children.[15]

The lives of women were transformed. The family became a separate entity, a private sphere with fierce loyalties and impermeable defences. Sex roles became exaggerated so that instead of women being *mostly* in charge of children and the domestic sphere, and men being *mostly* in charge of earning but with duties in the home too, women became responsible for all that lay within the walls of the home and men all that was on the outside. Home became an enclave away from the sweat and filth of daily toil on the railroads, in the factories or down the mines (for the working classes) or the office (for the middle class). It was the woman's job to create that place of sanctuary, to become the 'hearth angel' who created a nest for her children and a refuge for her husband. Gradually, men's involvement with children tailed off entirely until the responsibility for moral teaching was taken away from them and placed in the hands of women. The metamorphosis from the indifferent mother, absorbed in politics and culture, of whom Rousseau wrote, into the Victorian maternal ideal, the good woman at home with her brood, her piano and her principles, was complete.

The split between the private and public worlds saw an end to the political aspirations of upper-class women. Instead of aspiring to active engagement in decision making, women became 'the hand that rocks the cradle' and 'the power behind the throne'. And men encouraged women to find contentment in their new sphere of influence by assuring them of the power of this uniquely feminine role. By being convinced of this inimitable, maternal role women were, and are still, discouraged from encroaching on external male domains where the real political, social and economic gains are to be made.

Women of the bourgeoisie took on a decorative role not seen since the heyday of the Italian Renaissance. Victorian writers, clergy, politicians and poets, especially the Romantics such as John Ruskin, Matthew Arnold and Alfred Lord Tennyson, were quick to eulogize women, especially mothers, and place them on a pedestal from which they have collectively never quite succeeded in descending. The matriarch, in the form of Queen Victoria, rose to prominence. Among the burgeoning middle class the measure of a woman became her ability to master the feminine arts – quiet conversation, needlepoint, dancing – rather than the speed with which she could milk a cow. Nurturing skills, not household budget management, became the qualities a man sought in a wife. Women wore crinolines and hoops, fainted at swear words, covered up the legs of pianos and became prone to mysterious fits of hysteria, a condition some modern psychologists consider to have been produced by the tight stays, the isolation and the emotional constraints of their circumscribed lives. As women and mothers, their ability to sacrifice themselves apparently knew no bounds, as one particularly ghastly offering from the period testifies:

> There was a young man loved a maid
> Who taunted him. 'Are you afraid,'
> She asked, 'to bring me today
> Your mother's head upon a tray?'
>
> He went and slew his mother dead
> Tore from her breast her heart so red
> Then towards his lady love he raced
> But tripped and fell in all his haste
>
> As the heart rolled on the ground
> It gave forth a plaintive sound
> And it spoke, in accents mild:
> 'Did you hurt yourself, my child?'[16]

Not the kind of sentiment inspired by Christopher Hibbert's story of Lady Abergavenny, one imagines.

Of course, this was a deeply hypocritical period. Upper-class women still left most of the physical care of their children to paid servants. Men revelled in uxoriousness and treated women (of their own class and race) like delicate vessels while satisfying their more earthly needs with women from the lower orders. It is extremely important to remember that the saintliness of motherhood was only accorded to women of a certain class. In England, although the crimes of Jack the Ripper (thought by many to be a nobleman) dominate our memory of the period, many working-class women on their way home at night were kicked to death by gangs of men in one of the vilest expressions of the misogyny of the culture of that period. In America the glorious days of the antebellum bore witness to the savage treatment of black women who worked in the cane fields up until the onset of labour pains, gave birth to their masters' bastard offspring only to have them taken away. Sojourner Truth, the abolitionist and feminist who was born a slave, saw her own thirteen children sold into slavery. The contrast in the experience of womanhood from the perspectives of black and white is the theme of her most famous speech, in which she asks the question 'ar'n't I a woman?'

The cult of the 'good mother' depended (and still does) on money, and on a male wage that was sufficient to support a wife and children, which was (and is) frequently not the case. The many women who continued to work during the Industrial Revolution found themselves caught in the trap, now so familiar to working women, of trying to match the requirements of work and motherhood. Many tried to limit their families or to stop having children altogether because pregnancy posed such a threat to the family's income and survival. Accampo's studies of specific communities during the period show that, among the poor, the rates of abortion and infanticide soared. Children of the poorer classes were sent out to work as soon as possible and usually were ruthlessly exploited, as described in the work of Dickens, Wordsworth and William Blake, author of 'The Chimney Sweep'.

Finally, the motherhood mantle de-sexed women. If Queen Victoria refused to believe that sex between two women was a possibility (and so refused to outlaw what did not exist), Victorian men simply could not tolerate the idea of mothers, perhaps even their own mothers, having sex. Whereas there are depictions of women of earlier generations enjoying hearty sexual appetites – from Chaucer's tales through to James Boswell's accounts of his sexual exploits with women of all classes in London in the 1760s – women were now stripped of their sexuality. From henceforth only men were to have a sex drive. Women were given maternal instinct instead, and in no time at all Sigmund Freud would give that view all the authority of science.

Scientific motherhood

It is no surprise to discover that, even among those women who benefited from all the changes so far, it took very little time for a downside to the new status of mothers to appear. The impetus was provided by science, which served to provide apparently objective justification for the social repression that was already taking place.

Childbirth was gradually being taken out of the hands of female midwives and delivered into the hands of male physicians, who previously had regarded such work as beneath their dignity. Now there was money to be made in attending births, particularly where they involved middle-class women, and the invention of forceps brought wealth to the men who devised them. At first, though, doctors killed more women and children than they saved by passing on diseases from their other patients. They also used unsterilized equipment and caused the horrific deaths of many women from puerperal fever, or childbed as it was then called. Gradually, with the discovery of bacteria, the development of inoculations and the introduction of standards of hygiene, doctors secured and held steady their power in the birth chamber.

At the same time, in the Western European countries, an understanding of demography led to a parallel fear that nations were effectively disappearing; an idea, as we have already seen, promoted by Jean-Jacques Rousseau and the *Philosophes* who blamed an apparently declining French population on bad mothers. Census-taking had started in the eighteenth century and a growing awareness of economics linked population size with national wealth.[17] Governments began to embrace pro-natalist politics and to elevate women's calling as mothers. In Britain, horror at the waste of infant life prompted the opening of hospitals and homes for foundlings, which were soon inundated. By the 1900s women who practised birth control were accused of racial suicide, but only women of a certain class, of course, for poor people were no more encouraged to procreate then than they are now.

Alongside these new ideas came a trend which has proved to have enormous longevity – that of publishing manuals for women telling them how to be better mothers.[18] Most of the earliest pamphlets were reasonably well-intentioned, aiming to bring to an end some of the most misguided childrearing practices and to save infant lives, but even Rousseau, whose stated aim with *Émile* was to improve the lives of children, couldn't help throwing in a few side swipes at mothers and women in general. He believed women needed an education only to make them better wives and mothers, which he regarded as their true calling, and not to encourage them in intellectual pursuits in which they persisted. To prove his thesis he pointed to the natural tendency among little girls to play the coquette and to display a fondness for dolls; an observation later rubbished by Mary Wollstonecraft who commented that little girls, who could not share in their brothers' education and with nothing else to do, would obviously entertain themselves in whatever way they could and with whatever they were given.[19]

Voices of reason were few and far between, however, as men lined up to give their tuppence-worth on the proper role of women, couched in the guise of maternal advice. By the nineteenth century, badgering mothers had become a popular sport. William Buchan, a Yorkshireman and supporter of Rousseau, published several immensely successful books: *Domestic Medicine* (1769), *Offices and Duties of Mothers* (1800), and *Advice to Mothers* (1803). *Domestic Medicine* was enormously popular, reprinted many times and published throughout Europe and in America. In it he warned women of the importance of remaining calm and ladylike at all times, and gave the instance of a woman who flew into a rage while pregnant and gave birth to a child with its bowels burst open.[20] Andrew Combe's *Treatise on the Physiological and Moral Management of Infancy* issued the same advice on the importance of emotional tranquillity to Victorian women, whose children's physical and mental health he warned would be 'a legible transcript of the mother's condition and feelings during pregnancy'.[21] And the famous Beeton's *Housewife's Treasury* cautioned women that ill-temper would sour their milk, turning babies' food into 'draughts of poison'.[22]

From that day to this, advice to mothers and mothers-to-be has proliferated, but the warning tone remains the same from Donald Winnicott in the 1950s to Penelope Leach in the 1980s. Indeed, many of the same old chestnuts – for example, putting pressure on women to breastfeed, the idea that unborn children react to their mothers' emotions, or that motherhood is women's true calling above and beyond other roles – appear time and time again.

Conclusion

So, in brief, that is how motherhood came to be as it is today: one of the most natural human states and yet one of the most policed; the sole responsibility of women; not simply a duty but a highly idealized calling surrounded by sentiment. Matters were bad enough for Victorian mothers, but they were set to become even worse during the twentieth century as science, psychology, politics and debates surrounding gender pushed the motherhood myth to its limits and beyond.

Viewing motherhood through the lens of time reveals details that are lost up close. Let's take the current debate over whether it is psychologically damaging for children to be placed in day-care, specifically the idea that work and good mothering are incompatible. During the Industrial Revolution changes to the system of work meant that women *could not* work outside the home easily as well as being responsible for family life within it. After the Second World War, when the government needed women to give up the jobs they had held during the war period for the men returning from fighting, it was said that women *should not* combine work and motherhood; the justification for that, as we shall see, was provided by psychologists in the second half of the twentieth century who claimed (and continue to claim) that children are damaged by their mothers' absence, even for a few hours, at work.

Rousseau, who incidentally put five of his own children into foundling homes, thought that caring for children was solely the job of women and blamed them alone for the plight of eighteenth-century French children. He argued that education and ambition distracted women from their basic function. So did the Victorians. Today, the legacy of those ideas continues to be reflected in attitudes to 'career women' who choose not to have children and mothers who work.

An historical perspective makes us redefine our most basic assumptions about human nature and motherhood. What seems 'natural' in one period appears unnatural in another. We would never want to return to treating children as they were treated in the eighteenth century, but it is interesting to speculate how those mothers who had so little time for or interest in their offspring, and who regarded breastfeeding as unpleasant and motherhood an unavoidable bore, would view the Victorian woman to whom motherhood was (expected to be) everything?

Elizabeth Badinter remarks:

> Mother love has been discussed as a kind of instinct for so long that a 'maternal instinct' has come to seem rooted in women's very nature, regardless of the time or place in which she has lived. In the common view, every woman fulfills her destiny once she becomes a mother, finding within herself all the required responses, as if they were automatic and inevitable, held in reserve to await the right moment.[23]

After her odyssey into motherhood in times past, Badinter casts doubt on the notion of any kind of universal, predictable and long-term 'maternal instinct' at all. Indeed, the term has now fallen out of use among professionals, be they psychologists or scientists, but presumptions about the biological make-up of women are nevertheless central to the discussions about how women carry out the duties of motherhood and what those duties actually are. A popular view of maternal behaviour includes a woman's sole responsibility for an infant right through to adulthood, and that is an idea that historical evidence simply does not sustain.

In the past many people knew, or thought they knew, why they had children. It may have been because they could not prevent conception, or because they needed extra hands to work the looms, or to care for them when they grew old, or because they had been instructed to 'go forth and multiply'. Nowadays those reasons appear redundant. In the context of modern times, children are as likely to be the product of our emotions – desire, passion, altruism, selfishness, love, boredom and vanity – as much as any deeply-rooted, biologically-impelled compulsion. Fuelling the modern obsession with motherhood are our efforts to construct a new rationale for it. Until we find one that is complex and subtle enough to satisfy us, we will continue to build myths around motherhood.

The final lesson of history, on which this chapter must conclude, is that mothering has varied over time. The style of mothering which we have inherited today, with its roots in the nuclear family, was fashioned in a particular way at a specific time in history out of necessity and expediency. The separate elements consist variously of genuine concern at the abandonment of children, a less wholesome view of the nature and the place of women (and of men) and a specific economic context. By coincidence and by design these elements intertwined to produce what we now think of as 'traditional' motherhood. The emphasis on romantic motherhood in the Victorian era would eventually give way to the new century and suffragist demands for the vote and women's liberation. For women, that sense of freedom would prove short-lived with the massive revitalization of the motherhood myth as the twentieth century moved forwards.

chapter 3

Pygmalion Mother: The Making of the Modern Myth

Testimony: Barbara

Barbara is forty-one years old, married, with two sons. A trained lawyer, she currently works for a charitable trust.

My mother stayed home with us, me and my two brothers – one a year and a half younger, one five years younger. My mother was always at home with us. Once I got into secondary school she began to do some volunteer work and she was always involved in activities in our school. My father was a surgeon and not at home very much. He was very involved in his practice, so my mother was pretty much on her own in terms of looking after us. She came from a big Catholic family, six brothers and six sisters. Her sisters would help out. Three sisters lived nearby, as well as her sisters-in-law who were happy and willing to help out from time to time. Other than that, I don't even remember her employing a cleaner to do the housework. She did it all herself.

I can't remember a single one of her friends who worked at that time. There were two women who had law degrees and didn't practise. I remember being so impressed that they had these degrees, but I wasn't surprised that they didn't work because they were mothers, and mothers stayed home. My father would not let my mother work. That's the way she put it. He just said no.

I never really gave children or motherhood much thought. I didn't have much empathy for the few women that I knew who had children before I did. I didn't have a sense of how overwhelming the responsibility and the time commitment would be. In recent years I've regretted that I didn't provide more support to my friends who had children. But I didn't get it. I didn't realize what a great thing it would have been for me to say, 'I'll take the kids for a day,' which I easily could have done, but I didn't. I just didn't get it. I would go and visit them, but I never suggested doing anything.

With my own kids, I planned to hire someone to come in, but then I decided I couldn't trust anyone. I couldn't monitor them. I was very protective. First I put him into daycare and I went back to work at five and a half months. Then I took him away from there, because I didn't think the woman was giving him the kind of stimulation I wanted him to have. So I put him in another daycare situation. Then when I had my second son I stopped working and stayed at home for two and a half years. Any help I had I got through agencies, or they were contacts through friends.

The worst thing was leaving my first son in daycare. I don't think he was hurt by it, but it was traumatic for me. I felt very guilty. I also hated not being able to find childcare people who have the same approach as I do to raising my children, which is constant stimulation. I always read to them, talk to them, tell them what we are doing. I say, 'Now we are going to go and open the window', 'Now we're walking across the room'. I felt tremendous frustration with my husband. I guess it wasn't his fault. I wouldn't say he was an uninvolved father. He was in career mode. But I guess I should not have expected too much. I think men are just not really conditioned to be that kind of parent. I think there really is a difference between mothering a child and fathering a child. Mothers are primarily responsible for the caring of the children. I feel it is and I guess I feel it ought to be, should be, the mother's responsibility. I know a child who lost his mother and was raised by his father. There is a difference in the way that child has come out.

An ideal father to me would be willing to step in and handle the everyday stuff, knowing what to do without being told. Is there a conflict in saying the mother is the primary parent and expecting men to take responsibility? I suppose so. I like things done the way I want them done, and I suppose that can have a chilling effect on my husband when he tries to do things, for fear of being criticized. The best way would be for women to be able to let them do things their way, but it's frustrating. If he does the lunches, he doesn't put the right things in, he puts yoghurt in they don't like and it ends up coming back.

An ideal mother for me stays at home with the children. Deep down I do think it's the man's responsibility to earn the money. Ideally a mother would be at home – always. She bakes cakes, she picks them up at the end of school, not later. She has two or three children, she has her first in her twenties and, yes, she is married. She's my mother, actually.

Why am I not like that? Well, I work because I always want to have the ability to earn money. My background and skills are such that now I could always find work if I needed to. I also have much more to give than just being a mother. I spent a lot of time becoming educated and becoming prepared to be a person who made a difference in the world and I'm really uncomfortable about giving that up. I define myself a lot by what I am in the community. I am a role model and a leader in some respects, I sit on a lot of boards, for example. This is a difficult world and I feel it's my obligation to do what I can. I try to strike a balance. When I'm at home I try to live up to my image of the stay-at-home mum. I bake, I make my children's birthday cakes. I never talk about work. I'm as calm and housewifey as I can be. I cook dinner every night. Some people can't believe I do that. So that's the way my boys see me when I'm at home. I'm never on the phone doing business. And that makes me feel better. I try to do that because I want them to remember mum that way.

Yes, there is a tremendous emotional cost to me in being a working person and trying to be a calm, patient wife and mother as well. It's very hard. It was worse when I was working as a lawyer. That was an even bigger shift. There's another cost, in that – I'm sure you've heard this from other people – I never have any time for myself.

I have thought so hard about what I would tell a daughter, if I had one. It's difficult because you always want your daughter to be *independent and self-reliant if she needed to be. On the other hand I would want her to be a loving wife and mother, and create the kind of home for a family that I have done. And it's very hard to do. I'm not sure what to say. I think I'd advise her to think about her goals very hard. My life is a paradox . . . I know that.*

By the start of the twentieth century, the major historical and economic structures were in place to create the background for the modern motherhood myth. Changes to work which swept in with the Industrial Revolution had left women holding the baby at home while men went to work in the new factories, mines and metal works. At the same time a burgeoning fascination with scientific discovery had begun to exercise people's minds. In 1861 Pasteur had published his theory of germs and the spread of disease was by now beginning to be clearly understood and controlled. In only twenty years' time Alexander Fleming would notice changes taking place in his petri dish and give the world penicillin. These developments had a radical effect upon childcare and the raising of children. If romance had characterized motherhood in the previous century, then the twentieth century gave rise to the scientific mother.

Childcare became the subject of study, analysis and theory and was taken out of the hands of mothers and placed in the hands of men, who henceforth would tell mothers what to do. These were the childcare gurus. Suddenly babies became a matter for the experts. Popular writers emerged such as Frederic Truby (later Sir Truby) King and D. W. Winnicott in Britain; and in America John B. Watson and Luther Emmett Holt. Between them they moulded modern motherhood in their own vision, dictating every detail from the emotional relationship between mother and child down to mastering the fine art of burping or winding (a practice which, incidentally, is virtually unknown in many parts of the world).

The legacy of the first gurus lives on both in ideas about what constitutes good mothering as well as in the continued reliance of Western societies on the words of experts and their personal philosophies. Winnicott's lectures broadcast on the BBC were replaced by Dr Spock's *Common Sense Book of Baby and Childcare* with which generations of babyboomers were reared. When they became parents, they turned to Penelope Leach's *Baby and Child*. It's a rare woman today who embarks upon motherhood without a manual in her hand, like an instruction leaflet for a new computer. Despite the fact that every mother knows that the theory and practice of raising children frequently do not coincide, there are few who dare to go it alone. The experts create and feed their own market by issuing dire and prophetic warnings of the untold damage inflicted upon children by uninformed parents who may think they know what is good for their own child. Of all the many ways guilt has been induced and exploited in mothers, the childcare gurus must rank high on the list.

A famous author, who is the mother of several children, once told me that she had each of her children in a different decade and raised each on the popular method of the moment, with a different and conflicting set of rules every time. If after every birth, as she embarked on motherhood anew, she had believed the words of the fashionable, new expert she would only have been able to conclude that she had utterly ruined her preceding child. Truby King, who influenced many generations of mothers up until the Second World War, warned mothers against touching, petting or 'spoiling' their children and decreed a four-hour feeding schedule. A Truby King baby would have had a very different infancy from that of his younger sibling born in 1950 and brought up with Spock's enthusiasm for displays of maternal affection and feeding on demand. From early on, experts emerged from various and often competing fields whose disciplines placed the emphasis on different aspects of the child's well-being. Some were doctors whose main concern was with exercise and nutrition; others were ethologists keen to apply their observations on animal behaviour to human subjects; still others were psychologists and psychoanalysts who were far more interested in the dynamics of the relationship between mother and child.

Early in the twentieth century, Sigmund Freud was expanding his theories of human behaviour and the development of personality. The resulting discipline of psychoanalysis has, at its core, the belief that early experiences in childhood set in place events and behaviour in later life. It is this idea, which was built upon and developed by Freud's disciples, that is central to the tendency, which later became endemic, to blame mothers for their children's misfortunes and to scrutinize the relationship between mothers and their children.

Freud, however, was actually far more interested in the relationship between boys and their fathers and the resolution of the Oedipal conflict which was the foundation stone of all his theories. He did not actually delve deeply into the personality or behaviour of the mother, nor was he concerned with specific childrearing practices, believing instead that babies are driven by powerful instincts and love their mothers who are the people who feed, warm and comfort them. But he did explicitly point to the direction in which psychoanalysis was to progress by describing the mother–child relationship as 'unique, without parallel, established unalterably for a whole lifetime as the first and strongest love-object and the prototype of all later love-relations – for both sexes'.

Freud's sexism is notorious and has been the subject of criticism both from within psychoanalysis as well as outside. He saw women as castrated men and wrote of their 'sense of inferiority' and of the blame young girls place on their mothers for their lack of a penis which has left them for ever 'insufficiently equipped'.[1] Motherhood was women's salvation and compensation for being without a penis, particularly if they bore a male child equipped with the prized piece of anatomy.

Only in relatively recent times, with the advent of feminist thinking in all disciplines including psychoanalysis, have Freud's

theories about women been properly addressed. In the 1970s
Kate Millett, the American feminist, accused Freud and his followers of overlooking in their entirety existing social structures
and notions of femininity which, rather than biology, might
account for women's social status. In other words, Millet argued
that nurture rather than nature might account for gender differences.

From within the therapy movement, psychologists Dorothy
Dinnerstein and Nancy Chodorow have both powerfully reinter-
preted Freud's theories on motherhood. In *The Mermaid and the
Minotaur*, published in 1977, Dinnerstein presents the idea that
small children develop a rage against their mothers (which is
never properly overcome) as the person who alone has the
power to grant or withhold what the child desires. Chodorow
says it is the girl's unconscious identification with her mother,
while boys see themselves as different and separate, that endlessly reproduces gendered divisions of labour and women's
exclusive responsibility for nurturing children: girls copy their
mothers mothering. Both women argue that society and the
position of women and mothers will improve only when men
take on their share of responsibility for their children.

So, in the first three decades of the century, while Freud
was producing his theories, the essential elements which would
eventually produce our modern maternal ideology were coming
together. The medicalization of motherhood – the result of an
increased scientific understanding – removed childcare from the
hands of women and placed it in the hands of experts. Soon
most babies in Britain would be born in hospital and this, added
to the creation of the welfare state in the post-war period, dramatically decreased the infant mortality rate. For the first time in
history, parents did not need to fear the death of their children.

Concern for the physical health of children was immediately
replaced by new considerations for their mental health and
psychological well-being. The psychoanalyst John Bowlby highlighted this concern with his theory of 'attachment'; in other

words, the biological bonds between mother and child urgently required that, in the post-war period, women should return en masse from the world of work to their rightful place, as he saw it, in the home. Between them these men – and with very few exceptions they were all men – created the ideal of the 1950s stay-at-home, full-time mother.

The gurus rose fast in their respective fields, amassing tremendous fame and influence, but one by one their theories have been reconsidered by subsequent generations and either debunked or rethought. Today, no one would dream of leaving a young baby to sleep outside on a cold night, as Truby King once advised. Bowlby's ideas have been revisited and watered down. In modern times, Marshall Klaus and John Kennell, two Bowlby followers, presented their theory of bonding to a receptive public, only to have their methods criticized and their findings overturned by their peers. Few were unmasked as spectacularly as Bruno Bettelheim, a world-famous psychoanalyst and expert on autism. Bettelheim's theory that autism, now recognized to have an organic genesis, was caused by extremely brutal treatment at the hands of the children's mothers gained wide acceptance, despite the protests of the accused women. Bettelheim's solution was to separate mother and child and allow no contact between them. Only after his death by his own hand in 1990, when an American investigative journalist Richard Pollack (whose own mother had been blamed for his brother's autism by the doctor) delved into Bettelheim's background, did the truth emerge.[2] Bettelheim had fabricated his credentials including his training as a psychoanalyst, faked research and claimed to have cured children he never even treated. In all, he was a fraud who tormented and vilified mothers, and influenced the way emotionally disturbed children were treated for decades.

Frederick Truby King

Most of the childcare gurus make one unequivocally positive contribution to childcare and with Truby King it was the revival of breastfeeding, which at that time had become thoroughly unfashionable. 'Breast is best' was his saying and his achievements, including halving the infant mortality rate in New Zealand, are undoubtedly due to that single premise. Otherwise posterity has not judged Truby King kindly. His approach to childrearing was strict, forceful and unyielding. He bullied, cajoled and threatened mothers whom he appeared to regard as the weak link in the entire process (he once commented in exasperation that if men had the capacity to breastfeed they would have the sense to do what he said) and he advocated for the care of small babies a regime of almost military harshness.

Babies were to be fed only every four hours and at no other time, regardless of how much they cried or however apparent their distress. He also forbade mothers to feed at night at all, urging them to let their babies 'cry it out' rather than give in. To do so would have been to spoil the child. The Truby King method also discouraged physical contact between mother and child, including kissing or cuddling which was considered unnecessary as well as unhealthy and highly likely to pass on germs. Playing with babies would only overexcite them and for that reason was frowned upon. Of course, many women broke the rules and hugged or played with their babies only to berate themselves about it afterwards.

A flick through his most famous book, *Care and Feeding of Baby*, reveals what has become the standard style for babycare books even today: the only two characters are Mother and Baby (fathers have no role except to earn money); baby is always a boy; the family arrangements are nuclear. The prose is classic 'carrot and stick'. The author uses his professional status to back up his mixture of inducements and warnings. Mothers would achieve peace and perfection if they followed his advice.

Breaking the rules resulted in indiscipline, a ruined child or even death as the eminent paediatrician remarked in speeches which were sometimes little more than rants against the failings of mothers: 'much wastage of infant life in our midst is due to self-indulgence and shirking of duties.'[3] Mothers frustrated Sir Frederick who would have much preferred that the care of infants was entirely taken over by specially trained nurses.

Despite a firm belief in gender roles and the place of women, Truby King did not appear to believe in the idea of maternal instinct. He considered motherhood a calling for which women had to be trained, because left to their own devices they would ruin the lives of their children. The closest he ever came to recognizing any kind of natural emotions was a reference to the additional advantage of promoting bonds between mother and child when breastfeeding. In general he regarded mothers as inadequate, ignorant and lacking in discipline. A mother was all that stood between him and the creation of the perfect child.

When Truby King died in 1938 in New Zealand, his long and distinguished career had earned him international recognition. His ideas lived on until the war years and just beyond; many of today's fifty-, sixty- and seventy-year-olds were Truby King babies, and many grandmothers still regard silence, solitude and timed feeds as the definition of a good baby.

The aftermath of the Second World War produced a new set of circumstances and a different agenda. Women, too, were ready to give up this gruelling and often heartbreaking regime. By the 1950s, Truby King's ideas were swept aside as a new era of motherhood rolled in.

John Bowlby

No other theorist had as powerful and as radical an effect on thinking about motherhood as Edward John Mostyn Bowlby who died in 1990 and whose ideas on 'attachment' and the effects of maternal deprivation form the cornerstone of modern maternal ideology. Unlike the other great 'gurus', Bowlby was not so much a popular writer as an academic and theorist. Nevertheless, his first book, *Child Care and the Growth of Love*, sold hundreds of thousands of copies around the world. It was a seminal work.

Bowlby came from somewhat elevated beginnings. He was distinctly upper class, the heir to a baronetcy who was raised by a nanny, followed by boarding-school and Cambridge. As with Freud, there has been speculation over whether it was Bowlby's early experience of being raised by a somewhat distant mother, who preferred to leave the children's care to a hired nanny, that established Bowlby's later fascination with mother–child relationships.

The 1940s were a critical period for Europe and for Bowlby, and most of his ideas were the fruit of this thoroughly atypical period. The Second World War bore witness to the large-scale evacuation of children from the cities to the relative safety of the countryside and sometimes abroad to other countries, such as Canada. Children were separated from their families for months, even years, often boarded with strangers and lived unfamiliar lives.

War changed the lives of women. In the previous decades women's work outside the home had been declining steadily, but conscription and the call to arms reversed the trend sharply. Women staffed the munitions factories, went to the countryside to work the fields and bring in the harvests, volunteered as nurses, raised funds for the war effort and joined the Wrens. For the first (and last) time in the history of the country, the government both condoned women working outside the home and provided extensive, state-funded nursery and daycare so that they could do so.

Britain and the world had undergone massive social shifts, the long-term effects of which remained unclear. Six years of fighting a war had resulted in population shifts and decimated

communities in the countryside and the city. Eventually, ter-
raced homes, with their narrow streets and facing backyards,
would be pulled down and replaced by modern tower blocks
and prefabs. While that was still to come, the social effects were
already felt, particularly by mothers who lost their support networks of kin and neighbours in one fell swoop. Women from
the upper classes no longer had servants to administer to their
children's needs and for the first time became wholly responsible
for their own offspring.

This is the context within which Bowlby produced his
studies of institutionalized childcare and his twin theories of
the instinctual bond between mother and child which should
never be broken, and the effect upon children if the bond is
broken.

Bowlby had been following with interest the work of Rene
Spitz who had made a study of institutionalized babies. Spitz's
findings then mirror the situation documented in state orphanages in China in the 1990s: children deprived of human contact
and isolated for long periods will fail to thrive, rocking themselves back and forth, hitting their heads repeatedly against the
sides of their cot, or staring in dull passivity for hours on end.
Bowlby carried out his own study of forty-four child thieves,
noting that seventeen of them had been separated from their
mothers for a period as infants. Struck by this fact he ascribed
their later problems to this single event, famously writing:
'changes of mother-figure can have very destructive effects in
producing the development of an affectionless psychopathic
character given to persistent juvenile conduct.'[4]

In 1950 the World Health Organization commissioned a study
from Bowlby on children orphaned or separated from their
parents as a result of the war in France, the Netherlands,
Sweden and Switzerland. The report, which was published in
1951, immediately caused an international sensation. In its
pages Bowlby condemned the cruelty of all institutional care,
arguing that children needed and were entitled to the love

and care of a mother. Anything less amounted to 'maternal deprivation', the effects of which would be seared on the child's psyche eternally and irrevocably.

Bowlby desperately wanted to close down or at least reform the system of large orphanages which were incapable of meeting the needs of individual children. In this he succeeded and he can be thanked for current social welfare policies which try to place a child with foster parents or in a family environment instead of in children's homes. But for women, for mothers, Bowlby's views, his high ideals and exacting standards as well as the way his work has since been interpreted, spelled disaster.

In *Child Care and the Growth of Love*, Bowlby declares that the mental health of a child absolutely requires 'a warm, intimate, and continuous relationship with his mother . . . in which both find satisfaction and enjoyment'.[5] No small order by anyone's standards, but that is the very least of it. He continues: 'we must recognise that leaving any child of under three years of age is a major operation only to be undertaken for sufficient and good reason.'[6]

In Bowlby's terms, not only should a mother be her child's constant companion, but she should find her fulfilment in the role, too. If she fails to do so, the whole exercise is useless. 'The mother needs to feel an expansion of her own personality in the personality of the child' – note *needs* to feel. 'The provision of mothering', he argued, 'cannot be considered in terms of hours per day, but only in terms of the enjoyment of each other's company which mother and child obtain.' Any woman who hesitated received admonishment in the very next paragraph. 'The provision of constant attention day and night, seven days a week and 365 days in the year, is possible only for a woman who derives profound satisfaction from seeing her child grow from babyhood, through the many phases of childhood, to become an independent man or woman, and knows it is her care which has made this possible.'[7] Of course, there weren't, and aren't, many women who would have dared to declare themselves anything less than absolutely committed to the healthy progress of their children.

Bowlby elaborated all kinds of emotional, psychological and character disorders which could result from maternal deprivation, from the creation of full-blown psychopaths to adults unable to function properly in their own relationships. Deprivation had many causes, including a child's stay in hospital. Ignoring a crying child counted as partial deprivation, this last much to the consternation of a generation of women who had followed the diktats of Truby King with their own children.

All the attention mothers were required to lavish upon their children facilitated their proper 'attachment' to each other. Bowlby was an early fan of ethology and from his readings on the behaviour of birds and monkeys, specifically ideas about imprinting (the way newborn animals automatically follow their mother), he concluded that an infant's attachment to its mother was both natural and instinctive.

Fathers, it will be no surprise to hear, once again had no significant role, save as earners. By placing so much emphasis on mothers and arguing that attachment was instinctive and natural, Bowlby left little for fathers who have struggled to find a place in their children's lives ever since. Bowlby himself was a father of four who, by all accounts, left the care of his children entirely up to his wife Ursula.

Bowlby's theories were seized upon and his conclusions, based on extreme situations, were glibly applied to the everyday. It is clear, too, that Bowlby himself, in his zeal, overstated his case. An immediate consequence was panic among women terrified they had already damaged children – an anxiety he was obliged to quell by softening his message slightly in later writings.

Another far more serious consequence was Bowlby's success in achieving the closure of not only the orphanages he loathed, but the vast proportion of nurseries and daycare centres which had opened up, with government approval and funding, during the war. In 1944 there were 1,559 nurseries in Britain catering to tens of thousands of children, but after the war the nurseries became an expensive wartime legacy for the government, which was also under pressure to provide jobs for thousands of returned soldiers. In 1951, in response to Bowlby's commissioned report, a WHO report claimed that nurseries and daycare 'cause permanent damage to the emotional health of a generation'.[8] Bowlby's findings swiftly became official policy. By the early 1950s virtually all the wartime nurseries had gone. It became accepted wisdom among health professionals, social workers and teachers that working mothers ran the risk of damaging their children.

It has been suggested by some historians and writers that more than a whiff of conspiracy surrounds what appears to be the remarkably fortuitous timing of mutually expedient concerns. From the point of view of the government, there does appear to be some truth in the suggestion that they had more in mind than the happiness of infants when they embraced Bowlby's theories so readily. But Bowlby probably also imagined he was elevating the status of mothers by bestowing on their task so much importance, rather than simply driving women back into the home. It is easy to see how his theories could have been a soft sell to plenty of women. Many had witnessed or experienced the wartime shattering of their families. They wanted time to re-establish relationships with their children and their husbands. These were the babyboom years when not only cities and economies were being rebuilt, but families too. Postwar prosperity in Britain, helped by billions of dollars of Marshall Plan aid from America, meant that even blue-collar workers could earn enough to keep a wife and family.

It is illuminating to see how certain of Bowlby's recommendations were taken up, while others were ignored. Bowlby was opposed to mothers with young children going out to work at all. Previously most nurseries were perfectly prepared to accept two-year-olds, but soon, thanks to Bowlby's warnings, they would only take children from the age of five. Bowlby, however, did recognize that most women who worked did so because they needed the money. By way of compensation he suggested a wage for housework to be paid by the government to mothers, to encourage and enable them to stay at home – a proposal that never made it to the statute books.

The train Bowlby set on track gathered pace in the years that followed. In time, researchers began to focus not just on the mother's relationship with her child, but even on her competence. Selma Fraiberg, a Bowlby devotee, invented a method for measuring a child's attachment to the mother and declared that children whose mothers were not sufficiently skilled or attentive were poorly attached and would grow up insecure. In her immensely popular 1959 book *The Magic Years*, she argued that nothing less than twenty-four-hour devotion would do, and that being cared for by persons other than their mother was actually harmful to infants. Notably, her calls for financial support for mothers to stay at home also went unheeded.

So the 1950s mother was actually Pygmalion mum, the result of one man's vision of the perfect mother. For a mixture of social and economic reasons, Bowlby's ideal of the loving, selfless, stay-at-home supermum became, and still is to this day, the established view of what constitutes 'normal' mothering. Motherhood became transformed into a rigid, rule-laden process, governed by dogma produced by so-called experts whose views were always framed in terms of what was best for baby, placing them beyond debate. By being so inflexible and so extreme in the application of ideas which had started as guiding principles, the new professionals put the interests of mothers and their children into conflict.

Typically, far more attention is paid to a controversial or radical new theory than to the subsequent critiques. If Bowlby and his followers were accepted uncritically by the general public, within his profession his views prompted no small degree of controversy. Many other critics came from fields outside psychoanalysis such as ethology, sociology and anthropology. One of his critics was the world-famous anthropologist Margaret Mead who had spent years chronicling childrearing methods in Samoa, Bali and the United States and elsewhere. She dismissed his ideas on the need for exclusive mothering and his ideas about attachment. Others pointed to aspects of Bowlby's research, in particular the methods he used, which would never meet the standards required of scientific studies today. He rarely, for example, used control groups to measure his findings or looked for other possible causes.

Perhaps the main and most constant criticism is that while Bowlby claimed to be making a study of the effects of 'maternal deprivation' on children, what he was really looking at were the results of institutionalization. The children whose case histories make up the bulk of his work were deprived of everything, including ordinary human contact and any kind of affection. They were placed in huge orphanages and had dozens of carers who often provided poor care. Many had suffered some kind of distress in the form of family conflict, or wartime loss, others had been abused. Simply put, these were deeply unhappy children.

The British psychiatrist Michael Rutter has significantly re-vised and rethought many of Bowlby's ideas. In his 1972 book *Maternal Deprivation Reassessed*, he shows that some of the symptoms of 'maternal deprivation' which Bowlby described, in particular stunted growth and poor speech development, had far more mundane roots. The children did not grow properly because of their meagre, vitamin-depleted orphanage diet, not because they lacked a mother's love. Similarly, they had poor vocabularies because of their environment, not their parenting. Indeed, children in large families often display the same problem. As for maternal deprivation creating 'affectionless psychopaths', Rutter showed that children whose mothers had died did not become delinquents. The root causes of criminal behaviour in children lay elsewhere.

The popular appeal of Bowlby's theory of uninterrupted

mothering lay in the fact that it seemed to explain something mothers already recognized – that children can be clingy. Bowlby took that premise several stages further and insisted that separating mother and child was actually wrong because it was damaging. Many psychologists now agree, however, that separation *per se* does not equal damage, even if the child cries when the mother leaves and even if the mother misses her child when she is apart from her. A child is not harmed by his mother working or by being left with other carers.

In his assessment of all the research since Bowlby, Rutter argued that attachment was neither exclusive nor irreversible, but rather a child could be attached to more people than just the mother and attachments could strengthen or weaken during the child's life. As far as the mother was concerned, it was not the quantity of time but rather the intensity of interaction during the time she spent with her child: 'mothers who play with their child and give him a great deal of attention have a more strongly attached child than those who interact with the child only when giving him routine care.'[9] Rutter still talked in terms of the duties of mothers as opposed to fathers and so did little to shift the weight of responsibility, although he did lessen the load slightly. One unanticipated result was to start the 1980s vogue for 'quality time' with which modern working mothers tried to assuage their feelings of guilt towards their children.

Neither Bowlby nor his supporters paused to consider the individual characteristics or needs of mothers. It was as though they regarded women as coming from some kind of mould like Stepford Wives, willing and able to accept all the many requirements of their role. Perhaps they believed that 'instinct' would somehow subsume every other personality trait and mothers would express towards their children only a bland, ideal type of love. But it seems evident that an aggressive, competitive woman will make a very different kind of mother from a bookish, withdrawn one; an exuberant, cheerful woman will approach her role unlike an anxious woman; a woman whose interests consist solely of classical music and intellectual discourse will doubtless find less pleasure in the company of a three-year-old than someone who prefers board games and walking in the park. When it comes to ideas about motherhood, common sense can sometimes appear to go out of the window. Women have their share of all mankind's imperfections, and yet to this day we expect to create perfect mothers out of imperfect humans.

Nancy Chodorow, a powerful psychoanalytical thinker, has taken the debate about attachment one stage further by saying that forcing mothers to spend all their time with their children, and to carry the entire emotional burden, guarantees the failure of the very relationship which Bowlby was trying to promote. Ann Dally, a psychiatrist, also points out that although mothers staying at home with their children remains a popular ideal, 'there is no scientific evidence to justify it on psychological grounds and . . . if one wanted to look for evidence one might even come up with the suspicion that the era of unbroken and exclusive maternal care has produced the most neurotic, disjointed, alienated and drug-addicted generation ever known.'[10]

What's more, the ideology of motherhood which Bowlby helped to create is almost entirely middle class in its aspirations, as well as being culturally specific. Although exclusive maternal care is often deemed to be natural – proponents of the idea usually point to baby monkeys clinging to their mothers' backs in the animal world – it seems as though, among humans at least, this way of raising children is not actually standard. A study carried out in the late 1970s of 186 non-industrial cultures by two anthropologists, Weisner and Gallimore, found only five societies where the mother did not share the care of her children with other people.[11] Similar conclusions were noted in the seminal study *Mothers of Six Cultures* by a team of American anthropologists carried out over almost two decades from the 1950s to the 1970s. They observed that the American mother was unique among the cultures they studied in having sole responsibility for her children.

Many of the greatest minds of child development and mothering, including Michael Rutter, Nancy Chodorow, Ann Dally and the eminent British psychologist Barbara Tizard, have all surmised that shared parenting or shared mothering is just as good for children. Some even consider it to be preferable.

Dally provides a closing thought on the theory of attachment and how it has become a self-fulfilling prophecy:

> Over the last forty years we . . . have been trying to condition babies to become attached to their mothers exclusively and, having done that, we . . . proceed to do research which reveals the undoubted distress caused when an infant who has been conditioned in this way is suddenly separated from his mother . . . This research is then used by academics and politicians to 'prove' that young children should be tied even more totally and exclusively to their mothers.[12]

Psychology has succeeded in creating what it originally set out to describe.

Towards a child-centred philosophy of childcare

Since Bowlby published his theories, childcare has become increasingly focused on the child whose needs now take centre-stage. Throughout the 1950s, the man who defined 'motherhood' was the British psychoanalyst Donald Winnicott who elaborated and built on Bowlby's themes of attachment and interdependence. Winnicott's influence gave way in the 1960s to America's Dr Benjamin Spock, who was regarded at the time as outrageously permissive in his 'let the child decide' approach to raising children. If greatness were measured in book sales and popular appeal alone, then Spock would stand head and shoulders above the rest of the gurus. Sales of his original volume *Baby and Child Care* reached 40 million and Spock continued to write until he died aged ninety-four in 1998.

Freudian ideas influenced both theorists. Spock and Winnicott emphasized the mother's unique and (as far as Winnicott was concerned) irreplaceable role in the emotional growth of the child.

Donald Winnicott made his name at a time when mothers were still reeling from the extremes required by Truby King in the name of discipline and training. Mothers neither trusted their own judgement nor did they have any faith in the advice of their own mothers who still believed in the value of four-hour feeds. Indeed, the 'gurus' of the twentieth century have been almost solely responsible for breaking down the time-honoured passing of wisdom and knowledge about childcare from mothers to daughters. Winnicott won women over with his sympathetic approach which stressed maternal warmth and love instead of rules, rations and timetables.

Most people in the 1950s came to know of Winnicott through his immensely successful BBC radio lectures on childcare. For Winnicott, just like Bowlby, a woman could not be with her baby enough and anything less than total devotion to the role of mother was an absolute dereliction of a duty bestowed by nature. Perhaps his most famous contribution to twentieth-century ideas about motherhood was to say that there is no such thing as a baby, only a mother–baby unit.

Winnicott praised women's efforts and their contribution repeatedly and self-consciously: 'I am trying to draw attention to the immense contribution to the individual and to society that the ordinary good mother . . . makes at the beginning, and which she *does simply through being devoted to her infant.*'[13] And he set himself apart from other professionals who sought to tell mothers what to do and interfered with the natural process of mothering which, according to him, women knew best. Women warmed to him. At last it seemed, here was someone who thought about mothers and not just children.

Winnicott was just as frequently patronizing, though, and the accolades came mixed with condescension. In his essay 'A Man Looks at Motherhood' he remarks: 'you do not even have to be clever, and you don't even have to think if you do not want to. You may have been hopeless at arithmetic at school, or perhaps all your friends got scholarships, but you didn't like the sight of a history book and so failed and left school early.'[14] The man who invented the notion of the 'good enough mother' concludes the paragraph with this observation intended to reassure his readers: 'Isn't it strange that such a tremendously important thing should depend so little on exceptional intelligence.'

Being a 'good enough mother' on Winnicott's terms wasn't so easy. A woman needed a saint-like capacity for patience, devotion, self-sacrifice and the ability to find fulfilment in even the most mundane tasks of motherhood. She had to delight in every filled nappy, every burp or fart or night-time wakening. 'All you need is love' might have been Winnicott's refrain, and that wasn't asking much because, according to him, women were like that anyway, it was simply part of female nature. The role of fathers, who were otherwise never mentioned, was simply to make baby love his mother all the more by being 'hard and strict and unrelenting, intransigent, indestructible'.[15] Trying to help the mother out would just interfere with his proper function.

In case any woman found her capacity to give waning, Winnicott backed up his sweet refrain with a few well-placed threats, promising stunted emotional development and psychological malfunction in the child if the mother failed. This is what happens when a mother doesn't pay attention and picks her child up without supporting the infant's head: 'There are very subtle things here,' listeners to the broadcast were warned:

If you have got a child's body and head in your hands and do not think of that as unity and reach for a handkerchief or something, then the head has gone back and the child is in two pieces – head and body; the child screams and never forgets it. The awful thing is that nothing is ever forgotten. Then the child goes around with an absence of confidence in things.[16]

The Winnicott child was a fragile bloom who, without showers of love and constant nurturing, would wither and fail.

Of course, everyone in Winnicott's world was white, middle class and lived in a nuclear family. With his emphasis on raising children in the correct environment, in his extraordinarily prescriptive world there was no room (and, one presumes, no hope either) for children with different family arrangements.

Winnicott also introduced the idea that, in addition to their mothers' continual presence, what babies needed most of all was familiarity in their environment. In other words, once a routine had been established it should not be changed, nor should the child be moved from location to location. So the woman who put her faith in Winnicott could expect to spend her time isolated at home with her child, unable and unwilling to do much more than make a trip to the shops for fear of playing havoc with her child's psyche. One wonders what he would have made of, say, Tuareg children who from the moment of their birth are on the move and do not see the same spot from year to year, whose tented homes are pitched in a different place week by week and who are cared for by several women and not just their mothers. Although Winnicott claimed that most mothers were 'good enough' mothers, the tone of his writing and lectures was every bit as rigid and moralistic as Truby King's.

In contrast, Dr Benjamin Spock's *Common Sense Book of Baby and Childcare* was cleverly titled and almost certainly struck a chord with women who were tired of the perfectionism demanded of them by men who had never looked after a child for a day in their lives. Spock's name became closely associated with 1960s' ideas of freedom from constraints and tolerance and at one point he was held almost solely responsible for the student riots of that decade, which his critics maintained were provoked by youngsters raised according to his permissive ideas. Right or wrong, the accusation nevertheless shows the extent of his influence.

Spock was himself raised on the standards of Emmett Holt (the American Truby King) but his own approach to childcare was just the opposite: sleep when the baby felt like it; potty training in her own time; feeding on demand and then as much or as little as the baby wanted; he didn't even insist on breastfeeding. While earlier approaches to childcare insisted babies fit in with adult schedules, Spock had it the other way around, but his relaxed approach meant that mothers had to be on hand twenty-four hours a day while baby did things in his own time.

The quantities of information from every quarter, the sea-changes in expert-led opinion, and most of all the apparently dire consequences of getting it wrong have placed mothers in a state of utter dependency on outside sources of information. Although Spock often urged women to trust their own instincts, as social historian Shari Thurer remarked in her historical account of motherhood: 'If a mother knew which of her impulses to trust, why would she have cracked the cover of these books in the first place?'[17]

Spock's era was a time of changing ideas and Spock, perhaps a little unfairly since he was scarcely the worst offender, took the brunt of feminist ire. Spock's assumption that parenting was women's work, backed up with remarks such as, 'Of course, I don't mean that the father has to give just as many bottles or change just as many diapers as the mother. But it's fine for him to do so occasionally',[18] inflamed the emerging ranks of sisterhood.

Like all good Freudian-influence theorists, he was also unhappy about the idea of women leaving their children to work and countered his recognition that some women may need or want to work with the guilt-inducing words: 'If a mother realizes clearly how vital this kind of care is to a small child, it may make it easier for her to decide that the extra money she might earn, or the satisfaction she might receive from an outside job, is not so important, after all.'[19] That was in 1958, five years before Betty Friedan awakened the consciousness of millions of women with *The Feminine Mystique* in which she challenged Freudian ideas of gender. Her 'problem with no name' was the mind-numbing routine of home and family life in which women were expected to find contentment, but which buried women alive. This state of affairs, she argued, was good for neither women or children: 'Strange new problems are being reported in the growing generations of children whose mothers were always there, driving them around, helping with their home-work – an inability to endure pain or discipline or pursue any self-sustained goal of any sort, a devastating boredom with life.'[20]

Adrienne Rich's problem had a name and its name was motherhood. She wrote with extraordinary candour about her experience of motherhood and her feelings for her children whom she confessed, from time to time, she had the urge to kill. She made it clear that the problem for her was the 'institution' of motherhood, 'the chaining of women in links of love and guilt'.[21]

A poet and academic, Rich, for a while, tried to become the archetypal perfect wife and mother. When she wrote of the experience she lit a charge:

I only knew that I had lived through something which was considered central to the lives of women, fulfilling even in its sorrows, a key to the meaning of life; and that I could remem-ber little except anxiety, physical weariness, anger, self-blame, boredom, and division within myself; a division made more acute by the moments of passionate love, delight in my chil-dren's spirited bodies and minds, amazement at how they went on loving me in spite of my failures to love them wholly and selflessly.[22]

Rich apart, popular feminism did little to address the issue of motherhood directly. In its vast literature, precious little has been devoted to the issue of motherhood which was seen as part and parcel of an overall package of oppression. This was probably really more an omission than a betrayal of women who were mothers. The feminist movement has always been dominated by white, middle-class, college-educated women who were themselves childless; the best known among them being Gloria Steinem, Andrea Dworkin and Germaine Greer. White feminists have recently been taken to task by writers such as bell hooks and Alice Walker for ignoring the needs and experience of black women, including black mothers. At the worst, perhaps, it was the potential for motherhood to be seen as a claim for 'special treatment' which caused some feminist thinkers, who wanted nothing to stand in the way of absolute equality, to look the other way. Those who did embrace the idea of motherhood mystified it, honouring the idea of great matriarchy in the past and of the future. They did not concern themselves with the daily trials of the ordinary, workaday mum. The omission left a glaring gap, and in time the institution of motherhood has become the neglected vulnerable spot of the Western women's movement.

The legacy of Bowlby, Winnicott and the others is a vision of motherhood in which stay-at-home, exclusive mothering remains the ideal and the presumed norm. Today, though, there are infinite sources of information from videos and television programmes to the Internet. The division and multiplicity of information distribution means that no single guru has arisen to inherit Spock's mantle; instead, we have hundreds maybe even thousands of experts each with his or her own line to pitch to mothers, including among the best known writers like Berry Brazleton in the USA, and Penelope Leach in the UK.

An analysis of eleven modern childcare books indicates that, if anything, childcare advice has become even more prescriptive than in the 1950s. 'The responsibility falls on to mothers', the survey concluded, 'for the "normal" development of a well-adjusted individual. To mother adequately a woman needs to be present with her child 24 hours each day and to be continually and actively engaged in providing stimulating and attentive company. If her child's development is not normal, the blame falls on the mother.'[23] The same mother-blaming mentality is evident in therapy rooms, radio phone-ins and the problem pages of magazines. 'Mal de mère' is the phrase the child psychiatrist Stella Chess coined to describe the tendency to blame mothers for all the ills that befall their children.

Some authors pay lip-service to equality and shared parenting by addressing their advice to 'parents' or to 'you', but that does little to disguise the fact that 'you' is really the mother. Often the underlying message is one which says, 'if you think mother nature is concerned with political correctness you're wrong; if you think that newborn babies respect your claim to equal rights, you're doubly wrong.' One author, Hugh Jolly, is quite explicit: 'You have to be a maternal rather than a sexual figure or an intellectual force, because this is the role nature meant you to play for the benefit of your child.'[24] It's clear that, for Jolly, maternity, sexuality and intelligence are mutually exclusive. If women won't do the entire job gladly, then they must be made to. Penelope Leach has been the frequent target of criticism for making working mothers feel guilty for not wanting, or being able, to stay at home. Across the board single parents, different family structures, other ethnicities or cultural heritages continue to be denied any existence in childcare literature.

Of all the modern gurus, perhaps the most prominent, due as much to her views as to the extent of her influence through books, television programmes and radio talk-shows, is Penelope Leach. Leach writes: 'For a woman, having a baby is the culmination of adult sexuality.'[25] Top of her list of concerns are working mothers. She is unhappy about daycare (she cites Bowlby and goes on to remind readers of what happened in the Romanian orphanages, warning 'any personal indifference is damaging'[26]). She is opposed to smacking or any kind of punishment, horrified at the idea of leaving babies to cry and otherwise depicts babies as immensely delicate and susceptible creatures easily damaged by unintentional neglect, disharmony or even loud noises. In her world, mothers must also enjoy their tasks or the whole exercise is redundant. When her latest volume *Children First*, in which many of these views are outlined, was first published in 1994, Leach's attack on the selfishness of modern mothers met with a bellow of protest from feminists and ordinary mothers alike. Leach had written: 'Every mother wants her baby to have the best and will deprive herself to buy it, but she dare not *give* him herself, the freebie that is best of all.'[27]

Few women in Britain could possibly meet Leach's standards. And modern beliefs about child development no longer support her views. Nowadays, most developmental psychologists will agree that infants and children are far stronger, more resilient, hardy creatures than Leach would have us believe – a point made in Scarr and Dunn's examination of the arguments for and against daycare, *Mothercare/Othercare*: 'The story of babies' fragility simply does not fit with what we know from careful research. There is no basis, in good research, for a fable that plays so disturbingly with mothers' anxieties and guilts.'[28] Indeed, the latest study on the subject of daycare published in April 1996 by the National Institute of Child Health and Human Development in Washington found (using Fraiberg's measure) that a child's relationship with its mother was not adversely affected by good daycare.

Despite a changing social climate and even in the face of conflicting research, the preferred form of motherhood, the vision that is sold over the counter to women expecting their first child, remains virtually unchanged. Mothers today endure a continually growing list of obligations, and run themselves ragged while the 'experts' crack the whip. The 'myth' about motherhood which produced the now legendary 1950s ideal has proved enduring and resistant because its followers have seized

for themselves the respectability of tradition and added to it
the authority of science, and also because their construction
of 'natural' motherhood offers a seductive simplicity which is
appealing even to women themselves because it has the feeling
of being pre-ordained, part of some wider, universal order. It is
from these roots in the 1950s that ideas about women, their
babies and the biologically determined nature of the relationship
between the two would spring again, revitalized, several decades
later and in a new social context.

Mother–infant bonding: the creation of a modern fable

There are any number of parallels between the story of the
theory of mother–infant bonding and the attachment theory.
First of all, in both instances an idea was promoted and treated
as gospel truth because it had the apparent backing of scientific
findings; on both occasions an initially reformist principle turned
into an oppressive doctrine, and once again women were being
told how they should mother, and their relationship with their
babies was defined according to an external social agenda.

Both theories purported to demonstrate an instinctual link
between mother and child and relied heavily on data from the
animal world to back their hypotheses. The difference is that
while attachment dealt with the child's connection to the
mother, bonding worked the other way around, from mother
to child. The theory of bonding was simply a rehearsal of old
ideas about maternal instinct dressed in the costume of scientific
research.

The notion of bonding first appeared in 1976 in an enormously influential book entitled *Maternal Infant Bonding* written
by two Australian paediatricians, John Kennell and Marshall
Klaus. Most simply put, their view was that in a time-specific
'sensitive period' shortly after birth, mother and infant become
emotionally tied if there is skin-to-skin contact; that is, if the

mother cuddles and cradles her baby for a certain amount of time. If attachment can be seen as invisible, elastic threads which link a mother and child over time and distance, bonding was the instant, modern version; a kind of emotional Velcro or superglue which instantly knit the two irrevocably together. Within a very short period, 'bonding time' became standard practice in most Western hospitals. Instead of being taken away to be cleaned and wrapped, babies were placed on their mothers' chests fresh from the womb.

What happened if for some reason a mother and a child 'failed to bond'? According to Klaus and Kennell's findings, women who missed the opportunity to bond with their newborns rejected them later, had a poor relationship with their children and sometimes abused them. The child itself would almost certainly develop less well than other children. It's no surprise then that in the maternity wards bonding became an absolute priority, a standard in which exhausted women were obliged to 'bond' with their babies for a minimum of ten minutes monitored by a nurse or midwife. Today it still is standard post-partum practice to ask a mother if she would like to hold her newborn straight away. And while it certainly does no harm – and a great many women do want to see their babies as soon as possible – no longer do hospital staff believe they must do so to 'bond'.

So how can a theory gain so much momentum only to be overturned and summarily rejected at a later date? The story starts with Klaus and Kennell, their work in neonatal intensive care units and their sustained efforts to make hospital practice more humane, more family friendly, less clinical and less austere. The two doctors noticed that many of the babies who spent their first months in intensive care often returned to the same hospital with problems associated with abuse, neglect or failure to thrive. They also noticed that the mothers of these infants seemed less concerned, less attentive to their children and less interested in their problems, in the opinion of the doctors, than other mothers.

The doctors also observed that when women whose premature or sick babies were in incubators went to visit them, the mothers seemed hesitant and unsure about touching or handling their newborns. They worried about feeding and taking care of them correctly and asked a lot of questions. From this Klaus and Kennell did not simply assume, as others might, that this was a perfectly logical response by someone faced with the daunting responsibility of caring for a fragile baby who might have died. They concluded instead that being nervous of touching a baby in an incubator was actually 'an aberration of the normal maternal behaviour'.[29]

John Bowlby developed some of his ideas about human mothers after he read about experiments with baby rhesus monkeys. Klaus and Kennell also began by observing human women and then looked to farmyard animals for the answer. They came across research carried out on goats which showed that if a nanny goat is separated from her newborn kid for as little as five minutes, she will butt it away and refuse to allow it to feed when it is presented to her. Klaus and Kennell asked themselves whether the same could happen with human mothers.

The doctors studied twenty-eight of the mothers in their care. Typically these were single, poor, inner-city women. When they published the results, they claimed that mothers who had sixteen extra hours of contact with their babies in the days following birth were 'more supportive and affectionate'[30] and were better mothers than those that did not. But what were the indicators of good mothering they used? One was how guilty the women said they felt if they left their children for a period of time (the guiltier the better) and another was how soon they returned to work (an early return was taken as a sign of bad mothering). The doctors tried to do follow-up studies of the mothers and infants for five years, but lost track of many. Nevertheless, from the remainder of their already small study they felt able to conclude that the babies who had the extra time with their mothers were better developed, more successful children, apparently all because of a few hours at a crucial time. On the basis of these findings, the theory of bonding was devised and it became the first study ever to claim to have found instinctual maternal behaviour common to all women.

The idea of bonding proved enormously popular, and in a short space of time made the leap out of the scientific journals into the popular press, women's magazines and childcare manuals. It became the buzzword of the 1980s. The notion was seized upon by social workers who, free from the restraints and caveats of academia, began freely to diagnose 'failure to bond' in instances of child abuse, family breakdown and parent–child relationships. Today it is often still part of the rhetoric of 'good' mothering. In an edition as late as 1991, long after the myth of bonding had been exposed, one of Vera Fahlberg's handbooks (almost the social worker's bible) devotes the first chapter to the importance of bonding, quoting Klaus and Kennell liberally. The post-partum bonding process as it should take place is described in detail: 'The newborn infant, when held horizontally, reflexively turns towards the person holding them. Parents are pleased when the infant looks at them. In turn they will usually gently caress the child.'[31] And so on. The section ends with the warning: 'Studies based on video-tapes of mother and child interactions made during deliveries and hospital stays indicate that when the mother does not take an active part in this claiming process, there is a high risk of severe mother–child difficulties in future months.'[32]

What about the mother who is too exhausted by a hard labour to hold her child? Or the woman undergoing emergency surgery? Or the woman who simply does not feel a burst of instant love upon the sight of her child? Or the woman who finds herself feeling distracted instead of elated? Or the hundreds of thousands of women who gave birth before hospital policy changed? They were now being told that their children's future happiness was at risk as a result of their inability or disinclination to perform a certain ritual in the moments after birth. As the bonding bandwagon gained momentum, 'poor bonding' was used as a cause of poor school performance, delinquency and autism as well as child abuse and neglect – all, apart from autism, viewed as social problems which were on the rise. Mothers were blamed for it all. Ideas drawn from Bowlby regarding psychopaths and thieves were revived and the terms 'attachment' and 'bonding' were used interchangeably.

Diane Eyer, a psychologist and academic, turned her attention to the bonding theory in the late 1980s. By then it had come under attack from any number of directions from within the medical and academic communities. 'The research on bonding', writes Eyer in a recent account of events following the publication of the bonding theory, 'is probably the most poorly conceived research in the entire maternal-deprivation canon.'[32]

First of all there were problems with Klaus and Kennell's study itself. Not only was the sample too small to be taken seriously, the methodology was suspect. The 'effects' the researchers used as indices were weak: how many times a baby is kissed or cuddled, the amount of eye contact, how many questions a mother asked. Their technique for quantifying or measuring behaviour was observation by the researchers themselves, who were far from objective. Michael Lamb, a British developmental psychologist, argued that the mothers who were the object of the study were likely to have received different treatment, namely more attention, from researchers. That might explain their willingness to, for example, ask more questions. Eyer herself points out that, astonishingly, Klaus and Kennell never tested women's hormone levels or conducted any kind of physical tests, even though they were claiming that bonding was a biologically-driven instinct.

Then there were the subsequent studies by other researchers. None confirmed Klaus and Kennell's claims, including a Swedish study[33] of fifty mothers and their babies and an exhaustive, rigorous 1980 study[34] of thirty women and their newborns. The literature which critiques bonding is extensive, compelling and conclusive. The theory did not hold up.

Central to the belief in bonding was the notion that women shared, along with other female animals, a common, predictable, instinct-driven form of maternal behaviour. Klaus and Kennell had freely lifted ideas and sought validation from the field of ethology but, as it later became evident, they misunderstood the research – specifically the research on goats and farmyard animals – on which they had relied so heavily.

Alice Sluckin is a social worker and an expert on psychopathology and child abuse. She is the widow of Wladyslaw Sluckin, a professor of psychology. The Sluckins, along with a colleague Martin Herbert, spent years investigating the bonding claims and came to the conclusion that Klaus and Kennell were simply wrong. In their book the three authors state: 'it is surely unprecedented to explain the acquisition of any other complex constellation of behaviours and attitudes in a *mature* human being in terms of imprinting. The idea of maternal bonding is deceptive because, on first acquaintance it is so simple and straightforward. Nothing could be further from the truth.'[35]

Wladyslaw Sluckin, who also specialized in animal behaviour, was convinced that there could be no such thing as a 'sensitive period' during which a mother bonds to her infant. He was certain that purely on an evolutionary basis it would be quite contrary to the needs of survival because so many mothers, in the past, died in childbirth. He held the opposite view to Klaus and Kennell: why would nature create a unique bond between mother and infant, if there was every chance that the infant might be raised by others? Research among different species of apes showed no evidence of bonding, and the success of adoption both in animals and in humans could only mean that bonding at birth is either non-essential or non-existent.

The three found that Klaus and Kennell had made a key error in their interpretation of animal behaviour. They thought that goats rebuffed kids who had been removed from them because a vital, instinctual process of bonding had been interrupted. They were wrong. The nanny goats rejected their returned offspring because they smelled different, they simply did not recognize these alien smells. In practice, outside the laboratory and in the farmyard, these odours would be the smell of another female. It was a simple olfactory labelling process at work. The goats perceived the kids, contaminated with the smell of the handlers and a different environment, to be the offspring of another female.

Looked at in the context of other cultures, the idea of bonding cannot be sustained. The anthropologist Nancy Scheper Hughes spent many years living and working among Brazilian mothers. She came to realize that the high infant mortality rate produced an expectancy among new mothers that the child would not survive; only when the child was old enough to be out of danger did the women allow themselves to become emotionally close to him or her. In the West we do much the same at an earlier stage. Women who first find out they are pregnant tend 'not to get their hopes up' and to keep the news quiet from family and friends until around the third month when the pregnancy is past the point where there is a substantial risk of miscarriage. The difference that the lack of health care makes to an infant's chances of survival makes the Brazilian mothers wait much longer before starting to invest emotionally in their child. So bonding, in so far as it can be said to exist, is not an instinctive process but a psychological one.

None of this explains why the idea of mother–infant bonding became so instantly popular and had such a massive impact so quickly. The idea struck a chord at a crucial time and appealed to different groups of people, from fundamentalists and family restorationists to feminists, for different reasons. Clearly for many it reaffirmed conservative views regarding the nature of women, but the social context of the early 1980s was more complex than that.

In those days hospital practice was almost completely consultant-led, becoming increasingly medicalized with the emphasis on efficiency rather than choice in childbearing. On the front pages of the newspapers, Wendy Savage, one of the country's few female consultant obstetricians, and champion of the midwives and of natural birth, fought the efforts of her male colleagues to oust her. Women were beginning to read the works of Sheila Kitzinger and the French obstetrician Michel Odent in favour of natural childbirth and to raise their voices against the often dehumanizing aspects (epitomized perhaps, by compulsory shaving and the stirrups) of giving birth in modern Western hospitals.

So, against that backdrop, evidence – actual scientific proof – that women needed time to bond with their babies after giving birth gave leverage and a big boost to the reformists' cause. Diane Eyer spoke to practitioners who kept quiet about their misgivings over the quality and findings of the research because they could see tangible benefits for women in changing maternity ward practices. These changes were effected in order to allow women to 'bond', for example as many caesareans as possible began to be carried out under local and not general anaesthetic. A whole new way of thinking emerged which emphasized women's choices in birth; it allowed women to be cared for by a midwife or a consultant; to be admitted into sitting rooms instead of wards near the time of delivery; and it moved families closer to centre-stage.

There was another reason why women were drawn to the idea of bonding. There had been a massive shift in the lives of women and many mothers of young children were now going out to work. From only a small percentage of women in the 1950s, by 1973 mothers were going out to work in 43 per cent of families, a figure which would rise to 60 per cent by 1992.[36] Women were suffering (and being made to suffer) tremendous guilt about leaving their children; politicians and social critics were talking about 'latch-key' kids; finding quality daycare was, and still is, a problem. Notice all the old attachment ideas resurfacing? Bonding offered an instant solution to all their problems. Just a few minutes spent after giving birth and their relationship with their child would be secure. No wonder the idea was so appealing.

Most of all, the theory of bonding was accepted without question because it conveniently fits a set of pre-existing assumptions about motherhood and women, in particular the idea that all women are inherently suited to motherhood. Bonding stated that biology was indeed destiny and that only when natural, instinctual processes are interrupted, do women fail at motherhood. The truth might be that not all women are natural, happy and devoted mothers.

The guru legacy

The modern maternal ideal was the product of a changed society. Today society is changing once more, but women who become mothers now, in an era where issues related to motherhood have become highly politicized, are told that in order to be 'good' mothers they have to fit an archaic mould ill-suited to their actual lives.

Even in what some people would regard as the golden days of the 1950s, poor women, immigrant women and black women didn't drop their jobs at Bowlby's command and return home to fix the supper in a twinset and pearls. They continued to work because they had to. In many parts of the world, where children are raised by several people in multi-generational households, notions of 'attachment' to a single, ever-present mother have absolutely no relevance whatsoever. Everything we understand about the family, child development and family relationships must be seen in that light. There are no rules, no absolute predictors, only context. What we are looking at, writes Nancy Chodorow, is 'a socially and historically specific mother–child relationship of a particular intensity and exclusivity and a particular infantile development that this relationship produces'.[37]

The truth is that an overpowering motherhood ideal creates problems in itself. When a particular way of being mothered, which requires money and a husband as well as the total commitment and fulfilment of the mother, is described as a birthright, it sets up a massive level of expectation. It is unrealistic, but is it even desirable? A growing number of professionals now argue that the close bond we have tried so hard to produce between mother and child has become stifling. Children now group up in tiny, private family units with minimal input from other adults. The wider community has freed itself of any responsibility regarding the raising of young children, leaving their care entirely in the hands of their mothers. Nowadays few of us will tackle youngsters misbehaving in the streets and we even hesitate before approaching a lost child. 'Where's the mother?' we ask instead.

The legacies of all the gurus remain. The enduring belief that mothers ought to be at home, and that children's well-being requires their absolute and unswerving commitment to the task of mothering is no accident, no twist of biology and fate. The idea was the product of a particular time and place in history. It was the result of beliefs held by a group of people who took one basic, simple and apparently unassailable notion – that it was natural for women to nurture babies – and constructed upon that simple premise a complex set of beliefs about 'good mothering'.

We continue to embrace the established style of mothering as the correct way to mother. It has become regarded as natural, as the standard against which all mothers should be measured. Over time the framework of this vision has been built upon, added to, the detail fleshed out and the ideology absorbed into every sphere of life.

chapter 4

Motherhood in
Popular Culture

Testimony: Rebecca

Rebecca, thirty-two, is an Englishwoman with a Finnish husband, whom she met while living and working in France. Together they ran the sales division of a company in the USA where their first baby was conceived in November 1994. After six months they returned to Britain.

When I had been pregnant for about a week we went to Florida for a kind of wild holiday just before a trade show. There were lots of bars, smoking, drinking and having a good time. [The show] involved taking lots of customers out and late nights. I felt tired but I thought it was just pressure of work. Then I missed my period and eventually went to the doctor when I was already about sixteen weeks gone.

When I actually realized I was pregnant I didn't give up smoking but I cut down. I gave up spirits but I was still drinking beer and wine. Every alcohol bottle you get in Massachusetts has a government warning on the label about pregnancy and drinking. Knowing that I was probably going to have the baby in America and knowing how strongly they feel I lied about the amount I was drinking. I told the doctor that I was drinking one glass of wine a week and she told me it was highly discouraged and I should cut out alcohol completely. I didn't mention smoking. I would brush my teeth well before I went because I knew in America, if the slightest thing was wrong, they would do an automatic caesarean. But also it was about how they might view you, whether they would give you a better or a poorer service because they knew you were drinking or smoking. In my mind I thought I might be discriminated against.

We were in a hotel in New York and I ordered an alcohol-free beer and mentioned to the person I was with that I was having a baby. Later I ordered a real beer. [The barman] said: 'I just heard you say you were pregnant', and said he had instructions not to serve alcohol to women who were pregnant. There was a huge sign up behind the bar.

When I was twenty-one I got pregnant and didn't realize. I was working in a wine bar and we drank heavily there, it was also a very smoky atmosphere. I remember I was frightened if I continued with the pregnancy the child would be damaged or have some kind of deformity. This time I was convinced up until the day Tara was born that she was going to be deformed in some way.

It's not being able to see, not being able to know. With a baby you can't check what's going on. If you could look into your womb you could measure your behaviour but you can't and there's so much pressure around you. I was careful what I was seen to do in public.

I bought a couple of books. It was like learning a new world. Suddenly you hear it over and over again. It was the same with articles and books on pregnancy. They're everywhere and you read them more interestedly than you did before. I remember it was very cold that year and as I lay in bed with my electric blanket on I read that [it] could damage the foetus. From then on I stopped using the blanket. Whether you become irrational when you're pregnant or whether it's because you have so much information thrown at you constantly, you start believing everything people say. When I came back to England I was talking to [someone] about car journeys and she told me a long car journey I was planning might 'dislodge' the baby. She said that in the late part of pregnancy the ligaments can become jostled and it can actually dislodge the foetus. It did start me worrying.

I think that in both France and Finland it's more relaxed. We went to Finland at Christmas after Tara was born. They don't have sterilizing equipment there, they just wash and air-dry bottles and teats, so I just went along with it. It was much easier and much more relaxed but I haven't admitted that over here. They would think I didn't care. The funny thing was that Tara got her first cold then, and my reaction was, 'Oh God, it's because I didn't sterilize the bottles.' I was in tears over that.

I think they'll get to the stage in some places where they put all pregnant women into an isolated room and feed them certain amounts of carbohydrate and protein and all the rest of it. You can't be pregnant and have a normal life trying to follow all the advice. In America you can't even drive after six months. There's a tremendous amount of worry about whether you're doing it right or not.

Tara was born 17 August 1995, and weighed 8lb 13oz.

If it was the 'experts' of the post-war period who first began to try to mould mothers in a particular image, then in the late twentieth century, and appropriately in our new 'information age', it is popular culture which has taken over the job of enforcing the boundaries of behaviour for mothers, deciding who should or should not be a mother, praising the 'good' mothers and admonishing the 'bad'.

Thousands of articles are published in the field of pregnancy, childbirth and childcare every year. It's routine material for the women's pages and health sections of daily newspapers. In addition there are a myriad of specialist magazine titles such as *Mother & Baby*, *Parents* and *Practical Parenting*. On the Internet the number of home pages and advice sources multiplies every day. Alongside the yards of advice issued to pregnant women are the stories of lost or stolen babies; the heroine mothers; the debates over who gets fertility treatment; the pack attacks on working mothers in the 1970s, then single mothers in the 1980s and in the 1990s on working mothers once again.

The river of comment flows inexorably in one direction and with one goal: to reinforce the narrow ideal of the perfect mother. That is reflected in the warning tone of many articles designed to provoke guilt or fear. Useful information is often lost under the sheer mass of material, accuracy has given way to hyperbole. The collective burden of all the advice which is offered on a daily, weekly, annual basis is intolerable and it would require someone of superhuman capabilities to follow it all. The futility of trying to conform to so many pressures means that many mothers feel like failures, and the lasting effect on almost all mothers is the battle with guilt which has come to characterize modern motherhood.

The pressure is being turned on just as women are trying to reshape their lives to adapt their role as mothers to the twists and turns of social change. Popular culture feeds off generally-held fears and anxieties and creates its own momentum. When Penelope Leach first published her new child-centred philosophy of the family and began to admonish career-oriented mothers and fathers, the women's magazines ran features which punctured the myth of 'having it all'. When the government, with an eye on social security cuts, turned its attention to lone parents, the press was quick to find examples of unfit single mothers. When, as a society, we began to agonize over what role had been left for men after feminism, the papers gave us stories about women who preferred the home hearth to their high-flying jobs. This isn't a world media conspiracy; it is the collective seeking comfort in familiar roles. Less benignly, it indicates a willingness to blame mothers for what is wrong in society, part of the same school of thought which teaches us to blame our own individual mothers (and their imperfections) for our problems.

Trying to control the behaviour of mothers is in essence a displacement activity for all the other things we cannot control, or (and perhaps this is closer to the truth) those we lack the will to change. Car fumes are burning a hole in the ozone layer and causing an asthma epidemic among our children, so pregnant women are told to avoid filling the car or using fume-filled underground car parks. Cigarette companies are targeting children *en masse* in the less developed countries of the world, but it is the pregnant woman who smokes a post-prandial cigarette in a Western restaurant who takes the flack. The seas are awash with toxic waste, chemicals leach into the rivers, hazardous dump sites border playgrounds and while the rest of us continue to consume obscene quantities, we ensure pregnant women eat only what is nutritious and don't 'poison' their bodies with alcohol or additives. We are risking the future of the world and of countless generations, but the woman who 'risks' the future of her unborn child has become the villain. The person of the mother-to-be has become a microcosm for the disintegrating social and physical environment.

The pregnancy police

In 1995 an advert appeared on British television which warned women not to argue with their partners while they were pregnant.[1] The commercial showed in graphic detail the distress caused to an unborn child while the parents were arguing. In the last century knowledge of the physical changes that took place during pregnancy was minimal; today, microscopic cameras can enter the womb and film a sperm fertilizing the egg. Science has logged the minutiae of pregnancy. Pity the pregnant woman! No sooner are the congratulations over than she finds she is subject to an endless stream of information, advice and warnings. Her every action will be observed and monitored, her every deviation noted. As medical advances identify ever smaller risks, the responsibilities of maternity grow until every aspect of a pregnant woman's behaviour is open to scrutiny, risk assessment and control. It's little wonder that women so often comment that they feel as though carrying a child has turned them into public property.

Playing Big Brother to pregnant women is a role that the media perform with relish. The dangers of caffeine, passive smoking, household cleaning fluids, sex, exercise (too much or too little), unpasteurized dairy products and spicy foods are catalogued. Every possible danger to the foetus is covered; new surveys and findings are gleaned for statistics to chill the heart of any woman concerned for her child; graphic descriptions are given of the deformities and foetal abnormalities that might arise if she neglects any one of the myriad instructions she is issued with.

In the late 1970s and early 1980s matters were quite different. Campaigning journalism still existed. Then the articles written about motherhood and pregnancy by women such as Jill Tweedie and Polly Toynbee focused on issues such as abortion and contraceptives; the unnecessary use of caesarean sections; childbirth choices; authoritarian hospital regimes. By contrast, today the focus has shifted away from the woman and is now directed entirely towards the foetus, and it is the unborn child who is seen to be in need of protection, not from over-zealous hospital authorities, but from its own mother.

This is the rhetoric of blame. Do this, the expectant mother is told, and your child will be healthy. Fail and the consequences will be your fault. Women's fears make them vulnerable and that vulnerability is a rich seam which can be exploited. In purely journalistic terms, it makes good copy because such stories are inevitably hard to ignore. In recognition of that fact, the tone of most stories is alarmist even by the usual inflammatory standards of tabloid journalism.

It's instructive just to read the first line of such stories. Here the laws of cause and effect are spelt out in such a way as to induce as much guilt as possible. So: 'A mother's diet during pregnancy may condemn her child to heart disease decades later'[2] is how an item on the environmental and genetic influences of heart disease begins. In the health pages of a broadsheet, a small column item starts with the ominous words: 'Pregnant women drinking three cups of coffee a day or more can substantially increase the chance of losing their baby or retarding growth of the foetus.'[3] 'Women who smoke during pregnancy may damage the fertility of their children',[4] warned another. 'Smoker mums kill babies' screamed tabloid headlines reporting the results of a study which linked cot deaths with passive smoking.[5] What readers don't usually realize is that the studies cited are frequently small scale and usually show a *correlation* between a certain behaviour and a certain result, but in scientific terms that is very different from showing a *cause*, let alone proof. What's more, where once academic rigour used to demand that studies be repeated before their findings were generally accepted, nowadays the Popperian view (that science is as much about disproving theories as proving them) has been abandoned. Researchers do not have the time or money for, or interest in, repeating other people's experiments. They have to move on swiftly to the next 'discovery' on which their future grant application depends.

The realistic chances of anything going wrong are not allowed to stand in the way of a good scare story. In March 1995 the *Daily Mirror* claimed: 'red tape puts babies at risk.'[6] The piece, by the paper's medical correspondent, linked a government restriction on advertising with the risk of giving birth to a disabled child. The argument went like this: taking folic acid during pregnancy has been shown to offer the child some protection from spina bifida, indeed the Department of Health advises women to take folic acid as a food supplement during pregnancy. But, said the *Mirror*, the same government refuses to allow manufacturers of folic acid to advertise such items of information because it is not a licensed drug. Therefore the paper draws the conclusion that 'millions of women are not taking the daily pill which could prevent the trauma of abortion or the agony of having a handicapped child'.

The truth is that in England and Wales there are around 1,000 spina bifida conceptions each year, of which three-quarters are spotted early and terminated. Women are routinely advised by their doctors and health workers to take folic acid. Any direct connection drawn between those births and the restriction which prevents manufacturers from advertising the benefits of folic acid is unproven and entirely spurious. Nevertheless, this did not deter the newspaper from running the article.

Another story spun from hot air and hype comes from the *Independent*, a broadsheet which, incidentally, prides itself on its refusal to subscribe to fads, as well as on its responsible reporting and its modern, emancipated readership. In 1993 it ran a lead article on the results of a new study of schizophrenia. Next to a silhouetted picture of a pregnant woman contemplating her swollen belly the headline read, 'When winter's chill is too much for baby' and the strapline below expanded: 'A new study suggests there is some link between flu in a pregnant mother and schizophrenia in her child.'[7] The piece began with the words: 'Pregnant women will inevitably be among those who catch flu in the current round: Could the result be a child who subsequently develops schizophrenia?' Yet after such an extraordinarily provocative start there proved to be little or nothing to back up such a claim. What the research had shown was that a woman's immune response to flu might have some, as yet unproven, link to perhaps 5 per cent of schizophrenia cases. One must ask oneself, in any other circumstances would a daily newspaper even bother to report such a minor medical finding let alone devote half a page to it?

How people assess, quantify and respond to risk is currently a question which is attracting academic interest. Western populations become more and more fearful of any kind of risk, demand greater controls, want a guaranteed risk-free environment. But how justified is our apprehension? How likely are the dangers, how real are the hazards? Minute chances become distorted, danger lurks in everything: in the food we consume, in the darkened doorway, in the air we breathe. To combat our fears we drive our children to school in ever larger and heavier vehicles, decline to have them immunized, refuse to go abroad. The pregnant woman, with the unborn child sheltering in her womb, finds herself at the sharp end of a growing, media-fuelled inability to find balance in a world where risk is unavoidable.

The fixation with maternal health and behaviour is not mirrored when it comes to male reproductive health. There are now a growing number of studies linking men's smoking, drinking and drug-use to the incidence of foetal harm, but in stark contrast these reports find little interest among magazine editors and TV news programmes. According to Cynthia Daniels, who has investigated media coverage of male fertility problems, 'men have been spared the retribution aimed at women'.[8] When stories are covered, the style is more often humorous, accompanied by cartoons which depict little sperm battling against chemical invasion, and they tend to focus on external, environmental harms rather than implicating men's lifestyles or habits. There's also a total absence of the kind of rhetoric and blame which characterizes texts on maternal foetal harm.

The expectant mother wants the best for her child, but what hope has she of assessing or quantifying the information she receives? The sheer scale of it makes it impossible to follow. Some of it even conflicts. Recent stories in British and American newspapers now report that babies are at risk from their mother's healthy eating.[9] According to those sources, carbohydrates such as cereal, pulses, rice and potatoes inhibit placenta growth and result in smaller babies who are in turn at risk of heart disease later in life. A woman's doctor may have advised an ultrasound or amniocentesis, yet she reads every week of the dangers with which those tests are associated. In the USA, in the same week as the national current affairs show *Dateline* aired a report telling parents to have their babies sleeping in the same bed for at least the first two years (to ensure proper attachment!), the Consumer Product Safety Commission published warnings to the opposite effect and revealed that a hundred children a year die of suffocation sleeping in their parents' bed.

A 'factoid' is a piece of information which people have heard at some point and believe to be true. Like its counterpart the urban myth, no one is quite certain of its origins. 'I read somewhere,' they say, or 'It was on TV'. 'Pregnant women who eat pineapples can miscarry' is an example of a factoid. The subject of pregnancy, so complex and mysterious anyway, is rich with half-baked ideas passing as fact and old wives' tales given as advice. Factoids are the light artillery of the self-styled pregnancy police. They know what the pregnant woman should or shouldn't do and they don't mind telling her because in their role as protectors of the unborn and defenders of 'good' motherhood, these ordinary citizens have earned the right to prescribe and control women's behaviour.

In addition to trying to avoid actually damaging her baby, there are also the 'extras' to contemplate. It is a modern mother's duty to produce a baby who is super-intelligent, stimulated and healthy and so she needs to start to think about early schooling. How early? Well, in the womb, actually; pre-school is already too late. Playing music, strapping on contraptions designed to provide sonic stimulation to the foetus, flashing lights against her belly and starting some basic vowel sounds are part of the pre-natal learning programme. Once her super-baby is born she may want to take the advice recently issued in the *Independent on Sunday* and consider eating the placenta for its invaluable nutrients.[10]

The obsession with the physical health of pregnant women and their foetuses illustrates a curious meeting of the minds of two apparently diverse groups. It is a bizarre and unwitting alliance between, on the one hand, those who would seek to control women's behaviour in small and in great ways, dictating how they can and cannot behave, and, on the other hand, those (of whom many are women), who subscribe to the yuppie ethos of 'having it all'. For behind the fussing over vitamins is the fundamentally unsound motivation of the child as product. If you do everything right, if you follow the rules, if you eat the correct foods, if you play music through the womb wall, the thinking dictates you will have the best child, the child of your dreams. A perfect baby is a 'result'. So although the advice and the warnings are framed in terms of what is 'best for baby', for many people the desires and needs being fulfilled are actually their own. Whose desires, whose agenda? Ours or our children's?

The foetal alcohol syndrome (FAS) scare

If there's one fact that most of us know, it is that pregnant women should not drink alcohol. Even if we are not clear about the exact facts, we know that alcohol in some way affects the development of the foetus and that, along with cigarettes and all kinds of drugs, alcohol is forbidden to pregnant women. It is also understood that any responsible woman who believes she might have conceived will immediately turn down the offer of a drink. Often it is the first clue friends pick up on. If the mother-to-be doesn't know the phrase by the time she makes her announcement, she will not get more than a few weeks into her pregnancy before she hears the words 'foetal alcohol syndrome'.

In the late 1950s and early 1960s French researchers had begun to investigate links between certain foetal abnormalities and alcohol consumption before and during pregnancy, but it was the findings of two researchers, Smith and Jones, published in the *Lancet* in 1973 that first brought attention to the problem of drinking in pregnancy and coined the phrase 'foetal alcohol syndome' (FAS).[11] Their study of the offspring of eight chronically alcoholic women identified certain abnormalities found in their children and directly related them to damage suffered in the womb caused by the mothers' alcohol intake.

There is no denying the appalling tragedy that results from foetal alcohol syndrome. FAS children are instantly recognizable. Their heads are often noticeably smaller than usual and their brains underdeveloped. They may suffer stunted growth, retardation and behavioural problems. Many share the facial disfigurements which typify the FAS child: small, wide-apart eyes, a short upturned nose, receding chin, sometimes a cleft palate.

Following the release of Smith and Jones's work, a myriad of small-scale studies and reports of individual cases flooded in from as far afield as Denmark, Hungary, Poland, Australia, France and Scotland. All confirmed the findings of the earlier study.

Foetal alcohol syndrome became one of the 'buzzwords' of the 1980s. Newspapers, television documentaries and women's magazines provided acres of coverage of the dangers of drinking alcohol during pregnancy. Most doctors in the USA and many in Britain routinely advise women to abstain from alcohol throughout their pregnancy. Dating from the early 1980s, state laws in many parts of America require that bars and even bottles carry warnings to pregnant women, or women who think they might be pregnant, not to drink. As recently as 1993 new laws required bars and restaurants in Toronto to display a sign with the words: 'Warning! Drinking beer, wine or spirits during pregnancy can harm your baby.'

The children in Smith and Jones's study, however, were the offspring of chronic alcoholics, women who, the researchers pointed out, were not at all typical in their drinking habits. Even while the research was being conducted, two were hospitalized with delirium brought on by drink. The fact is that foetal alcohol syndrome is associated with very heavy alcohol intake, that is 10 units (80g) a day according to a study carried out by Smith himself and published five years after the first.[12] Another study by Robert Sokol, now Director of the National Fetal Alcohol Research Center in Detroit, put the figure at at least 6 units (48g) a day, that is six drinks: six glasses of wine or gin and tonics or whiskies every single day.[13] An enormous amount by anyone's standards. Many of the women with affected children drank far more than this. One of the subjects was in such a drunken stupor when she gave birth that she had no idea what was happening to her. Another was admitted to hospital during the course of her pregnancy for treatment associated with alcohol dependency. It is worth noting that there were a significant proportion who drank in such quantities and produced unaffected children.

So how did such findings come to be translated into headlines which read: 'Two glasses of wine knock 7 points off unborn child's IQ', or 'Drink during pregnancy "can create murderers"'?[14] Why do many people now believe that a single drink can cause FAS and feel free to frown upon and even to abuse a woman enjoying a drink?

Popular baby books now warn even prospective parents of the danger of consuming any alcohol at all.[15] For example, *Planning for a Healthy Baby* advises both partners to drink 'no alcohol in the preconception phase for both partners and during pregnancy for the woman'. According to the same volume, women who want to be really safe should consider becoming teetotal during their childbearing years. *The Complete Handbook of Pregnancy* goes even further. Again, both partners should give up drinking, this time for six months before conception. The author feels no compunction about extending an already tall order to include avoiding the lead from petrol fumes, aspirins and caffeine, too.

A typical advice leaflet for pregnant women illustrates the kind of extreme pressure placed on women when dealing with this issue. The document is illustrated with cartoon images of a foetus pleading with its mother (humanizing the foetus is a classic way of maximizing feelings of guilt). 'Mum, please don't put me at risk', says the unborn child. Over the page the text of the leaflet warns: 'Alcohol even in moderation could possibly interfere with the growth and development of your child.' Below those words is the drawing of the child with the words, 'I feel awful – my Mum's drinking again.'[16]

How did such a moral panic about foetal alcohol syndrome come about? In a paper for the World Health Organization published in 1990, Moira Plant, a leading authority on foetal alcohol syndrome at Edinburgh University in the UK, traced the history of how FAS came to be so misrepresented in the public mind. After Smith and Jones's research was made public, she writes: 'What happened after this is difficult to understand . . . yet soon generalizations appeared from specific problem drinking women like those in Jones et al.'s study to all women who drink, even in moderation.'[17]

In her account, a turning point came in 1981 when the United States Surgeon General issued an important statement on FAS. It said: 'Each patient should be told about the risk of alcohol consumption during pregnancy and advised not to drink alcoholic beverages and to be aware of the alcoholic content of food and drugs.' That is, women should not drink at all. According to Plant, the controversial statement was highly influential, not simply because of its source but also because it coincided with the publication of the first major studies on FAS in the United States. Nevertheless, the statement was groundless. 'This statement had extended concern from women who drink heavily to women drinkers in general. There was little or no good evidence at that time to warrant so sweeping a warning,' Plant wrote.

By doing this, the US authorities, in the particular political climate of the time, gave official sanction to those moralists who sought to control the behaviour of pregnant women. In the 1980s, during the Reagan administration, the moral majority was at the height of its powers and the struggle over abortion rights between the moral majority and feminists and liberals dominated the political agenda. The propaganda of the Right, in attempting to overturn federal abortion legislation, asserted that women could no longer be trusted to protect their unborn children. Closely tied in with the idea that women were capable of killing their children was the notion that they were also capable of harming their children in other ways, either through wilfulness or neglect. Foetal rights and women's rights came into conflict in a way which had never been seen before.

Partly, too, it was the fault of the medical profession who were too quick to diagnose the new syndrome to cover a multitude of sins. Kenneth Jones, whose original research brought FAS to the attention of the world in 1973, was one of a number of experts who put their name to a paper in the professional magazine *Paediatrics* in September 1994 to criticize the recent use of the term 'foetal alcohol effects' or FAE, a less severe form of FAS:

> Unfortunately, within a few years after its introduction, the designation fetal alcohol effect (FAE) began to be applied more or less indiscriminately to children with a variety of problems, even those with simple growth deficiency or isolated behavioural aberration, based almost entirely on the knowledge (or suspicion) that their mothers drank alcohol during pregnancy. Not only clinicians, but concerned teachers, social workers, and foster parents, seeking explanations for the problems of children under their care seized upon the 'diagnosis' of FAE.[18]

And, of course, there was no doubt who was to blame: the mothers. Jones summarized the problem: 'Women are stigmatized for having damaged their children by drinking during pregnancy when it is by no means certain that they have done so.'

The fear and the worry inflicted on some women by misinformation regarding FAS have sometimes had devastating results. In Toronto, as the state debated the mandatory posting of signs warning pregnant women not to drink, an obstetrician at the Hospital for Sick Children reported that many women were seeking abortions on the grounds that they drank before they discovered they had conceived.[19] Typically these women were moderate drinkers whose unborn children were highly unlikely to have been harmed.

Jones was not the only one of the original FAS experts who has since tried to calm the hysteria. Doctors Henry Rosett and

Lynn Weiner published a book on FAS in 1984 entitled 'Alcohol and the Fetus'.[20] At that time, noting the excesses to which fear of FAS was being carried in wider society they remarked:

> In our society people have intense feelings about alcohol abuse, maternal responsibility and child welfare. Consequently there has been a tendency for research findings to be seized upon, interpreted and used by well-intentioned groups with a variety of social goals . . .
>
> Whatever the reasons many pregnant women have had sleepless nights and worry over exaggerated risks of small amounts of alcohol harming the unborn child.

Although Dr Rosett has since died, his former colleague Dr Weiner has subsequently gone on record to say that nothing that has happened since has tempered her conclusion that moderate alcohol consumption during pregnancy is harmless.[21] Today, in countries like Britain and New Zealand if not in the United States (where doctors give advice aware of the threat of a malpractice suit), there has been some reassessment of the risks of FAS and attempts by responsible health professionals to correct the inaccuracies. It is now also thought that the true figures for FAS births are much lower than were at first reported.[22] Once estimated at around 1 in a 1,000 in the Western world, that figure has now been reduced to 0.33 per 1,000. There has even been new evidence casting doubt on whether FAS should actually be called foetal *alcohol* syndrome at all. In other words, the link between alcohol and foetal harm may not even be as clear as was previously thought. One carefully controlled study showed that women of lower economic status with poorer nutrition who drank heavily during their pregnancy were almost sixteen times more likely to have children with FAS symptoms than middle-class women who drank the same amount.[23] In fact, the middle-income women had only a minimal chance of giving birth to an FAS child. The crucial factor was food. One group of women ate sufficient quantities of food, and enjoyed a balanced diet. The other group frequently missed meals and ate only small amounts of meat and fresh vegetables.

Despite these findings, the public perception is little changed. The layman prefers the wisdom of 'better safe than sorry', and sorry the expectant mother will be made to feel if there is anything wrong with her baby when it is born.

Low milk and yuppie mothers

On 22 July 1994 the *Wall Street Journal* ran a front-page article entitled: 'Dying for Milk, Some Mothers Trying in Vain to Breast-Feed Starve Their Infants.' At the top of the piece was the story of Chaz Floyd who suffered irreversible brain damage caused by dehydration after he failed to receive enough milk from his mother's breast. 'The lack of milk those first few days means that Chaz will never lead a normal life,' the attendant neurologist was quoted as saying. Remarks from Chaz's mother Pamela were included: 'I can't stop asking myself "Pam, why didn't you ignore all the experts and give him a bottle?"' Kevin Helliker, the author of the piece, continued: 'Days old babies are returning to hospital dehydrated and starved.' He estimated that there were a thousand cases nationwide and the 'numbers are rising rapidly'.

Breastfeeding is already a highly politicized issue. In some quarters the pro-breastfeeding lobby have been seen as over-zealous in emphasizing the benefits of the breast and condemning formula. The attention a baby requires of its mother during the period of breastfeeding is constant, as feeding typically takes place every few hours. Making women feel that in order to be a good mother they must breastfeed, sometimes for up to two years, ignores the demands and realities of a woman's life.

At first sight Helliker's article might appear to support women in pointing out that breastfeeding is not necessarily best. Indeed, he even touched on the debate, but his story had quite a different slant: he blamed the mothers. Central to Helliker's article and flagged in the strap-line below the heading, was the idea that the mothers responsible for starving their children were yuppies. They were, 'A generation of perfectionists' who approached childrearing as they approached their careers; determined to score highly on all points, they were blinded to the terrible suffering of their babies. 'The more intelligence and education the parents have, the greater the danger seems to be,' declared expert opinion.

It was an irresistible story, another angle from which to attack working women with children as 'bad mothers'. The sub-text was clear: these were women whom exposure to a man's world had robbed of the natural ability to mother. They neglected their children by going out to work and then they risked their babies' lives by being so emotionally detached that they had to learn their mothering skills from books and compounded the problem by ignoring the cries of their malnourished infants. The story was picked up and carried by newspapers and television programmes throughout the USA. Many local papers published rewritten versions of the *Wall Street Journal* piece; the NBC programme *Prime Time* carried a segment and *Time* magazine brought the story to the international forum.

By the time it appeared on the other side of the Atlantic, the facts of the story had become totally distorted and inflated. The 'Scandal of mothers who risk starving their babies' told of 'casualty wards around the States' reporting that 'thousands of babies are being rushed in gasping for sustenance'.[24] They were almost entirely the children of 'well-to-do professionals'. The source was given as a 'major study carried out in US hospitals' which, as things turned out, would prove to be completely untrue.

At the offices of La Leche League (a campaigning organization which provides advice and practical support on breastfeeding) in Chicago, the telephone calls began. Most were from anxious mothers requiring more information on the risks associated with breastfeeding. Despite the advice from La Leche workers, some insisted they were switching to formula immediately. Around the country doctors stopped actively promoting breastfeeding and hospitals began telling mothers to supplement their infants' feed with formula.

From their own knowledge of breastfeeding and of insufficient-milk production, La Leche workers Betty Crase and Mary Lockton were convinced that such fear was groundless and that the true figures of women who failed to produce enough milk could never be as high as the 5 per cent quoted. Holes were already beginning to appear in the original story. Pam Floyd, mother of the brain-damaged infant, had revealed on television that her son had suffered gestational diabetes as well as being born with a broken clavicle. He had been a very sick child from the beginning. A Florida newspaper which ran Helliker's original article added a note from the editor to the effect that checks with state hospitals had revealed no cases of low-milk syndrome locally.

Betty Crase decided to track the origins of the 5 per cent figure. The article referred to a Denver paediatrician who put the figure of women affected by 'insufficient-milk syndrome' at 5 per cent of mothers or around 200,000 a year in the USA. The figure of 1,000 babies at risk of starvation was based on this information and the fact that, according to Helliker, 'some emergency rooms are reporting dozens of severe cases a year'.

The Denver paediatrician quoted in the *Wall Street Journal* was Marianne Neifert, whom Crase knew professionally. Neifert specialized in the area of insufficient-milk production and had co-authored a specialist book on breastfeeding. She said she had drawn the figure from other literature and added that it appeared to correspond with a count of women at her clinic (not particularly representative since the clinic specialized in 'problem' women) which she put at 4 per cent. Well, that could just about pass as a 'guestimate' but it's hardly the 'major study' claimed by the *Mail on Sunday*.

The low-milk scare went as it came, but like other stories of its kind it left a mark. At a conscious level these stories are designed to play ruthlessly on the guilt and anxiety which mothers today experience routinely. Journalists often find support from a medical establishment constantly chasing funding and looking to justify its own work. The experience of the low-milk scare is evidence that these glibly-told stories do have an effect. They attack at a subconscious level, leaving imprinted on the public memory the idea of working women as freaks of nature and their children as the sad victims of modern motherhood gone awry. Mary Lockton of La Leche observes of the current attitude to mothers: 'There's a lack of belief in women, an automatic assumption that women today can't deliver.'

Selflessness, selfishness and the rise of maternal correctness

'Maternal correctness' came of age in December 1994 when the tabloids were able to report with unconcealed glee that Penny Hughes, the thirty-five-year-old head of Coca-Cola in Britain and rumoured to earn in excess of £250,000, was giving up her position to be a stay-at-home mum. The story was manna from heaven for the growing number of family restorationists in the media with a special interest in reviving the traditional mother's role.

The tabloids were captivated. Working mothers had been untouchable for years – after all, any number of the women's page editors rushed home to nannies after work – but now here were career women themselves giving up, claiming that they really didn't want the trappings of success, only the trappings of maternity. And no one had to point the finger. Esther Oxford, writing in the *Independent* soon after the Penny Hughes story broke, coined the term 'maternal correctness' to describe the apparent new fashion among career women to exchange their jobs for full-time motherhood.

It was an ingenious line of attack. First of all it brought the argument about whether mothers really belonged in the workplace back into the spotlight. It also brought the motherhood debate, as played out in the media at least, full circle by co-opting women to the side of tradition. Hughes's story came to typify the media's new morality in motherhood.

A year before, the focus of interest had been quite different. In Italy, a sixty-two-year-old woman became a mother assisted by modern scientific techniques. In the papers the story ran throughout most of July and August. Rosanna della Corte and her husband Mauro, whose only son had died in a car accident some years earlier, had a 7lb baby boy. Rosanna even said she would like another child one day. The doctor who helped her had pioneered fertility work with older women at his clinic in Rome, including some British women. In fact, the previous year (1992), Dr Severino Antinori had been forced to call off a trip to Britain to answer his critics after the publicity surrounding his work had resulted in a death threat.

'Could it ever happen here?'[25] asked the *Daily Mail* as the public debate on whether post-menopausal women should be 'allowed' to have children in this way gathered momentum. It did happen here, less than a month later. Sally Adams, using the name Jane Ward, sought fertility treatment at the age of fifty-seven. 'Defying nature to become a mother', wrote Lisa Sewards in the *Daily Express*.[26] Nearly every newspaper carried a report. One Sunday paper headlined its piece, 'This lonely woman who wants a baby for the wrong reasons'[27] (alongside a picture of Adams looking, in fact, remarkably youthful). The writer, Lorraine Fraser, went on to discuss the 'doubtful motives behind the wish of a 57-year-old to bear a child'. The article questioned more than Sally Adams's motives; it questioned her sexuality as well as her relationship with her own mother.

These women were condemned as selfish for wanting children, as though their age affected their ability to parent or to love. In the course of the debate some commentators accurately pointed out that no one queried a man's right or wish to parent in his fifties, sixties or even seventies. Indeed, we often look admiringly upon such men.

For mothers it is different, as Elizabeth Buttle discovered when she became Britain's oldest mother at the age of sixty in 1998. She found her name and reputation smeared across the popular press when it was alleged she had attended a private clinic for fertility treatment. Questions were also raised about the well-being of the child. Attitudes to older mothers reflect commonly-held assumptions about the roles and duties of motherhood. It is precisely because all the responsibility for children is left with the mother that an older woman with a child is viewed with disapproval in a way that a father is not. The fact that a man might not live to see his child's fifth birthday is regarded as virtually immaterial. It is the woman who is labelled 'selfish'.

In sharp contrast to the villain mothers are the mothers who are portrayed as saints. Top of the list of the qualities that these mothers enshrine is selflessness. In media terms, the ultimate 'motherhood' story is an exclusive on a woman who has made the ultimate sacrifice: a woman who has died in childbirth, or died trying to bear a child, or, best of all, who has died so her child could live. These stories are run regularly, the prose is heavy with pathos and the picture content is high.

'Whose life, hers or her baby's? Gaynor could not have both,' was the story of woman who declined both a termination and treatment for inoperable stomach cancer so that she could become a mother.[28] 'No greater love, a remarkable story of one woman's courage, devotion and sacrifice', read the caption. On the BBC, *The Labours of Eve* chronicled personal stories of pain, danger and the extremes of childbearing. In the minds of commissioners, film-makers and viewers, motherhood like religion is inextricably linked with themes of sacrifice and dedication, and thus the 'good' mother is one who endures. These are the mothers who are venerated. They are tragic creatures whose image is held up before us. They prefer death to childlessness, they choose motherhood over life.

Women who cross continents to adopt the children of women poorer than themselves are also 'good' mothers in media terms. So is the woman who has a child for her infertile sister. These are the women whose actions, even the illegal purchase and smuggling of a child, are right because in the eyes of the media they underpin the strength and 'naturalness' of maternal longing, the essence of maternity as sacrifice. The commercial surrogate is a 'bad' mother for she flies in the face of what is considered natural. The 'good' mothers and the 'bad' mothers, whom we know only through what is written about them, are as clearly drawn in our collective psyche as the Madonna and the Whore.

But back to Penny Hughes, Ms Coca-Cola. She offered something different to the media writers and she ushered in a whole new phase. Penny Hughes was the *redemptive* mother.

It is no coincidence that around the same time as the Penny Hughes story broke, numerous articles, radio and television programmes were discussing the future of men and the 'redundant male'. A few months before, the newest of the policy think-tanks, Demos, had published a revolutionary document on gender entitled 'No Turning Back'. Their main assertion was that the power balance between men and women had irrevocably and fundamentally altered. They argued that changes in the workplace, greater economic power and confidence had put a younger generation of women ahead of their male counterparts. The report painted a sorry picture of young men as under-achievers and facing long-term unemployment as the traditional masculine heavy industries were replaced by 'women's jobs' in the service sector. Men had lost their core function as bread-winners.

The women at the centre of maternal correctness were members of the progressive middle class and generally successful women. In the redemption-seeking style, several of the pieces were written in the first person by women returning to the fold of motherhood. Feminism had let mothers down, they argued. It was feminism's fault that people looked down on mothers because feminism had taught women that they could find self-worth only through a career. In *Bazaar* magazine, the foreign correspondent Geraldine Brooks wrote in July 1997 about how she had given up war-reporting for ever to become a mother, and had never looked back.

A mother who continued to want to work would have trouble ignoring all the warnings of the danger in which she was placing her child, as well as the suggestion of neglect. In *Vogue* (1995), Antonia Kirwen Taylor told how she gave up her job of twelve years after the family GP diagnosed stress in her young daughter following Kirwen Taylor's return from a business trip to Japan. At the end of the piece the magazine gave the address of a well-known clinic specializing in children's psychological disorders. A *Sunday Times* piece concentrated on the risks of placing children with childminders and described a recent case in which a child had died.[29] This theme was replayed a thousand times louder in reporting of the case of Louise Woodward, the British nanny convicted of killing her employer's baby. In *The Times*, an article on the successful relaunch of television presenter Esther Rantzen's career was entitled: 'I am driven, and my children have suffered.'[30] Three months later the news broke that Esther Rantzen's daughter suffered from ME or chronic fatigue syndrome. 'Esther finds a cause at home,' said the *Daily Telegraph*.[31]

When the Everest climber Alison Hargreaves was swept to her death by a blizzard in August 1995, the newspapers devoted most of their space to discussing whether or not a mother had the right to practise a dangerous sport. Alison Hargreaves was one of Britain's greatest climbers. Motherhood was not what consumed her. Yet it was through her children that she was identified after her death. Later, writing in the *Telegraph Magazine*, Raffaella Barker described how she fell from her horse and gave up riding because 'it was unfair to my children'. She wrote:

'I brought them into this world without consulting them and it is my duty as well as my privilege to see them through their formative years.'

The *reductio ad absurdum* is: If you are a mother, what is an acceptable risk? What about skiing, riding pillion on a motor-bike? What about scuba diving? Visiting foreign lands? Travel-ling on motorways? Must women cosset and protect themselves in every possible way, denying themselves every pleasure or activity because they are mothers? Perhaps some would say yes, because in our modern, urban society and in our imploding nuclear families the mother is now and increasingly the *only* person responsible for her children; only she can be relied on, or made, to stay.

Fifteen years ago we were reading about househusbands and role-swapping couples. Then women posed no particular threat in the workplace. In articles expounding the virtues of maternal correctness, husbands were not even mentioned (except, not-ably, when a writer remarked that staying at home allowed her to take better care of her husband too). In fact, those women who chose to give up work to stay at home were describing what has become a genuine modern dilemma. Those lucky enough to have jobs often work long and unsociable hours which leave little time for the family. Women working under these con-ditions frequently find, too, that their career prospects are limited by the 'glass ceiling'. Other people can't find jobs at all. In Britain there is a scarcity of affordable, quality childcare. It is absolutely true that in many ways the choices we enjoy some-times appear to make our lives more complicated instead of simpler, more fraught instead of more enjoyable. It can appear easier just to go back to the way things used to be.

The same dilemmas were highlighted by the stories of women like Nichola Horlick, the Morgan Grenfell fund manager whose high-profile suspension drew the media spotlight towards her home life. The public were fascinated to find out how she man-aged a pressurized career as well as a husband, home and five children. In September 1997 Brenda Barnes, one of Pepsi's most powerful female executives, also bowed out to spend more time at home. Both women gave interviews in which they talked about the conflict between the total commitment expected from them as employees and their own need and desire to look after their children. Nichola Horlick eventually took another job, Brenda Barnes didn't.

Most women don't work for status or to be able to boast of a classy career. They work, quite simply, for the money. The public self-martyrdom of a group of well-heeled women married to wealthy men is as offensive a gesture to them as it is vacuous, but it does mirror the opinions of many people on the right of the political spectrum, and it reflects the private thoughts of many others. The message is clear. If women would stay at home then men could have back their role as breadwinners and society would be set to rights. Indeed, social critic Melanie Phillips said exactly that in *Sex Change State*. And women who are mothers, more than anybody, are the easiest targets to make feel guilty about the 'luxury' of working by playing on the concerns they have for their children.

The war against single mothers

At first glance what could Penny Hughes, and the ideal of maternal correctness that she came to epitomize, have in common with a single mother? The British media have consistently reviled the single mother. The campaign against her has been led by, but is by no means confined to, the right-wing tabloid press. She is portrayed as promiscuous, obscenely fertile, man-hating, sitting in her council flat raising a generation of criminals for the future. She is a sponger. She takes from the state and gives nothing. The single mother and the maternally correct mother are media opposites but together they illustrate perfectly the link between economics, morality and maternity.

A well-off woman abandoning work to stay at home is regarded as virtuous, in a poor woman it is a crime.

For the single mother it was ever thus. In the mid-1970s there was a brief period of public sympathy which coincided with changes in welfare rules to benefit single parents. The good-will was generated by a campaign which drew attention to the fact that many single mothers were widows or women abandoned by their husbands. Single (never-married) women accounted for a very small number of lone mothers and their dilemma was explained by campaigners in terms of lack of proper contraceptive advice and availability. The introduction of free contraceptives appeared to change nothing, however. As the numbers of women raising children alone grew and with them the benefits bill, that moment of sympathy lapsed and the single mum resumed her mantle of media bogey. It is illuminating to note that, while the issue of single mothers has generated thousands upon thousands of articles, leaders and comments in Britain and the USA, despite similar increases in the number of lone parent families in many European countries, the topic has received scant coverage.

In Britain in the early 1990s, public distaste for single mothers was being fed by a Conservative government keen to cut its welfare bill. In addition the public heard the word 'underclass' for the first time. Social psychologist Charles Murray in his essay 'What to do about Welfare' and later in his bestselling book, *The Bell Curve*, warned in strident tones, which some people found convincing, of a growing and violent body of poor, disenchanted and disenfranchised people, most of whom were single mothers or the product of one-parent families. At the Conservative Party conference in 1992, Peter Lilley the new Secretary of State for Social Security referred to 'young ladies who get pregnant to jump the housing list'. The following year the spotlight focused on the 'home-alone' mother.

There were a number of 'home-alone' mothers, but Yasmin Gibson was the first and remained the definitive version. She was an attractive blonde fun-lover who left her eleven-year-old daughter behind in their Hammersmith flat while she holidayed in Malaga with a male friend. After several days a neighbour brought the child's predicament to the notice of the local authority and Gemma Gibson was taken into care while social services, Interpol and the British and Spanish police searched for her mother. The tabloids found her first and the story broke on Valentine's Day.

At first Yasmin Gibson remained defiant, insisting that she had done nothing wrong and would continue her holiday, but that soon became impossible. Followed and questioned every moment, she eventually accepted the offer of a flight home from one of the newspapers. One of the most enduring images of that year, printed large on the pages of several papers, was of Yasmin Gibson, tears of mascara streaking her face and her blonde hair awry, shouting at her tormentors as she was led away by the police at Gatwick airport.

Exactly what the circumstances were that led to the child being left alone were and have remained unclear. Yasmin Gibson insisted all along that she had asked a neighbour to look after her daughter. Certainly it looked as though there might have been some genuine confusion. Gemma herself was a self-possessed child who took herself to school each day and did not seem to have been noticeably damaged by events. Yasmin Gibson, particularly in her naïve dealings with the newspapers, struck one as an unfortunate character. She was immature and foolish rather than malicious. In her relationship with her daughter, the latter often seemed to be the dominant personality. Nevertheless, the tabloids ran headlines of the kind of vitriol usually reserved for killers: 'YOU BITCH' shrieked the *Daily Mirror*.

One of the most striking aspects of the media representation of Yasmin Gibson was how much of what was said and written dwelt on her sexuality. Sexuality and notions of 'good' motherhood are viewed as incompatible. Yasmin Gibson was portrayed, quite simply, as a slut. She was described variously as a 'dancer', 'actress' or 'model', almost always in quotation marks. Aspersions were cast on her relationship with her holiday companion, suggestively referred to (with undertones of racism) as an 'Arab benefactor'. Nor did the papers shy from running publicity shots of her dressed in lingerie and pouting for the camera alongside shocked editorials recounting her failure as a mother. She was also greedy: 'guzzling champagne' on the flight, 'tucking into her food' and 'ripping open' envelopes stuffed with cash offers from the papers.

Greedy, promiscuous and irresponsible – Yasmin Gibson had been turned into the archetypal single mother by the press. She was in an impossible position. In the *Daily Telegraph* Lesley Garner pronounced: 'If a woman chooses to become a full-time parent she must sacrifice her independence, income and career.'[32] While some commentators criticized her for her acting ambitions, which it was suggested she put ahead of her daughter, others condemned her for living off benefits. The publicity was doing Gemma more harm than being left alone. The mêlée was ended only when Hammersmith and Fulham local authority sought a High Court injunction to prevent anyone reporting on the case until Gemma was eighteen.

A lone voice of reason amid the baiting was Suzanne Moore, the *Guardian* columnist, who wrote of the real, everyday trials of being a single parent in modern Britain and the impossibility of admitting it for fear of being found wanting as a mother: 'Yet while we live in a society in which the idea of motherhood is sanctified, the price of this involves a wilful denial of reality.'[33]

Heidi Colwell knew a bit about the hard dilemmas and choices which face the single mother. In the summer of 1993 she became the next high-profile 'home-alone' mother after it was discovered that she abandoned her two-year-old daughter all day with just sandwiches, drinks and the television. Initially she received much the same press treatment as Yasmin Gibson and, to the satisfaction of some and the surprise of many, unlike Gibson against whom no charges were ever brought, Heidi Colwell received a six-month jail sentence. It soon transpired that her case was different, at least as far as public opinion was concerned, for Heidi Colwell left her daughter at home by herself for nine hours a day so that she could go out to work.

Heidi Colwell's case provided one of the rare occasions for the media to do some real soul-searching. Here was a woman who, far from being just another irresponsible single mother living on handouts, appeared to be trying to provide for herself and her daughter. The father was nowhere in sight. After a year in bed-and-breakfast she was eventually given a job by her uncle but it was many miles from where her family lived in Essex. She applied to social services for low-cost housing and a child-minder but was told that none was available. On what she earned, which amounted to little more than £100 a week, she had been unable to afford the £50 for a childminder. Such was the outcry over her sentence that Heidi Colwell was freed by the end of the month.

Colwell's case embodies all that is judgemental, hypocritical and selfish about modern Britain's attitude to mothers in general and single mothers in particular. There were more home-alone mothers after Heidi Colwell and every one of them was a woman raising a child or children on her own. Where was the community, where were the neighbours, the family who might have helped Heidi Colwell? Where was the father? Stephen Waine, who defended Heidi Colwell, points out that she had a boyfriend who knew all along what was going on. Why was he considered devoid of responsibility? Where were social services? Why is there a double standard of mothering which tells wealthy women that they are good mothers if they give up work to stay at home with their children but encourages poor women to work even if they have to abandon a toddler for hours on end to do so?

By now it was late August and the season of political party conferences was around the corner. John Major had taken over as Prime Minister from Margaret Thatcher three years earlier, but the party had been in the doldrums ever since. Major was looking for a big idea and a theme to ensure the success of the conference. Throughout the summer, usually a quiet period, he and his ministers had worked hard to push the family high up the political agenda and to declare the Tories the party of the Family. At Number 10 they were preparing to launch the ill-fated 'Back to Basics' campaign.

One of the prime movers behind family values was the young, ambitious right-winger and Welsh Secretary John Redwood, who would later challenge Major for leadership of the party. Two months before the conference he visited the St Mellons estate in South Wales. In a televised speech he described what he had seen there: large numbers of never-married, single mothers living without men and without jobs and with no prospect of either. They survived on state benefits. It was, he said, an unacceptable and growing state of affairs.

In the offices of the BBC's flagship current affairs programme *Panorama*, the editor Glenwyn Benson heard Redwood's claim and put producer Barbara Want and reporter Margaret Gilmore on the story. The programme aired in late September just before the 1993 Tory party conference. The opening sequence was unforgettable. It featured a woman with four children by different men and pregnant with her fifth child enjoying a day out at the funfair. The backing track was the popular song 'All That She Wants Is Another Baby'. Like John Redwood the programme-makers also visited the St Mellon's estate in Cardiff. Layer by layer, over the next forty minutes, the reporter built an uncompromising picture: a growing number of young women had babies for handouts and status. They were promiscuous but were uninterested in relationships with men. 'It's not just the amount they're costing the taxpayer,' said Margaret Gilmore to camera, 'it's the effect they're having on the family system and in the long term on society.'

In the American state of New Jersey, a scheme had begun to cap the benefits of single mothers who had another baby while receiving welfare. The proposals had caused much debate and attracted a huge amount of media and political attention. *Panorama* investigated its success and revealed startling results: the number of babies born to single mothers had halved, 'proof that people's behaviour can be changed simply by removing free handouts,' said Margaret Gilmore.

At home, watching with growing dismay, was Sue Slipman, then head of the National Council of One Parent Families (NCOPF). She knew that the BBC was making a programme about single mothers because she had been approached for help and had been interviewed (although she did not appear in the finished film), but she barely recognized the story she was now watching. She described Michelle Ellis, the mother of five with whom the show opened, as a 'statistical freak', highly atypical of most lone mothers. The next night she and a colleague, Anne Spackman, hosted a fund-raising event for the NCOPF. It was a performance of *Hamlet* in West London. She recalls that night she spent two hours persuading reluctant guests that they should attend. Even the charity's patron, the Duke of Devonshire, considered withdrawing his support. They had all seen the *Panorama* programme, and, so it seemed, had every right-wing politician. The programme's findings were quoted in Parliament[34] throughout the Tory party conference, even in a briefing issued by Central Office[35] as well as on radio and on television. Several cited the programme's findings as proof that young women were deliberately getting pregnant to jump the housing queues.

Also central to the debate was the New Jersey scheme and its extraordinary success. Many people wanted to know if withdrawing benefits, effectively punishing single women who have another child, would work in Britain. In deciding to launch a formal complaint against the programme with the Broadcasting Complaints Commission (BCC), Anne Spackman said: 'We had to nail that 50 per cent figure.' They began making calls to the state authorities. No one could verify the figure at all or even trace its origins. The *Panorama* team later claimed that the figure had been given during an off-the-record briefing by an unnamed official in New Jersey. The actual success rate was much lower – around 16 per cent – and even that figure was in the process of being revised.

Then Fay Shepherd, one of the single mothers from the *Panorama* programme, accused the programme-makers of deliberately misrepresenting her. She claimed she was filmed in a pub apparently having a good time without her children. What the commentary failed to mention, she argued, was that she was an organizer at a charity fund-raising event. Most importantly, she was described as relying on the government for 'housing and cash' when the truth was that Fay Shepherd was in receipt of maintenance from her former partner. The programme-makers also asserted that she was single by choice and didn't want a man around permanently. In fact, as the transcripts of her interview later revealed, Fay Shepherd said she had had children only because she thought her relationship was going to last.

It took a year for the hearing and the final BCC judgment to come. The BBC defended *Panorama* vigorously. Almost a year to the day, the National Council of One Parent Families heard they had won hands down. It was a remarkable victory by two women against one of the biggest broadcasting networks in the world. The BBC refused to let the matter rest and some months later succeeded in overturning the ruling on the technical grounds that only an individual and not a charity could take a complaint to the BCC. They did not, however, seek to revisit the substance of the ruling.

For the Conservative Party, the 'Back to Basics' campaign proved a disaster. Over the following months the private lives of their ministers would be scrutinized and subject to allegations of 'sleaze'. One by one the resignations would be proffered, starting with that of Tim Yeo, whose lover Julia Stent was found to be pregnant with his child and about to become one of the single mothers the Tories so reviled. The roll-call of those who fell short of the family values ideal would continue and included Stephen Norris and David Mellor.

There are 1.4 million single parents. Never-married mothers comprise 36 per cent of all lone parents. The majority by far, as Sue Slipman and Anne Spackman point out, are divorced or separated. Women like Michelle, with four or more children, represent a mere 3 per cent. Today Anne Spackman wishes the organization had not used statistical evidence to argue the case. 'I think we should have defended them *per se*,' she says, 'not on the basis that most were respectable and the never-marrieds were only a few.'

The fact is that the whole responsibility for children in our society falls on women and many men either will not or cannot take responsibility for their offspring. This cannot be totally separated from the way the benefits system works, whom it pays and whom it prioritizes. Since the days when women who gave birth outside marriage were hidden away in mental institutions, the lone mother has been a politicized figure, the embodiment of a threat to the family, to patriarchy and to conservative motherhood. In the words of Sue Slipman, 'Today we've made the lone parent into a symbol of total social disintegration.'[36] The present debate focuses on lone mothers and welfare costs. But the truth is that payments to single parents still account for only a fraction of total government spending.

We hold up the beauty of motherhood to all women, but when poor women reach for it we scorn them and strike them down. We talk only of the bond, love and sharing between mother and child and we confine fathers to the role of breadwinner. When women cannot find working men, do not see the point in marrying and have their babies alone we are horrified. We pretend we are shocked, we wonder at their motivations. Their real and only crime is to become mothers when their circumstances dictate they can never be the kind of mother of whom the majority of us will approve.

The rest is history. In 1995 the British government froze the one-parent benefit and the lone-parent premium with a view to phasing them out altogether in the near future. In 1995 Ms

S, a single mother from Liverpool, was jailed for abandoning her children. She claims she asked their father to take care of them while she was away. In autumn 1995 the Conservative MP Alan Howarth defected to the Labour Party over the government's social policies. In February the following year he told the House of Commons that there had been 'A hideously orchestrated campaign of vilification against single parents, which I think was one of the most shaming episodes in modern politics.'[37] He referred to the start of the campaign as the 1993 Tory party conference and added: 'I do feel that what we are seeing is really the expression of a certain set of values, a certain set of moral purposes, which to my mind are harsh and unjust and do smack of scapegoating.'

In 1997 one of the first acts of Tony Blair's New Labour government was to push through changes which would cut extra benefits to single mothers against the wishes of many of their own backbenchers. The job was given to Harriet Harman, the new social security secretary, who in opposition had vociferously argued against planned cuts by the Tories. One of the successes of New Labour was to retrieve and claim the Family as a political banner from the shambles of Tory sleaze. Today, in that context, motherhood has become a fixture in the landscape of politics, and attacking single mothers has become a legitimate and commonplace pursuit.

Images of mothers are created by popular culture to reflect and sometimes to manipulate a set of values about what constitutes exemplary mothering. Behind each individual depiction, good or bad, lies the model of the perfect mother. Private decisions about work, relationships, fertility and behaviour become public property because women are mothers. The mothers who are the subjects of press stories are judged by that standard, and so are women in the general populace who do not or cannot fulfil society's expectations regarding what a mother should be. They are all found guilty.

chapter 5

Future Perfect

Testimony: Afton

Afton is in her mid-fifties. She works as a child and family therapist on the West Coast of America and has a seventeen-year-old son as a result of donor insemination.

I always knew I would want children, but that wasn't my top priority in life. I was exploring relationships and they weren't going very well. Then I got near to forty and the child became more important than the relationship. I decided to make it happen and thought of different ways. Essentially it came down to two choices, either a sperm bank or find somebody who I thought would co-parent with me. I asked a couple of people, but the more I thought about it, the more I didn't want to share my child at all. Well, because, for one thing, when you're bonded as a mother you don't want to part at all when your child is little, it psychologically is not OK. So if you're not living together, how do you co-parent? I couldn't see it. If you don't have children, you don't understand. It felt right for me to go to a sperm bank. I checked two, the first was very mercenary, money-oriented and with no choice. Then I discovered the Repository.

When I first inseminated I used one donor, but then another one came on the scene and he seemed like somebody who would have been right out of my family background. What we would do, friends of mine, we would line up the résumés and at that time [we were given] pictures, so you'd find yourself falling in love, getting all excited, arguing about this one or that one. But that was before this donor came. After he came everybody agreed he was the one to use. I still have the picture. What I especially liked was his love of the outdoors and his musical ability. My son definitely has his musical ability. He didn't get a love of the outdoors, but he definitely is musical. [The donor] was fair, I guess he was Pennsylvania Dutch. But the first one I chose was an Ashkenazi Jewish man, so it wasn't physical characteristics. I also went for perfect vision, because I have very bad vision. Although my son has just started to wear glasses. I love music and I would love to have been musical, too. I am thrilled that my son thinks he's going to go to music graduate school. The donor was renowned in computer science. He's supposed to be famous. I don't know who he is. I know how to find him and if my son ever wants to find him I'll leave him to do that. I can't tell you much about it.

I have a close friend of mine who also [used that donor], my son has a half-sister. She's very bright. She looks like her mother, my son looks like me. We joke that sperm-bank babies tend to look like their mothers. There was one other child, I don't know if it was a boy or girl, that was born around the same time. My son has been told everything.

The absence of a father has only made it easier. I think any single mother with a single child, who intentionally has that child, has the kind of bond that I have with my child. I think it cannot happen with more than one child and it cannot happen with a husband around. I think that it has to be only the two of you and that creates the bond. I've spoken to other people who say it's the strongest relationship they've ever had. I prefer it like that and my son will tell you the same too. There is no greater intimacy than that relationship. There are disadvantages. I have a gentleman friend, I didn't have one until my son went away to school, but when he came back at Spring it was very hard. He was not used to sharing. I felt torn the whole two weeks. I think it's very hard for these children to share their mother, because they want their mother all to themselves. But his self-esteem is phenomenal. He loves his looks, he loves life, he has great time management, he's grounded because he hasn't had anybody to tear that down. The end result is that my son said on the phone, 'Maybe he won't be there this summer', and I said, Maybe he won't be. And my friend too said maybe he should get his own place because he thought he got in the way of my relationship with my son. So he realized.

[My son] is very intense and he's always been very strong-willed. He came home one day and told me he was going to go to one of two schools for gifted kids. They deliberately go around the world recruiting the cream of the crop of gifted kids. My son was already in a program for highly gifted children. Every year scouts from a school come recruiting, they go to the math class and give them a sales pitch. He came home and told me, 'I'm going to go there'. I said, no way, I'm not parting with you until college and he just said, 'Well, you've got two years to get used to it, mom.' I'm just giving you an example. His whole life he has just told me how things will be. People get upset with me because I have not put limits on him, or done discipline because you can't with him. But he's a beautiful kid, he's such an incredible kid you don't need to. He's so self-motivated. He's talented at everything. He's good at athletics. He's top of the math class. He's in the accelerated math class. He hates it, but he does have a choice, he always says 'No, I have this talent so I might as well cultivate it.' He plays the piano, he writes his own compositions which he plays at recitals. He plays electric guitar and sitar and he wants to take the cello or violin. Now he wants to be a musician, but when he was nine he wanted to be president. But I just want him to be fulfilled and happy because [those] people make contributions to society. My mother on the other hand says, 'Oh, you're so gifted at physics, the world needs physicists.' She says musicians don't make any money. But he makes money. He makes $800 per interview and he gets quite a few. If you were wanting to see him instead of me, that's what he'd ask you for.

He does things his way. At times it can be a problem. He got kicked out of pre-school when he was four, we were asked not to come back. They described him as wild. And this was a liberal kind of school. I made a decision to follow my intuition with him, to model, to talk to, to reason with and trust in my vision that everything would go fine. So he was a bit slower than many in following the rules and being civil.

I did consider adoption at the start. And I considered it again for a second child. I did try very hard to have a second child, although I'm glad now I didn't. Well, I've accepted the advantages of not having a second child, but I tried for several years for a sibling. He wanted one, when he was about five or six and he really wanted one. So then I began to think of adoption, but then he was about six or seven and I saw some of my friends going through such hell trying to adopt. They were flying down to Mexico and discovering the child they thought they were going to get was severely retarded, or flying to Romania and not getting a child at all, when they've been promised one after spending thousands and thousands of dollars. I just missed one child I would have loved to have had. My doctor told me that she almost called me about a baby, an interracial baby, born to a girl at the highly gifted program. I said 'Why didn't you call me?'; she said, 'I didn't think you were quite ready.' But ready or not, this would have been the perfect child! I was so upset she didn't tell me. Evidently the boy had also been in the program. It took me a long time to get over missing that one.

I have no regrets. My child was very wanted, very consciously wanted. He slept in my bed until he wanted his own. I breastfed him until he was five; people couldn't believe we were still doing it but I think it has paid off. As a mother my job is encouragement and guidance. I never worry that we are too close or worry if anything happened to me. I feel the opposite. The more one has the love of the mother, the more you have the feeling of a good mother inside you and the more you succeed in life.

Today most new mothers expect, with the help of their doctors plus amniocentesis and ultrasound techniques, to deliver a child which is, in every way, as complete and as exquisite as they, and their partners, have hoped. Infertile couples, too, are being helped to fulfil their dreams of a family using techniques such as artificial insemination, IVF, egg retrieval and surrogacy. Each new medical advance is greeted with a flare of publicity, debate, and finally some degree of acceptance. The pace of discovery is gathering momentum. Not content with trying to perfect mothers, our society is beginning to try to perfect babies as well. The perfect mother now requires a perfect child, one that is genetically her own, free from disease or deformity, full of hope and bright prospects. For if motherhood is an art, the sculptress mother requires quality clay to mould. Children are increasingly seen as a 'choice', and so couples search for reproductive meaning in childrearing – that is, children who will grow up to reflect their own philosophy, talents and creativity – and not just an heir to carry their name forward. Today it has become increasingly possible for science to fulfil the desires of couples to choose the gender of, even genetically to design, their child. Motherhood has entered the marketplace.

Infertile couples are at the forefront of these changes because of their contact with the world of reproductive technology. To them, in exchange for cash, the marketplace holds out a dream of parenthood, specifically a dream of an idealized form of motherhood built on a set of assumptions about genetic links, love and the relationship between parents and their children. The contradiction is that the marketplace is being used in an attempt to supply the one thing that can't be bought: human relationships. Parent–child relationships are cherished precisely because they offer qualities which lie outside the commercial sphere, such as love, giving, freedom and trust.

One Saturday in the spring of 1996, an advertisement appeared under 'Wanted' in the classified section of a British daily newspaper. It read: 'Are you univ/medicine educated, fair haired? We are a professional couple trying to have children. Our only chance is with the help of women willing to donate eggs.'

Let us imagine for a moment what the couple who placed this advertisement are like. They have already told us that they are professional, let's say urban. Yuppies. He is, say, thirty-seven. She is thirty-five. Like any number of modern couples they have delayed having a family while they both worked hard at their respective jobs and no doubt they were happy, too, to enjoy the substantial fruits of success without the responsibility of children. With the benefit of a sizeable double income they live in a large, semi-detached house and have already converted the attic into a small studio apartment for a nanny. Another room adjacent to the master bedroom has been decorated as a nursery. But that was eighteen months ago, and since then the baby has failed to show up. We have been led to understand that theirs is an increasingly common modern predicament.

The wording of the advert is framed to win our sympathy: 'our only chance . . .' What do we feel? Are we supposed to worry about this pair of over-achievers with their swollen bank balance? Surely it was their choice to set childrearing aside while they both scaled the walls of the meritocracy? In an age characterized by the prizes of acquisition and individual achievement, some dissenting minds see a kind of divine justice in the knowledge that a woman's fertility begins to decline in her thirties, just when the job is going so well.

Let's look at it another way. Perhaps our couple see themselves with fewer choices than we imagine. After all, most women who work don't do so to stack up Pulitzer prizes or see themselves profiled in the newspapers. They work quite simply for money and self-sufficiency. They need to because the divorce rate is sky-high and even if it wasn't, one of them still needs to be able to earn if the other is laid off by the firm at the age of forty-five.

Their jobs are likely to mean they have moved to London, or Birmingham, or Edinburgh – some big urban centre where everyone lives self-contained, private little lives. Our couple think they want children, they assume they do because, well, doesn't everyone? But the truth is, neither of them has spent more than a few hours at a time in the company of a child in the last decade. Their brothers and sisters with children live a distance away, and those among their friends who have started families seem to have simply 'disappeared'. The world seems to have become divided into the new 'haves' and the 'have-nots'. Those with children and those without. The 'haves' organize group activities in which children are included, like Sunday lunch and picnics; they holiday together; they talk babies and help with each other's children. When a 'have' is invited over to the home of a couple of 'have-nots', they dare not 'impose' their offspring and so they call the babysitter. Requests for child-minding or other favours are asked only of other 'haves' because then they can return the favour.

The modern manners of the urban West today dictate that we cannot force our 'lifestyle choice' on anyone else. Those who chose to have children must keep them to themselves. The 'childfree' enjoy their pristine apartments and the company of adults. It's a new kind of self-imposed lifestyle apartheid. One drawback is that many people now live their adult lives with little contact with children until they have their own. It also means that if a couple for any reason cannot have their own child they will not even be consoled in their childless lives by the presence of nephews, nieces, and the children of friends and neighbours. This heightens feelings of isolation, frustration and exclusion.

When the baby does arrive, there won't be anyone from the family or friends willing or expected to help. That means they'll have to hire a nanny. And that will cost a basic of £8,000 to £10,000 plus accommodation, national insurance and tax. So the new mother might well end up foregoing the extra months of maternity leave and going back to work.

This is all just speculation because at the moment they're sitting in their spacious house, which now just seems empty, and they are contemplating how they are going to bring a child into their lives. They don't have the biological apparatus to create the family they desire themselves, but they do have the money. Their doctor has talked them through the range of options available to people in their position and has given them hope.

Today, there is a growing industry in reproductive technology which aims to provide children for infertile couples. Test-tube babies now appear quaint when compared to sperm banks with a range of donors covering a multitude of physical characteristics; frozen embryos stashed away to provide a 'twin' sister or brother years later; surrogate mothers carrying babies to which they have no genetic link. This massive, ever-expanding industry exists because of couples like the one who placed the ad, and it has been built on their dreams. All the myths about motherhood are condensed and collapsed into one. What is being offered to infertile couples is a child of one's 'own', one who has certain desired characteristics, one who can bring the hopes of parents to fruition. To infertile couples, the reproductive industry holds out a promise of perfect, achievable motherhood with a perfect baby.

The commercialization of reproductive technology

In 1993 a report published by the market research company Frost & Sullivan on the potential of the emerging markets in fertility treatment and reproductive technology noted the effect of social factors such as delayed childbearing on the assured profitability of the fertility product and pharmaceutical market: 'It is projected to grow steadily over the forecast period, because of the growing number of baby-boomers who will try to conceive and seek solutions to their infertility problems. Additionally, the emergence of new assisted reproductive technologies will support growth in the fertility pharmaceuticals and products.'[1]

It started with animal husbandry. The technology now used for human reproduction was actually first developed as a cheap and efficient way of impregnating breeding cows. Later it came to be used, even more lucratively, as a way of improving the genetic stock of farm animals to improve milk yield or produce

leaner meat or thicker wool. For many years farmers have artificially inseminated their cows with the semen of prize donor
bulls, a product which itself is bought and sold across the world
for significant sums. Soon afterwards the eggs of the best cows
and ewes were removed and fertilized. Then they were placed
in the wombs of other animals of inferior stock who would
gestate the embryos. Using all that science had to offer, farmers
have for the latter part of this century been able to outwit the
pace of nature and break the natural breeding cycle to produce
better animals at a greater rate.

None of this had any particular application to humans until
the 1970s when certain key social changes came into being. The
first change was, of course, the widespread use and availability
of the contraceptive Pill; access to abortion services was the
second; and the third came in the form of a new range of benefits
for women bringing up children on their own. Contraception,
abortion and state support for single mothers have had a
phenomenal effect on the number of babies available for adoption by infertile couples. In 1974 figures from the Office of Population and Census Statistics reveal there were 22,502 adoption
orders made. Today in England and Wales there are only around
300 baby adoptions each year.[2] In the late 1980s and 1990s
came another social shift, as noted in Frost & Sullivan's report:
women began to wait before having children, but by then their
fertility has begun to decline and conceiving may be difficult,
and adoption virtually impossible. Of paramount importance to
those in the reproduction business, this growing group of childless couples are typically middle-class, professional people with
good incomes. The most elementary law of the marketplace is
supply and demand. In not much more than a decade, the
demand for babies increased just as the supply dwindled.

The problems of infertility and of infertile people have
received an enormous, arguably disproportionate, amount of
attention. There has been talk in the media of an 'infertility
epidemic'. Let us be clear. Thanks to modern health care and

preventative medicine, fertility in the West is extremely high. Next to levels in some parts of the world where half the female population is infertile, figures of less than 1 in 10 couples in the UK who experience some kind of difficulty conceiving seem less significant. In 1990, the US National Center for Health Statistics investigated claims of widespread infertility and reported: 'The increased use of infertility services, the increased number of childless older women with impaired fecundity and other factors may help to account for the perception that infertility is increasing or is more common than it actually is.'[3] In Britain, the Human Embryology and Fertilization Authority does not recognize any suggestion of an infertility epidemic and neither does the British Medical Association which says the problem has simply become more visible because solutions are now available. The real issue here is not 'how much' infertility, but 'who' is infertile, namely a significant number of older, better-off couples.

That childless couples could and would pay considerable sums to have a child was evidenced by the enormous increase in babies being adopted from developing countries by Westerners. According to United Nations figures, some 20,000 children are adopted in this way annually.[4] Markets opened up wherever there was a good supply of healthy, preferably white- or pale-skinned babies who could be adopted by couples in Western Europe, the United States and Australia. Commercialization of the process began early with the introduction of intermediaries and entire adoption networks. Babies began to change hands for large sums of money. Figures of up to $50,000 have been reported for highly adoptable Russian children.[5] Abuses of the law and the sale of children, as well as the exploitation of women and families, have been flagrant and wholesale and have been documented by international agencies such as Defence of Children, Interpol and the United Nations.

Reproductive technology seems to offer a preferable alternative to adoption, with fewer variables. No wonder this is big business, globally worth many millions of pounds ($1.3 billion in the USA alone[6]), which has attracted giant pharmaceutical multinationals such as Abbott Laboratories, Ares Serono and American Home Products which already dominate the market in contraceptives and related products. The reproduction business now extends far beyond the laboratory. It involves patents of techniques as well as products; high-level investment; speculators and venture capitalists operating in the volatile and potentially highly lucrative field of biotechnology; stock-market takeovers; share ratings, sales and purchases – everything you would normally find in a commercial enterprise.

The profits in creating dreams are enormous and have even greater potential. In the USA and Australia, private insurance covers a proportion of the costs of fertility treatment. Some policies will pay for specific items such as the drugs. In Britain the question of whether the NHS will pay for fertility treatment is central to how much profit the industry, presently constrained by individuals' ability to pay for costly treatment out of their own pockets, can generate in the future. Pressure groups such as Child and ISSUE campaign on behalf of couples to have infertility recognized as an illness and treatment paid out of the public purse. On behalf of the industry two pharmaceutical companies – Ares Serono (owners of the prestigious fertility clinic Bourn Hall and manufacturers of the IVF drug Pergonal) and Organon Inc. – retain a company of parliamentary lobbyists to place NHS funding of fertility treatment on the parliamentary agenda. They call it 'benign self-interest'. Unsurprisingly, many fertility specialists also support funding for treatment by the NHS.

Given a free rein and a free market, there are a thousand ways to make money in the business of human reproduction, from the manufacture of drugs and equipment to the conception services themselves. On a single day one company files a $510,000 marketing application for a catheter for transferring fertilized human eggs into the fallopian tubes; a second invents and patents a new high-density video laproscope for retrieving eggs from the womb; another wins a highly lucrative exclusive contract to become sole providers of assisted reproductive technology to the 3 million couples of the US Armed Services. Infertility is a huge market, with a captive audience and big potential. Sales tactics can be brash as sellers compete for customers; several clinics have recently started to offer 'a baby or your money back' guarantees (only to selected clients with easy-to-treat problems, of course); one advertising executive hired to promote a clinic's services described her tactic as 'go for the jugular'.

Reproductive technology is also a global business, operating within the shifting and frayed boundaries of medical ethics. Operators owe as much to shareholders as to the fragile emotions of their 'customers', the infertile couples.

While the industry markets the wholesomeness of motherhood and apple pie, business practices can be exploitative and sometimes criminal. In Canada, the USA and Britain, a fast-growing market exists in the sale of human gametes to be used for IVF or surrogacy. Young women are frequently offered several thousand pounds to give up their eggs. Middlemen and agents advertise in university magazines for college-educated donors who are hard up for cash, but whose eggs would be considered high quality. At the University of California at Irvine, three millionaire fertility specialists, Ricardo Asch, Sergio Stone and Jose Balmacedo, collectively known as 'the baby-makers', stole eggs from patients, implanted them in others and used frozen embryos of some couples to produce pregnancies in other, unrelated women. Bernard Lo, who chaired the task force to determine the future of IVF programmes at the university, has blamed 'the intense competition for patients, and the compromising of ethics by business interests'[7], for the scandal. Human eggs, sperm and ultimately human babies have come to be treated as commodities to be traded.

The difference between creating human babies and piglets, calves or lambs is the complex ethical questions surrounding the former. Another difference is motivation. Animal husbandry is unarguably an industry, but should making babies be one too? In order to justify the creation of vast amounts of wealth and the potential exploitation of human beings, those involved in the reproductive industry must market their image carefully. They do so by associating the values of their industry with the ideology of motherhood. Furthermore, their ultimate, self-serving, goal is to maximize the desire to become a parent, to make the absence of a child felt more keenly, and to tailor their services to realize a dream. They have become the new myth-makers.

People often accuse those involved in creating human life artificially of 'selling babies'. The truth is they sell something else first, something far less tangible, they are selling an idea. They are not selling families, but the *idea* of families. It's the idea that gave birth to the industry. Now the industry takes it and shapes it. IVF was originally developed to help women with damaged tubes to conceive a child, but today assisted conception techniques are far more refined. Science is being used to create nuclear, biological and genetically-perfect families.

The industry does much more than offer a child where one might not previously have been possible. A large number of women submit to IVF, not because they cannot have children but because the low quality of their husbands' sperm makes scientific intervention necessary. Techniques are being used to screen out imperfect foetuses. Donors are screened, not just for physical characteristics, but for their IQs and artistic abilities as well. Where will we stop? Scientists claim to have isolated genes causing fatness, baldness, dwarfism and intelligence. Should they be screened out? Technology is used to eliminate imperfection. As Robyn Rowland remarked in her recent book *Living Laboratories*: 'women will be placed under more and more pressure to use all technological means offered to secure perfection. Less and less assistance will go to those who make the "mistake" of having an imperfect child. So in the age of the perfect product, difference (named "defect" or "abnormality") will be less and less acceptable.'[8] The reproduction industry is flourishing on wish fulfilment.

In this brave new world of parenting, we begin to lose sight of children, their unique needs and our collective responsibility towards them, and to see them as objects and as assets. In the words of one American legal scholar of reproductive rights: 'the whole definition of normal is being changed, the issue becoming not the ability of the child to be happy, but rather our ability to be happy with the child.'[9] In Canada, Patricia Baird, whose Royal Commission on Reproductive Technology made 293 recommendations and issued strong warnings against the use of reproductive technologies, commented: 'We used to think that children were the luck of the draw. That will be a fundamental change over the next decades. For the first time, as a species, we will be able to choose the kind of children we have.'[10] And it seems we choose not just to insist upon perfection in mothers but also in children.

The baby trail: IVF

Let's return to the couple who placed the advertisement. By now their doctor has set up an appointment with a fertility specialist. Today these men (as they mostly are) are modern stars, latter-day saints. They are interviewed for magazines; made the subject of fly-on-the-wall documentaries; invited on to radio and television to debate and discuss their art. They are revered by those to whom they have given children and carry the prayers of those who still hope. It puts a whole new gloss on the phrase 'playing God'. In the new mythology, the 'barren' woman has been banished. Infertility is no longer tolerated.

So what have they just embarked upon? Given the details that are revealed in the advertisement, it is likely the woman in the couple does not produce eggs of her own. Assuming there is no medical reason why she shouldn't carry the child herself, the treatment she is most likely to be offered is IVF (in-vitro fertilization) using a donor's egg and her husband's sperm.

There are now over 100, mainly private, clinics in the UK licensed by the Human Fertilization and Embryology Authority, the statutory industry watchdog. Each provides prospective customers with brochures and information on the clinic's own success rate (called the 'take-home' rate). The price lists read like a menu, treatment option on one side and cost on the other, with or without extras.

The sales pitch isn't hard to miss. On one of a number of regular open days at Bourn Hall, prospective clients are treated to a slide show and presentation by the medical director Neil Brinsden. The marketing angle has clearly been thought out. The talk majors on the science and technology, the range of treatments, new techniques and Bourn's expertise and commitment. 'Take comfort, many members of this team have spent their whole lives trying to make women pregnant.' Two couples near the back of the hall are discussing the relative cost of IVF in Britain and America. Meanwhile, the slide show ends with a cartoon drawn by a child conceived by IVF. It is entitled 'A Magic Doctor Making Babies'.

The walls of this Jacobean country house, with its wood-pannelled dining room and acres of garden, are adorned with hundreds of framed photographs of children and babies. Couples on their initial visit turn to look wistfully at them. The same kinds of photographs of big-eyed toddlers, contented babies, or mother-and-child-together bliss are used in the brochure distributed by the London Gynaecology and Fertility Centre. These are the photographs of those couples who have been successful using IVF, not of the many who failed. Behind the sheen and smiles of staff and satisfied customers are more sobering facts. Couples intending to embark upon IVF would do well to look closely at the so-called 'take-home' rate.

Callers to ISSUE, the help group for people with infertility problems, will be encouraged to hear that they are as likely to become pregnant using IVF as they are through natural inter-course. Much of the literature distributed on IVF by hospitals and clinics says the same, but although the comparison is broadly accurate it is nevertheless misleading. A woman stands a 33 per cent chance of conceiving through ordinary sexual intercourse in the first month, and around a 20 to 25 per cent chance each month throughout the following year. The average live birth rate for IVF nation-wide between 1995 and 1996 was 15 per cent![11] Of the 30,216 IVF cycles carried out in that year, there were only 4,609 births. Even the very best clinics have take-home rates of only around 20 per cent. These are not encouraging odds by anyone's standards. 'Still poor results for an allegedly established procedure,' wrote Professor Anthony Dyson in *The Ethics of IVF*.[12] Even Professor Robert Winston, star of the 1996 BBC series *Making Babies* and a fertility specialist at Hammer-smith Hospital, has called IVF 'a divine throw of the biological dice'.[13] Gambling is an excellent analogy for assisted conception. People are attracted by the promise, they may be desperate and they have everything to lose because IVF is a game with high stakes.

For the procedure to which the pair who placed the advertise-ment are submitting themselves – IVF with donor egg – prices start at around £2,200 to £4,500 (not including the cost of initial tests and consultations) for a cycle. An average couple might try IVF four times before either conceiving or abandoning the attempt. After three cycles the odds start to decline. At this point many give up. But some, just like compulsive gamblers, simply become obsessed and find themselves unable to stop. Robert Winston admits treating a patient who had tried IVF twenty-two times. A sister at Bourn Hall tells of one patient who clocked up eighteen cycles. In her opinion the patient, whose marriage nearly collapsed, had lost sight of the purpose of what she was doing. Although medical staff and counsellors told her it was useless, significantly they did not refuse to treat her.

Nowadays embryo freezing is used as a way of keeping costs

down and avoiding repeating the first 'retrieval' stage of the IVF process. Freezing an embryo costs around £250 a year and implanting it into the woman at a later date a further £1,100.

The couple must also budget for the cost of drugs not included in the price. A bottle of the hormone suppressant Buserelin is £18 and an injection of Goserelin is £75. The daily ampoule of Pergonal costs £6 and Metrodin is £10. Then there's the overnight accommodation in hotels in the early days of tests and appointments as well as the travel costs. Couples who try IVF are likely to spend all their savings or may finish up with a second mortgage.

So, as the facts are made available, why do people do it? One reason is everyone thinks they are going to be the lucky ones. Lorraine Dennerstein and Carol Morse, eminent Australian psychiatrists specializing in infertility, reported the results of one study: 'most couples overestimated their chances of having a child, and half of them expected pregnancy within a few months.'[14] The majority of couples 'predicted that they had a higher than 40% chance of achieving a pregnancy despite having been informed that the chance of successful conception with IVF was about 10%'. Another researcher who spent many months interviewing and observing patients and staff at a fertility clinic noted that what was in fact a 20 per cent chance became exaggerated in the patients' minds and also that: 'Patients viewed probabilities in the best possible light: I will be in the 25% not the 75%.' Equally frequently people claimed, 'I will be the one out of four.' One patient remarked to the researcher, 'I figure I have a 50–50 chance.'[15]

In IVF, a donor's egg is removed, fertilized in the laboratory with the sperm and then placed inside the receiving woman. It sounds simple, but in truth it is very far from it. Few women who have been through IVF treatment would describe it as anything other than uncomfortable and at times painful, time-consuming, stressful and frequently degrading. In the culture of reproductive technology, however, part of the proof of commit-ment is a woman's willingness to submit, uncomplainingly, to the procedure. It is considered to be the price of motherhood, and women who are unsuccessful are urged to go on and on trying. One woman for whom IVF was successful, nevertheless confessed to me that she found the experience so traumatic that, except for her husband's wishes, she would not agree to go through with it a second time.

The process of IVF begins after initial tests and checks. In the case of a couple using a donor egg, the menstrual cycles of the donor and the recipient will need to be co-ordinated. For the recipient this is usually a fairly simple process involving taking oestrogen or contraceptive pills. In the case of the woman from whom the eggs are to be taken (in our example the donor, but just as often the infertile patient), it is far more complicated. She will begin by taking different hormone-based drugs. One, a nasal spray or an injection given daily for the next month, will suppress her natural menstrual cycle. Another drug, again either a daily injection or tablets, will stimulate her ovaries into producing many more times the number of eggs they normally would (superovulation). Photographs of the ovaries of a woman going through IVF show visibly distended, swollen sacs. Some-times her husband or partner will be taught to give the injections into his partner's hip, but if the donor is single, she must visit her local hospital or GP every day. Recently at least one member of the industry has gone on record to criticize the treatment of women. Dr Robert Edwards, a fertility specialist, accused doctors of using too many expensive hormones and producing unneces-sarily large crops of eggs. He called for fertility clinics to treat women more gently.[16]

Many women find the injections painful. Pergonal, one of the most commonly used superovulatory drugs, contains human menopausal gonadotrophin extracted from the urine of post-menopausal women and commonly produces symptoms associ-ated with the change of life, including depression and irritability, headaches and hot flushes. In some women cysts may develop on the ovaries. In one in a hundred women the drugs will cause a massive number of eggs to develop and her ovaries to swell painfully, requiring immediate hospitalization. If all goes well, however, she will be asked to go to the hospital late at night on the eve of the day on which the eggs are to be harvested for a final hormone shot to ripen the crop.

Human eggs are retrieved one of two ways. The first involves using an ultrasound-guided needle which is passed through the bladder, then urethra, and then the vaginal or abdominal wall and the eggs are removed one by one. It can be a painful procedure, requiring drugs and causing bleeding. The second is via laparoscopy, which is far more complicated and requires a general anaesthetic. The woman is cut just below the navel and a needle inserted to remove the eggs. Common side-effects include painful stomach, chest or shoulders and bleeding. Laparoscopies have also been linked with infections, haemorrhaging and even bowel damage.

Assuming there are sufficient eggs of good quality – many women fail to produce enough and have to start again – the eggs can now be fertilized using a fresh sample of semen which the male partner must produce beforehand. The sperm and eggs are mixed and a day or so later, if they have 'taken', up to three embryos are inserted into the womb using a catheter. Nowadays new techniques can inject a single sperm straight into the egg. Then probably the most tense period of the entire process begins, for the couple must wait to see if the woman becomes pregnant. There is an 85 per cent chance that she will not.

The shortcomings of reproductive techniques like IVF beg the question whether assisted conception is really viable as a solution to infertility. Should we be encouraging large numbers of people down this path at all when we know that only a few will succeed and all of them will lose a great deal of money in the process? In some ways it actually deters people from coming to terms with their infertility. Many speak of the need to 'exhaust all the options' before giving up. But how far does one go before then? How many tries? Three, four, a dozen? How much money? £3,000, £10,000? Is a child worth selling a house or a business for?

Questions like these have prompted psychologists who work closely with infertile people to take a more challenging look at the notion of 'curing' infertility through treatments like IVF. By law in Britain everybody must be offered counselling before embarking on a programme of fertility treatment, but few counsellors stop to ask couples to think about their answer to the simplest, most fundamental question: why do you want a child at all?

In 1991 a study by a group of Canadian psychologists into the motives for parenthood held by people who put themselves forward for IVF treatment contained the initial observation: 'There has been no investigation into the beliefs or motives underlying couples' decisions to pursue IVF, other than the obvious recognition of a desire for children. This seems to reflect the current consensus in our society that parenthood is inherently both positive and desirable.'[17]

The accepted solution to fertility problems is the provision of a child. That's the first suggestion offered by most GPs. James Monach, a Sheffield lecturer and an infertility counsellor, believes that this is not necessarily the right way forward. Many infertile people 'want the choice to be able to have a child' and not necessarily an actual child. Sometimes a reproductive problem is discovered before the decision to start a family has even been taken. Before they know it, the couple find themselves enrolling in a medical programme, taking the first step down that arduous and expensive route without stopping to ask whether they want a child that much. Nowadays, with the scientific choices on offer, we don't stop to look closely enough at the alternatives.

In one chapter of his book *Childless: No Choice*, Monach examines an aspect of our culture which he calls 'pro-natalism' as the reason for assuming the validity of the desire for children as well as the cause for the existence of the desire itself.[18] We are all part of a society that assumes, encourages and rewards parenthood while disapproving of those who do not have children. Evidence of pro-natalism is everywhere from the doctrines on procreation of the Islamic, Christian and Judaic faiths to government tax breaks for families; from advertising images to the question 'When do you plan to start a family?' Indeed, pressure from family and friends has been cited by study after study as a major reason for wanting a family. Having a child or children is still very much seen as the natural and inevitable result of marriage.

Unsurprisingly, women feel it most, but men are also under pressure to prove their maturity and even virility by having children. In his survey of 2,388 patients at an infertility clinic, Monach found: 'The stigma of infertility for men closely relates to the prevalence of this "folk belief" that fertility and virility are inseparable.'

For women, the desire to have a child can be deeply bound up with perceptions of the feminine role and the stronger the woman's wish to conform to that stereotype, the stronger her wish for a child. In an Australian study, women on an IVF programme were found to have 'described themselves in more traditional terms, seeing themselves in terms of traditional feminine attributes much more than did other women'.[19] Those women, as compared to a group of mothers and other women who remained childless out of choice, 'judge themselves as meeting the ideal image of the good mother'. Motherhood has traditionally been such a revered state that failure to attain that status is especially bitter for the woman who wishes to, but cannot. Her condition makes her apt to view an already romanticized institution with even more longing. The same study also demonstrated that women seeking IVF displayed higher expectations about being loved and being needed than voluntarily childless women or mothers. What research of this type indicates is that the compelling force which drives women to try to become mothers through artificial means may be more psychological than biological.

There are times when the myths associated with motherhood and women's desire for it simply overrule basic common sense. I was told another story of a woman who flew to America, in this instance to use the services of a surrogate, and tore up and flushed the child's American passport down the toilet of the aeroplane on the way home. Ever since then she has denied that the child is anything other than her own, despite her husband's vain attempts to secure her co-operation in regularizing the baby's adoption and citizenship. I was expected to feel sorry for her, and I did, desperately, but not for the reason the story-teller imagined. Here was a woman who was patently unwell, who needed psychological help rather than simply being handed a baby. If her compulsion was expressed in some other form, she would have received help years ago. I recounted that story to a psychologist specializing in the treatment of infertile people, who remarked that one could be almost certain that her problem, whatever it really was, would re-emerge in another guise and at a later date.

The power of maternal ideology and the constraints of the mother's role have even led some researchers to point to the prevalence of such ideas as a reason for infertility in itself. Around 15 per cent of couples who are infertile show no apparent medical reason. Some psychologists believe that the reasons may be psychosomatic and that for some women, although by no means the entire 15 per cent, it is the either/or nature of modern motherhood and the tensions which seem to have become woven into the role which cause them consciously to choose motherhood while subconsciously rejecting it. In a review of the findings in this area, Dennerstein and Morse say: 'For the woman with a strong intellectual drive, choosing between an ambitious competitive career or domesticity and motherhood has been suggested as another source of conflict.'[20]

So what are the reasons people want to have a child? Susan

Rice, spokesperson for the support group ISSUE, cited the most common motivation among people contacting her organization is the wish to have a baby as a 'gift' within a relationship. Timothy Hedgely of the same organization, who counsels couples and has a child of his own through assisted conception, described wanting 'immortality through children' and confessed to a fear of being 'genetically dead'. Wanting to pass on one's genes as a form of life after death is a reason given over and over again, particularly among men who seek infertility treatment. Snowden, Mitchell and Snowden's psychological study of men whose wives were receiving donor insemination quoted one husband: 'My major hang-up really was based on this rather metaphysical notion of genetic immortality. What depressed me most of all, and overwhelmed me mentally, was the idea that at this point my genetic channel stops.'[21] When a man cannot produce sperm of good enough quality, this concern for immortality has even led to the highly controversial practice of mixing his sperm with donor sperm in order to allow him to believe that the resulting child might be his.

Arlene Westley, a marriage, family and child therapist who specializes in treating couples with fertility issues, refers to a notion that commonly crops up in sessions with her clients called 'outliving the self'. Some people leave their mark on the world with accomplishments – sporting, intellectual, cultural or political – but for the majority of people a child serves the same purpose, someone who can carry forward their own achievements, values and beliefs. 'The child is a project which they can leave behind,' Westley explains. So people increasingly want a child that is their own both biologically and also in the sense that the child's characteristics, qualities or talents reflect their input and effort.

This is why many people, even those who could adopt, prefer to use artificial reproduction methods. In fact, adoption as a solution to infertility has rapidly fallen out of favour. Assisted conception has become a choice in its own right because it offers something 'better' than adoption. Aside from the genetic link, it also, and perhaps even more importantly, promises a *baby*. Organizations like the British Agency for Adoption and Fostering continually point out that there are still many children looking for adoptive and foster homes, particularly older children, black or mixed-race children, or children with special needs. To many of the couples at the fertility clinic, these are compromise choices. They want a baby of their own. In the words of one patient: 'At the beginning there seemed to be so many options: tubal surgery, IVF, adoption. We have been accepted for adoption, but there are no babies available, only older children and we really want a baby.'

In their investigations into artificial reproduction, Snowden, Mitchell and Snowden write that almost all the couples interviewed believed AID (artificial insemination by donor) to be preferable to adoption, citing the reasons above and adding fears that adoptive children might have undesirable characteristics and that this way the child would be more 'theirs'. The wish for quality control is becoming increasingly prevalent. A fact sheet available on the Internet explaining the advantages of IVF with a donor egg, advised prospective clients: 'Your nutrition, psychological input, and what you do or don't do during pregnancy are significant: areas you may not be able to control with adoption.'[22]

Snowden, Mitchell and Snowden also discovered that many people who have children with the help of reproductive technology plan ever to tell those children that they were born through AID. In fact, in their study of fifty-six couples only three had positively decided to reveal the child's origins to him or her. This allowed the majority of couples to pretend the child was all theirs and that they were an ideal family, as well as maintaining the assumption that the husband was fertile. The question of secrecy touches ethical and practical concerns from the right to know, to the need for accurate medical information. The desire for secrecy highlights reproductive technology's appeal to some people as a choice over adoption. Secrecy used to be part of the philosophy of adoption, indeed the first Adoption Act in 1926 advocated the 'fresh start'. Today people think quite the opposite, believing that openness and honesty are absolutely essential to a happy family in the future. Surely the same must apply to families with children born through AID or IVF?

The bottom line is that reproductive technology simply reinforces the most conservative family values and ideas about biology and parenting. Making babies artificially is not nearly as radical as it first appeared; that is to say, it is radical in form but not in content. Judith Modell, an Australian anthropologist who has conducted interviews with both prospective adopters and IVF patients to compare the two, writes: 'while in-vitro fertilization may be technologically innovative, it is conceptually conservative in upholding existing cultural assumptions about parenthood, sex and marriage.'[23] At one end of the spectrum, reproductive technology appears to defy conventional beliefs about motherhood by allowing lesbians or older women to become mothers, although not without opposition (in fact most clinics in Britain decline to treat unmarried women and women over a certain age), but in reality the reproductive industry supports and actively promotes deeply conservative ideas about mothering, namely the primacy of biological over social parenting and the overweening importance of the genetic link. And that is the foundation of many of the most entrenched myths about motherhood.

Let's go back to the couple who placed the advertisement. They're a long way from giving up the dream of achieving the ideal family. Let's imagine that, for them, IVF failed to produce a child. There is another option which more and more people are choosing and that is to use a surrogate mother. It is perfectly possible that the advertisement seeking an ocyte donor was placed with the express intention of fertilizing that egg with the husband's sperm and implanting it into the womb of a host woman.

Surrogacy

Surrogacy was once considered unnatural and immoral. It was regarded as at once futuristic in its possibilities by some, and by others as regressive and exploitative. Today surrogacy is a highly commercial, structured, global industry. It is consumer-driven, using the best that science has to offer to provide couples with exactly what they want. If IVF is 'better' than adoption, surrogacy offers a range of choices and infinitely more control than submitting to the vagaries and low odds of IVF treatment.

For a start, in commercial surrogacy the 'raw materials' will be the best that money can buy. The carrying mother will usually be a woman selected for her ability to bear children with ease. The sperm that is used may be that of the husband or it may be specially selected donor sperm. Today, the ability of doctors to achieve a pregnancy in one woman with eggs from another offers up an even better range of possibilities. Ocyte donation means that if an infertile woman is still able to ovulate she can have a child which is genetically her own, although carried by another woman. Using a donor egg, from whatever source, also means that the woman who carries and bears the child need have no genetic tie with the baby at all, broadening the pool of potential surrogates enormously.

The best aspect of ocyte donation in surrogacy, from the point of view of potential parents, is the fantastic potential for selection and quality control. Let's take another look at that classified advertisement. 'Are you univ/medicine educated, fair-haired,' it says. What does that mean? Presumably the woman is fair or blonde and they want as many characteristics between her and the donor to match as possible. Or perhaps they both just prefer fair looks, perhaps the woman always wanted to be a blonde and is going to bestow that gift, like a fairy-godmother, on her child, courtesy of science. What does 'univ/medicine' mean? Given that they are professional people, does it mean they only want eggs from a woman who is a graduate and whose intellectual abilities are proven? It would seem so. The added stipulation of medicine would suggest they want someone with a medical or scientific qualification or background. Their own specialist subject, or once again just a whim?

With so many possibilities surrogacy is now a boom industry in the United States, where it is legal in several states including California. No agency collates figures on surrogate births either here or in America, but the US-based international Organization of Parents through Surrogacy estimate that there have been well over 8,000 commercial surrogacies in that country since 1979.

Commercial surrogacy is forbidden in the UK, but it can only be a matter of time before restrictions are lifted. Under the Surrogacy Arrangements Act 1985 voluntary agencies are not prohibited. Nor does the Act rule out payments to mothers who can and do receive in the region of £12,000 in 'expenses'. The 1990 Human Fertilization and Embryology Act smoothed the path even more for people who use surrogates and donate their own gametes by making it easier for them to adopt the child. And in November 1995, for the first time, a British court ruled against the right of the surrogate mother to keep a child conceived using the infertile woman's egg and donor sperm. The court also upheld the terms of the surrogate arrangement, including the fee for £8,000 in expenses. In February 1996 the British Medical Association, previously firm in its anti-surrogacy stance, performed a policy volte-face and permitted, even encouraged, doctors to look upon surrogacy as a solution for childlessness and to help with such arrangements. In the same month, the NHS approved the first ever use of a surrogate paid for by public money, using IVF at King's College Hospital.

In its policy document the BMA also acknowledged the growth of 'medical tourism' – people going abroad to use the services of a commercial surrogate.[24] In the future, this is the way many British couples will circumvent the country's restrictions on commercial surrogacy. In one instance a surrogate mother flew from Britain to Holland to bear the child of a Dutch couple. Since February 1997, America's prestigious Center for Surrogate Parenting in Beverly Hills has been recruiting British couples. Staff fly to the UK, carry out all the necessary tests and collect the requisite gametes from the new clients. They then return to the USA where the waiting surrogate is implanted. After nine months all the British couple have to do is hop on a transatlantic flight and claim their newborn baby (and pay the Center's $50,000 fees). The Center estimates that, at present, at least a quarter of their clients live in England, Europe, Australia and Japan.

It is all a very long way away from the days of Kim Cotton, the first British woman to bear a child as a surrogate mother in 1985. Then the ethics of the arrangement were almost unanimously agreed to be questionable. There's no doubt that our attitude towards using women as surrogates for infertile couples is becoming more relaxed and there is a greater willingness within the courts and the authorities to recognize and validate such agreements.

In the United States, despite the legitimacy of commercial surrogacy in some places, courts have nevertheless been reluctant to enforce agreements, but that is changing. The landmark case, which was finally decided in 1993, was that of Anna L. Johnson, an African-American woman living in Orange County who agreed to carry a child for a white couple, Mark and Crispina Calvert.[25] It was a private arrangement, under which the couple agreed to pay $10,000. Johnson was impregnated using Crispina Calvert's egg fertilized with sperm from an anonymous donor.

Before the child was born, the couple fell out with the surrogate, for reasons which are unclear. Anna Johnson declined to hand over the child. Both women filed claims of maternity. The entire surrogacy industry watched and waited as the case reached the Supreme Court. The judges decided that Crispina Calvert, the genetic mother, was the true mother of the child over and above the woman who carried and bore the child. Who knows how much the race of the child and his two mothers affected the decision-making process. The only dissenting voice among the seven judges was the one woman, Justice Joyce Kennard, who warned them against failing to protect women and children and their 'uncritical validation of gestational surrogacy'.

Today the courts are prepared to award a child to a woman on the strength of her genetic contribution, even though she did not carry or give birth to him. This is extraordinary in many ways, not least because an unmarried man still has no legal rights at all with respect to a child he fathers and to whom he contributes half the genetic make-up. Surrogacy has gone a long way to redefining modern motherhood purely in terms of ownership – that is, who owns the genetic material of children who have been designed and commissioned.

Clinics which offer surrogate and IVF services are self-serving in their reinvention of myths about motherhood to sell their product. When I called the Center for Surrogate Parenting, I was told in the course of the conversation that the 'real' mother in a surrogate arrangement was the woman with the genetic link with the child. The lack of a genetic link, the speaker continued, made it easier for the surrogate to give up a child she had merely carried because she would not bond with that child. Conversely, in similar conversations with organizations marketing IVF technology to infertile couples, I was told the opposite: that the true mother is the one who carries the baby, and genes are unimportant. Of course, it's important for each supplier that their potential client swallows their line on motherhood. Motherhood is being redefined by the demands of the sales pitch.

The late Noel Keane was known as the grandfather of surrogacy. A lawyer based in Michigan, the centre he founded (operating out of Indianapolis where the laws are more favourable) has produced over 600 babies and has up to 4,000 surrogates on the books at any time. After the initial consultation the international clientele, including many British couples, visit the centre to select a surrogate and often an egg donor from his files. Apart from physical attractiveness, Keane told me, most couples also look for evidence of sportiness and musicality in the donor or surrogate. For special requests such as an Ivy League education, Keane would advertise. When we spoke in the summer of 1996, he was offering a fee of $50,000 for the eggs of a woman who he said must possess 'particular good looks and an exceptional IQ' at the request of one client. He admitted the idea of genetic quality was 'of primary importance' to professional couples. His statement has been borne out by the success of another centre, the Repository for Germinal Choice, a select sperm bank founded by Hermann J. Muller, the 1946 physics Nobel Prize winner. There interested parties can obtain the sperm of Nobel Prize winners and, more recently, Olympic athletes and outstanding sportsmen. Their brochure contains the CV of a typical donor. He is a six-foot, blond-haired, blue-eyed Austrian Olympic athlete and geneticist. Surely I am not alone in questioning the taste of promoting the institution's services with an example so eerily reminiscent of Hitler's dream of a master race?

Typical surrogacy contracts make no concessions to maternal sentiments on the part of the woman who is to carry the child. She must agree to undergo genetic testing and be willing to have an abortion if there is any abnormality. Contracts issued by the Woman to Woman Fertility Centre also stipulate that the surrogate must agree to a selective termination if she is found to be carrying twins. Should she miscarry, a standard clause declares she will be paid pro rata for her time.

In the past, the most common objection to surrogacy, coming especially from religious and right-wing groups, is that the practice undermines 'the family' and the institution of motherhood. Yet what is remarkable about talking to people who run and use the industry is how deeply conservative their views of the family and the role of women as mothers are. While others see surrogacy as challenging these norms, they see themselves as upholding them. The shared view throughout the industry, which the industry uses to justify its existence, is the same: a woman has a right to mother, therefore the end justifies the means. Yet the maternal interests of the surrogate who carries and bears the child are summarily dismissed; the notion of maternal 'instincts' in surrogacy is argued from a highly selective perspective, which cannot be divorced from class. Rich women have them and poor women don't. Discussing the case of Anna Johnson, one woman who used a surrogate to bear both her children became impassioned: 'The child wasn't hers! That wasn't her egg. She had no genetic link whatsoever. The child had nothing to do with her.' In the world of artificially-conceived children genetics have become king.

The reproductive industry holds a particular responsibility for the fetishizing of genetics and in particular, the fetishizing of a shared genetic link with a child. In order to sell their 'products' large parts of the industry have successfully exploited the extraordinary grip ideas about genetics have rapidly gained on the public imagination. Faith in genetics has a reverential quality. The genetic child, the fantasy child, becomes irreplaceable as the receptacle for the hopes and aspirations of the parents. Meanwhile the concern for real children blurs and fades.

In surrogacy the idea of 'family planning' takes on an absurd and undesirable new meaning. When a surrogate hired through Noel Keane's agency produced twins, the prospective parents took one child home and placed the other in a children's home for adoption. In another incident, through the same agency, prospective parents and a surrogate ended up in litigation when the surrogate reneged on the deal and refused to abort a disabled child. In 1983, Judy Stiver, a twenty-six-year-old surrogate, bore a child with microcephaly, an abnormally small head. Both she and the prospective parents refused to take the child which languished in hospital while the two parties went to court. The New York accountant who hired Stiver sued for $50 million claiming the child was not his. In the final analysis the question was settled when the results of a blood test were announced live on a television chat show and the child was shown to be that of Stiver's partner.

Finally, the exploitation of women through surrogacy seems to have slipped off the political agenda. Commercialization and profits have renewed the incidence of abuse. In Canada a Royal Commission into the practices of commercial surrogacy found that newly-immigrant women were being coerced into bearing the surrogate child of their sponsoring families. In 1995, twelve Polish women were taken to Holland to be used as surrogates and paid £14,000 (the equivalent of around two years' salary in Poland). In the same year John Davies, a British adoption specialist who sold children from Eastern Europe to wealthy Western countries, developed plans for a global market in surrogacy using Eastern European women impregnated with the sperm of American men and flown to the USA to give birth. Before his arrest for baby smuggling he had drawn up a business plan and had already lined up a team of gynaecologists and obstetricians. He called surrogacy 'the perfect solution for childless couples who don't want to go through the hell of adoption'.

What of the future? One day reproductive centres intend to extend their repertoire of available options by hiring geneticists to screen out inheritable diseases or conditions, and eventually to screen in desirable traits. Despite all the attention such ideas have received we still have no idea if polygenetic traits such as musicality can be isolated and passed on, but scientists are already claiming to have discovered a gene for intelligence. Laboratory technicians working in IVF clinics already perform embryo selection; they pick only the best and healthiest embryos of a fertilized crop and discard the rest. There is no reason why gender selection should not become as straightforward as implanting an embryo of the chosen sex. In China, couples who are restricted to having only one child have already begun to turn to IVF techniques to guarantee results. 'If I pay the doctor more, will I get a better baby?' one woman was reported as asking at an IVF clinic.

The cloning of Dolly the sheep in Scotland, followed by the cloning of two monkeys in the USA, sent shock-waves of excitement through the reproductive industry. So far, it has proved possible only to try to match the genetic specifications of couples as closely as possible through third-party gamete donation. The potential to clone a human being using their own DNA opens up a myriad of opportunities, for it offers people exactly what it is many of them admit they are looking for: genetic immortality. In the USA, Canada and the UK, lobby groups for the reproductive industry pressed their respective governments to open up the possibility of allowing cloning of human beings as an option for infertile people. In the USA, National Institute of Health Director Harold Varmus asked Congress to make an exception to any ban on human cloning so that it could be used to help couples who could not conceive or bear their own genetically-related offspring. In January 1998 Richard Seed, an unemployed physicist, announced his intention to set up a private clinic to clone human beings.

As a society we have begun to place mounting emphasis on genetic make-up, yet the truth is we still know very little about how genetic manipulation or enhancement might work. Paul Billings, a Stanford geneticist, has said: 'That genes will be on tap in the future is the current myth, but they will be on top.'[26] There is every sign that what has worked in laboratory mice will not necessarily work with human genes, and we also have very little idea what the long-term effects of genetic manipulation might be. Furthermore, the idea that a single unique gene produces a single unique effect is being overturned as the anomalies to the rule grow. For example, identical genomes can produce up to 250 different cell types. Similar species, say two kinds of monkey, may have very different DNA; and species with very different forms such as humans and chimps may have very similar DNA structures. Finally, rather than solving the nature/nurture debate, new discoveries in gene science suggest that the issue may be even more complicated than we ever imagined. It is now becoming evident that environment, that is to say habits and lifestyles, can actually change genetic expression over time. The DNA of athletes who train hard and regularly over a period of years actually alters. So environment remains a significant part of the equation.

The new faith in genetics moves us even further down the line towards individual responsibility for decisions and their consequences and even further away from any kind of societal or collective responsibility for children. Pre-natal diagnoses already place women under pressure not to bear a child with a disability. And just as 'choice' has become a reason not to help people with their children (they chose to have them), 'choice' will become an excuse not to aid or empathize with a woman who goes ahead with a pregnancy under such circumstances. The great irony is that just as maternal influence is used to blame a child's condition on his or her mother, now genetic knowledge will allow us to do the same. People used to imagine that homosexual men became that way because of their emasculating mothers. The possible discovery of a 'gay gene' will overturn that theory, but for those looking for someone to blame, it won't change anything. I once saw a slogan on a T-shirt sported by a gay man which made the point: 'Thanks for the genes, mum.'

Do we have a 'right' to children?

The notion of rights is central to the debate over access to reproductive technology and all that it entails now and in the future. In the 1990s the increasingly influential infertility lobby has co-opted the language of feminist campaigns for women's reproductive rights to use for its own ends. Campaigns for reproductive choice such as the right to have a termination have traditionally asserted that every woman has a legal right to choose whether or not to become a mother. If that is so, shouldn't that right be extended to people who are infertile? Shouldn't they also be given the right to control their own fertility by having a baby employing any and every possible means to do so?

In law, there is some evidence to say yes, it is a universal right. Article 12 of the European Convention on Human Rights states: 'Men and women of marriageable age have the right to marry and found a family.' The 1974 World Population Plan of Action has no particular legal status but nevertheless affirms: 'all couples and individuals have the basic right to decide freely and responsibly the number and spacing of their children and to have the information and education to do so.' So there is some evidence to say that we recognize the existence of a human right not just for couples, but also for individuals, to become parents.

In the United States, there is evidence of legal precedents dating back to 1942.[27] Several other and more recent cases have established the right to choice and privacy from intrusion in matters of family and child, specifically Carey v. Population Services International 1977, which cited the Fourteenth Amendment on 'liberty' as extending to 'freedom of choice in certain matters of marriage and family life'.[28] That finding was reaffirmed by the Supreme Court in 1992 in Casey v. Planned Parenthood.[29]

However, legislators could not foresee the situations to which those 'rights' might be applied. If we say a woman has a right to become a mother, are we also saying that every man has a right to become a father, whether or not he has a partner to bear a child? Strictly speaking that is exactly where the argument leads us, as the case of William Austin illustrated in the most graphic way possible.

William Austin, a twenty-six-year-old single man from Pennsylvania, decided he wanted a child and hired a surrogate through the surrogacy centre run by Noel Keane. The establishment regularly provides surrogates for many single people including, in the past, about eight single men. Austin was not offered, neither did he receive, any counselling. By law in those American states which allow surrogacy, only the surrogates, not those who use their services, must be psychologically assessed. A woman was inseminated with Austin's sperm and the child was born in the winter of 1994. Five weeks later Austin battered and shook the child to death. Austin was jailed. Later, in a legal hearing, the agency was absolved from any wrongdoing in providing Austin with a child and the court upheld the absolute right of any citizen to have a child regardless of the circumstances.

Where does this trail of 'rights' end? First the right to have a child, and then the right to have a healthy child, followed by the right to have a child with all the traits of one's choosing. In other words, the right to have a perfect child. These are the commandments of the reproductive industry. The maternal ideal has become more than something to which we should all aspire; it has become something we *must* have. From simply wanting the best for our children, we increasingly seek to have the best children. The so-called reproductive revolution has actually served to entrench the myths about motherhood even more deeply in the common psyche. The casualties are those women (and men) for whom infertility is a permanent fact of life and whose hopes are exploited until they become unquenchable needs; but the greatest disservice is to our children. Our collective responsibility for children has been replaced by the need to fulfil the individual desires of adults. Think not what you can do for your children, but what your children can do for you, could well be the motto of the reproductive industry.

chapter 6

Persecuting Mothers:
Motherhood and the Law

Testimony: Karen

Karen Henderson, twenty-four, is a fuel station cashier and a mother of two. In 1993 she had a third child by another partner. At birth the baby tested positive for drugs. He died two months later and minute traces of the drug methamphetamine (a party drug) were found in his bloodstream. Karen was arrested and tried for murder, accused of passing drugs to the baby through her breastmilk. At her trial in September 1994, despite the testimony of expert witnesses that her baby had died a cot death, she was found guilty of child endangerment and was jailed.

I grew up in Bakersfield. I had a sheltered life, I guess, a strict life. Nothing special. My mom's disabled and my dad's a mechanic. [I] stayed home and took care of my sister's kids. She was eight years older than me.

My own life was kind of like the way I grew up. I just had the kids at home, played and just stayed home and lived a sheltered life. I met their father when I was thirteen. We lived together from when I was sixteen until I was twenty. While we lived together he worked on a drilling rig and we had a good life, the kids were happy. He was home every day, he played with the kids although as a father he was scared [laughs] to stay home with them and look after them on his own. My kids were never out of my sight. They were two and three then. They're six and seven now, a boy and a girl.

I didn't really decide to have a third baby, but I got pregnant in '92, and I had him in '93. He was only with us for nine weeks, but he was a good baby. [My daughter] was only three but she just loved him. She would sit on the couch and feed him his breakfast. She took it hard when he died.

The day before he died we were at my [new] boyfriend's mom's house and we had gotten into a fight and Jason threw hot coffee at me and the baby. He was the father of the baby. The father of the other two is Brendan. I handed the baby to my daughter and I hit [Jason] a few times for doing it and we left. We went home and the baby was tired and took a nap. My daughter helped me feed him and give him a bath, and we put him to bed at 10.30. The next morning my oldest son was at my bed crying to come in bed with me. It was six in the morning. I checked on the baby, because his leg was sticking between the [cot] bars. I said, look he must have moved in the night, he got stuck, how cute or whatever and I picked him up and that's when I noticed he was blue and I told Jason that the baby was dead and I was screaming. Then I ran across to my mom's and called 911 and did CPR on him. We called an ambulance and went to the hospital but he died.

One day, later on, my mom came over to my house and said, 'What's going on, what's wrong?' and I said, 'What are you talking about?' She said, 'A detective called and wants you to call him back.' So I called him back. He answered the phone and he said, 'Detective S., Homicide.' He said, 'I want to talk to you about Jason Alan,' and I said, 'My baby?' and he said, 'Yes' and I said, 'My baby's dead.' And he said, 'Oh, we know that. I want to talk to you about his death.' I said I don't know why he died, I haven't got the death certificate. You need to talk to the Coroner's Office, so he said, 'We've already talked to them. We want to talk to you now.' So I said, OK, I can come in right now. And he said the next day would be fine. So when I got off the phone I asked my dad, I said 'What does homicide mean?' and he said it means murder. I said, 'Oh, my god, why do they want to talk to me?' I just figured then they were going to accuse me of killing him.

It was just like TV, one was nice and one was mean. I told them everything. They asked me did I use drugs? And I didn't lie, I told them I'd used them off and on for five years. So then he started asking me about that last year, '93. And I told him I found out I was pregnant in December '92. I had the baby in July and he died in September. That's all there is to it. The baby was born positive, I had used drugs on the Fourth of July. So, they tried to put everything together. When he was born positive I had called CPS (Child Protection Services) and told them myself, you know, that they had kept the baby in the hospital, he was born positive and what should I do? They checked him out, they said he was fine, that it wasn't that much and that he could come home to me. I told them, 'You guys can come right here and test me, I'm not going to do it no more.' They never did.

[The policeman] said I killed my baby because I breastfed him drugs and that I didn't care because I wasn't crying. I told him I had cried because the baby was dead, but I'm not going to cry because I killed him, because I didn't. And then he said I had to have my kids out of my house by 5 or he was going to take them to CPS. So they went to my mom's across the street and I got arrested two weeks later. Later CPS took my kids away, anyway.

I started using [methamphetamine] when I was about fifteen, just because some guy introduced it to me and my sister. We did it to get high, off and on, on the weekends. Then we'd do it, you know, when payday came. We didn't do it often. We didn't do it alone. That was the only drug I used.

When I got pregnant, in December, that was it. I just quit using it. I wasn't strung out. I was never addicted to it. I don't know what I was thinking when I took it that last time. I can't say I was talked into it, because I can only do what I want to do. But, I was there with my kids' father and the baby's father. We were over at my mum's. Brendan was visiting because it was the Fourth of July and they were saying: 'Oh, let's just do one line.' I went into labour the next day. The baby was a month early.

Jason, the baby's father, provided the drugs. He'd always get mad *if he didn't have it. Sometimes I'd have to go and get it for him. I don't know, I'd want to be happy. I didn't want to fight. So I didn't say nothing about it afterwards.*

After I went to see the detectives two weeks went by and I just forgot about it. The day I got arrested I went to my mom's. By then CPS already had my kids. I went into the front room and I looked up and I saw a car and a white jeep [outside my house]. I went, 'Mom, they're here. They're here!' They didn't know my mom lived opposite me. I went out the back and left. I knew, I knew why they were there. I just knew it. And I went and got Brendan and me and him spent time together. We went up to the cemetery. That was at nine o'clock in the morning. At one o'clock I went and turned myself in at the Sheriff's department. The same detective who had questioned me before told me I was under arrest for second degree murder and child endangerment.

I was in custody up until my trial. I had never been in a prison before. It was terrible, but nothing that you can't live through. I was in protective custody, so there were nine girls at the most. They were all in there for something to do with children, some kind of baby case or something. When I first went in, there was one girl who had her baby in a trunk for five years. I had heard about [it] on the TV before I got arrested. There was another one whose baby starved to death, and another one who got hit over the head. The first day I was arrested somebody beat on the door 'You baby-killing bitch!'

I was in County [Jail] for ten months and the trial lasted four weeks. They lied. The detective who arrested me, he lied. The ambulance driver who took my baby to hospital lied. He said I had sores all over me. But I had shorts and a tank top on, I mean if I had sores all over me I sure wouldn't be walking around like that. They were trying to make out that I was strung out on meth. The detective said that I was late for my interview because I was scared that I was going to be drug tested because I was dirty. But I'd told them, 'You can test me right now.'

I was nervous the whole time. I just kept thinking I'm going to be there for ever. Until the very last day when they dropped the murder charges. It was a hung jury. They said they were going to refile, but they didn't. I was convicted of child endangerment and they gave me six years. In the end I served three years and three months.

They said the drugs were passed through the breastmilk, but I wasn't using drugs. The night before [the baby died] my neighbour was over while my son was taking a nap. I had breastfed him and bottlefed him too. Jason had made the bottle for him. I didn't use [drugs] at all.

I don't know where the drugs [in my baby's bloodstream] came from, maybe from before when I was pregnant. That's the only place it could have come from. Even in the newspaper they said that I had taken a line or a quarter of meth that night and took my baby to my breast, but I didn't. The coroner had three different causes of death. He said a hole in the heart, then he said SIDS, and then he said methamphetamine intoxication. He couldn't make up his mind.

While I was in prison my kids were sent everywhere: to an aunt on my dad's side for a while, then they went to my sister's. Then my daughter finally went to my mom's while my son went to his aunt on his dad's side. For the last two years now he's been with his dad's mom, his grandma.

I think it was hard on them because they hadn't had nobody but me. I think that's why my daughter's a little hateful now. But they see me. I visit them all the time. They are six and seven now. I still love them. But [my daughter's] just a little bitter at life. My mom told me that she'd always cry, just lay in her room and cry that she wanted her mom. All they know is that I was in prison for drugs. I'll [tell them] later. I don't know how I will. But I know that I'm going to. Later, later, later. They're going to be OK. We're all good people. Mommy's nice. They're not going to think that I'd go and do something like that. They know I love them and I loved the baby. I just get real mad [sometimes] because I feel I should never have been involved with any of this. I'm not a criminal.

For more than ten years a war has been waged against mothers through the courts. Women are being punished for their actions specifically because they bear children and are responsible for children. Women are being prosecuted for their behaviour during pregnancy as well as for decisions they make regarding their own bodies and their children, born and unborn. Reproductive freedoms are being challenged by new laws and by reinterpreting existing laws to find mothers culpable. Up until now debates around motherhood have concentrated on reproductive choices – whether to become a mother, when, under what circumstances, as well as the politics of motherhood. Today, of all the legal assaults on mothers, the emergence of a body of law establishing separate rights for the foetus pits a woman against her unborn child in a way never seen before.

America invents foetal rights

Women first began to be prosecuted for their actions during pregnancy in the USA in the late 1980s. Since then the appearance in the American courts of women who have taken drugs, drunk alcohol or declined to follow their doctors' orders while they are pregnant have become commonplace.

A pregnant cancer patient is forced to undergo a caesarean section in an attempt to save the life of the child she is carrying; both the child and the mother die.[1] Another woman is charged with child abuse for drinking alcohol.[2] A court rules in favour of a husband who wants to force his wife to undergo a cervical operation so that she won't miscarry.[3] A thirty-year-old crack addict is sent to prison for ten years for taking drugs while she is pregnant on the grounds of child neglect.[4] There have also been high-profile prosecutions of mothers of young children. The case of Shirley Draper, a Texan woman, made international headlines after she was charged with both child endangerment and injury to a child, when a car driven by her drunken husband plunged over a ravine. Draper was neither in nor anywhere near the vehicle at the time; she was prosecuted for failing to stop them from driving away, for failing in her duty as a mother.

These are all true cases, and many other prosecutions like these are taking place today.

Sometimes the decision to prosecute is clearly absurd. At other times, particularly when illegal drugs are involved, it may seem reasonable to think that a woman should be held responsible if she causes harm to an unborn child. The issue of foetal rights raises a multiplicity of moral and social dilemmas because the successful prosecution in the courts of any one woman on any charge, whether she is a 'sympathetic' figure of a 'hateful' one, opens the doors to the prosecution of any pregnant woman for any action which might harm her unborn child, whether that action in itself is actually legal or illegal. The social and political context which has already given rise to the creation of foetal rights makes it probable that the future will bring more prosecutions. This should be a matter of concern to everyone.

Cases like these seize the headlines as part of a wider malaise, an emerging social mythology that women are no longer fit to be mothers. As women increasingly gain control of their own bodies, from one particular vantage point it can seem as though women have it all. As well as having careers and becoming mothers at the same time, they can now decide when to become mothers, choose to be single or lesbian mothers, and abortion rights have given them the choice of whether they even want to be mothers at all. Some people find this degree of autonomy on the part of women deeply threatening to a degree not seen since Rousseau observed that the independent-minded women of his day seemed intent upon abandoning the institution and duties of motherhood altogether. This sentiment is at work in the courts today in the minds of prosecutors and ordinary citizens alike, and it says that although it may not yet be possible to prosecute women for exercising their freedoms, they can certainly be tried for their transgressions.

The fact that women bear and raise children has meant that, historically, they have been judged by altogether different standards than those applied to men. Nowhere has this become more starkly evident in modern times than in the attempt to establish foetal rights to protect unborn children from the actions of their mothers. Since the 1980s a number of cultural, social and political shifts have combined with medical and technological advances to produce an idea of the foetus as an autonomous individual, separate from its mother. In the USA attempts have been made by judges, law-enforcement officers and elected officials to crystallize that perception in law by prosecuting pregnant women under existing laws – for example, laws relating to child abuse or neglect – and to win for the foetus a set of rights distinct from those of the woman in whose body it is growing. This notion has thrown the interests of women and children into conflict with each other and generated a deep crisis over the civil liberties of pregnant women as patients, as individuals and as citizens.

The foetus as an image, as a personality and as a person in its own right has become familiar. Once the progress of a pregnancy was hidden from view, in the darkness of the woman's belly. Now parents-to-be see their growing offspring thanks to ultrasound; fibre-optic images show the limbs and emerging features of tiny, budding humans; we now know at precisely what stage each element of the growing child develops.

Among the very first to make use of the humanizing of the foetus were anti-abortionists who have employed the notion of the 'glass womb' (if women could see their unborn children they wouldn't have abortions), and used films such as *The Silent Scream* to spread their message. In addition, technological advances enabling doctors to remove eggs from women, fertilize them individually and incubate them in another woman have served psychologically to divide foetuses from women. In an atmosphere of profound social unease about motherhood in general, these social forces have combined to generate a sense of the foetus as a 'symbol of hope and fear',[5] and have served to obscure the image of the woman behind that of the unborn child.

As our knowledge about foetal development increases along-side scientific capabilities, the boundaries of when we see 'personhood' beginning have been moved farther and farther back, with implications for foetal rights. In Britain, controversy has surrounded whether and how to dispose of frozen embryos, which had been stored and then abandoned by couples undergoing fertility treatment. In several states in America, frozen fertilized eggs have been given legal status as people. The abortion debate in both Britain and America has come to hang on notions of foetal 'viability', that is, the point at which an unborn child can survive independently outside the mother's body. The enormously aggressive American pro-life movement has fought vigorously to push the time limit for an abortion earlier and earlier. It has also re-interpreted the ruling in Roe v. Wade (the seminal case which provided American women with the right to seek abortions) to use as a weapon against women by arguing that the viability line established in the case marks a point after which society can override a woman's rights. Incidentally, pro-lifers have also worked hard to portray women who have abortions as over-ambitious, as rejecting motherhood and as misusing their procreative liberty to make choices on the basis of lifestyle and convenience.

In the 1970s the slaughter by Charles Manson and his cohorts of a heavily pregnant Sharon Tate in California prompted a massive national debate over the need for 'feticide' laws. At the time, Manson could be tried only for Tate's murder and not the killing of her and Roman Polanski's unborn child. Since then, many American states have enacted feticide laws intended to allow the prosecution on charges of homicide of anyone who intentionally kills a woman's viable foetus. Feticide laws were supposed to compensate a woman for her loss at the hands of a violent husband or negligent doctor. It was not envisaged that laws of this type would most often be used to prosecute mothers themselves. In the intervening years a growing awareness of how a woman's actions might harm her foetus has combined with a deliberate push on the part of pro-life prosecutors and over-zealous doctors to make women who, for example, take drugs or refuse medical treatment, culpable. The particular enthusiasm for charging mothers has its foundation in beliefs about the sanctity of motherhood and a profound moral disgust at women who do not appear to uphold those values.

In 1986 in San Diego, Pamela Rae Stewart, a twenty-seven-year-old mother of two, became the first woman to be prosecuted under California's feticide and child abuse laws for her conduct during pregnancy. She was warned by her doctors that there were problems with her pregnancy, essentially that the placenta supporting the foetus was becoming detached, and that at the first sign of bleeding she should immediately seek medical attention. She was also told to abstain from sex for the duration of the pregnancy. Pamela Rae Stewart went home, had sex with her husband, took amphetamines and started bleeding, but she ignored her own condition for twelve hours before going to hospital. The baby was eventually born with brain damage and died two months later. Stewart was arrested and charged, but the prosecution was eventually thrown out by the courts on the grounds that the statute was never intended to apply to a woman who failed to follow her doctor's orders.

Three years later, the foetal rights lobby won its first victory in the conviction of Jennifer Clarise Johnson, a crack-cocaine addict, who was sentenced to fifteen years' probation for delivering drugs to a minor, her newborn son Carl, in 1987, through her umbilical cord. Stringent controls were placed upon her liberty during those fifteen years: she was to stay employed or lose her children permanently, she was to report to the courts if she became pregnant, she was forbidden to go anywhere where alcohol was served and she was to be randomly tested for drugs and alcohol. These are more stringent conditions than any drug addict would normally be required to meet, certainly any male drug addict whether or not he was a father. Alcohol, for example, is not an illegal substance and yet Johnson was not even allowed to enter a bar. The Johnson case demonstrates how the foremost concern of the courts is in controlling *mothers*. Multiply this concern hundreds of times over to cover any mother who transgresses, and you have the makings of a police state. Of course, children cannot be left alone with drugged, incompetent mothers but controlling motherhood by using court sanctions is not an appropriate course of action.

The Johnson case came at a time of growing concern over the increase in the use of crack-cocaine, its links with inner-city crime and public awareness through the media of so-called 'crack babies'. For some people the idea of a crack-addicted pregnant woman evokes feelings of pity and concern, but in the minds of many the image provokes disgust, contempt and the spectre of spiralling public-health costs for treatment for these women and their babies. Few people have any interest in defending crack-addicted mothers, but by all accounts Jennifer Johnson was concerned about her drug problem and its effects on her pregnancy and reported her condition to doctors. Although Johnson's conviction was eventually overturned, to this day drug-abusing pregnant women have become the main target of prosecutions for foetal rights violations in numerous states.

If the welfare of unborn children was the primary concern, one might expect, in the USA where women are being imprisoned for taking drugs while they are pregnant, for there to be more research on the effects of smoking crack on women, and in particular on pregnant women. In fact, there is a dearth of such information. All the research is conducted on men, and the majority of rehabilitation facilities cater only to men. In fact, internationally, most drug companies won't even allow fertile women to take part in drug trials, on the grounds they might become pregnant. The truth is that drug-addicted mothers, because they attract so little public empathy, have become scapegoats for public rage over welfare, drugs and crime.

In fact there is no sudden rush of women out to harm their

166 · *Mother of All Myths*

unborn children. In fact, women probably take better care of themselves while they are pregnant than ever before. To assume that any significant number of women actually set out to harm their unborn children by taking drugs or refusing an operation is wilfully to ignore the complexity of their lives and the issues at the heart of the question. The public wrath that errant mothers inspire is rooted in beliefs about the nature of women, namely the idea that maternity, or simply the knowledge of maternity, is enough to change the behaviour of even the most heavily drug-addicted woman. That this is not always the case can appear to undermine the whole institution of motherhood.

The arrest and imprisonment of pregnant drug addicts has produced a fight of enormous proportions between civil liberties organizations such as the American Civil Liberties Union and feminist groups on the one hand, and conservatives and right-wingers on the other. The latter insist that women should be made responsible for their actions. The former defend women's autonomy and the right to procreate and ask where it will all end. If a woman can be prosecuted for failing to follow doctors' orders, what about the woman who smokes, drinks alcohol, swallows aspirin, fails to eat properly, or doesn't do up her seat belt? Alan Dershowitz, the celebrity lawyer who made his name defending high-profile clients such as Claus von Bulow, is one of many people who favour a broadening of the scope of the law on foetal rights, and dismisses the 'floodgates' argument. But the evidence so far is that the number of cases is indeed multiplying rapidly.

According to the New York-based Center for Reproductive Law and Policy, estimates based on news reports, court documents and attorneys' records show that at least 200 women in thirty states have been arrested and criminally charged for their behaviour during pregnancy. The range of charges displays an imaginative use of existing laws. A woman whose newborn tested positive for cocaine was charged with assault with a deadly weapon (the drug);[6] another was prosecuted under a child support statute for failing to take enough bed rest and, once again, having sex with her husband against the advice of a doctor;[7] a woman in Charleston who tested positive for drugs in the seventh month of her pregnancy was put under house arrest for the duration of her pregnancy;[8] a woman in California convicted under child abuse laws was ordered to be temporarily sterilized using Norplant.[9]

The range of activities for which women have been arrested and charged has diversified beyond 'using illegal substances' to include actions which on their own are perfectly legal; for example, taking prescription painkillers. In instances of illegal drug use, the burden of proof does not even require that the child has been harmed in any way, simply that the mother smoked marijuana or crack, or took heroin while she was pregnant. So, theoretically, a woman can now be imprisoned for doing something which is legal and which doesn't harm her unborn baby, but which is considered undesirable. Even if harm can be proved there is a terrible risk involved in criminalizing mothers. In the future, women who are afraid they might be prosecuted for smoking or drinking will avoid the medical services or have abortions rather than risk prison.

In addition to rounding up pregnant women whose conduct during pregnancy isn't deemed to meet the required standards, women have been forced into medical treatment including prenatal foetal operations and caesarean sections. All Western countries regard jurisdiction over one's own body and the right to refuse medical treatment as sacrosanct. Except, it seems, if the person in question is a pregnant woman. As the most common kind of legal coercion, court-ordered surgery poses a serious threat to women's civil liberties and right to self-determination in the name of foetal rights. The case of Angela Carder pricked the conscience of an otherwise indolent public; in the words of Janet Gallagher, it was 'a nightmarish scenario that would have been labeled a paranoid feminist fantasy if suggested as a possibility by opponents of fetal rights'.[10]

Angela Carder had suffered from cancer since she was thirteen years old. Her fight against the disease had included the amputation of one of her legs, but eventually the disease went into remission and had been for three years when she decided to try to have a baby at the age of twenty-seven. Angela was only twenty-five weeks pregnant when a routine check-up showed a massive tumour in one of her lungs, which left her only days to live. She was immediately admitted to hospital. Despite the objections of Angela herself, her family and her husband (who had taken advice from their own doctor that any attempt to save the baby would hasten Angela's own death and was unlikely to be successful), the hospital authorities decided to try to rescue the unborn child. By this time Angela had already been given the last rites and her family had gathered to say goodbye.

Angela Carder died two days later. The tiny baby girl, which even the hospital gave only a 50–60 per cent chance of survival, also died. Official records admit that the surgery contributed to her death. Despite a successful suit by the family against the hospital, as well as the overturning of the decision to allow surgery in the Court of Appeal, despite even the public outrage the Carder case provoked, until 1994 when the courts deemed forced caesareans unlawful,[11] dozens of pregnant women were forced into surgery. In such instances women were regularly portrayed as stubborn and unconcerned over their babies' survival, or too ignorant to make a decision themselves. Hospitals, ever wary of the possibility of a lawsuit, sought the sanction of the courts to impose their authority under the guise of foetal rights. Invariably, judges accepted the opinion of obstetricians over the wishes of the woman (and often her husband and doctor, too).

There are many instances, however, which show that hospitals are not always right, including the case of an African couple who resisted the pressure to have a caesarean.[12] In this case, the woman had had an almost identical experience with her first child, but succeeded in giving birth naturally. The couple argued that it was important that she try to deliver vaginally because when they returned home, there would be no hospital for a hundred miles to have a repeat caesarean (when a woman has had one child by caesarean, later babies usually have to be delivered the same way). Fortunately, just before the court order was issued, the mother delivered successfully.

Rarely do cases of foetal rights illustrate genuine concern for the foetus itself. Hospitals try to cover themselves legally; pro-life state prosecutors want to punish crack-addicted women and advance their political careers. The notion of 'foetal protection' has also been used by multinationals to restrict women's access to jobs, particularly those which are higher paid and unionized. Digital, the computer company, banned all pregnant women from certain categories of jobs manufacturing microchips on the basis of a methodically dubious internal study on women's miscarriages; Johnson's Controls, a battery production company in Vermont, insisted that women be sacked or sterilized, even when they were post-menopausal; five female employees at a paint company, American Cynamid, underwent surgical steriliz-ation in order to keep their jobs, only to be made redundant a year later (they sued successfully and their story was made into a TV movie entitled *For Their Own Good*). In the United States, many international household names have at one time or another barred women from certain jobs purely on the grounds that they are capable of conceiving. They include: Eastman Kodak, Union Carbide, Firestone Tires, General Motors and AT&T.

Today, American companies are prevented from introducing policies which exclude women on the basis of their childbearing capabilities. The whole wave of foetal protection policies was in reality designed simply to protect large corporations from the possibility of a lawsuit if a child was born deformed, according to Cynthia Daniels, a Rutgers law professor and author of *At Women's Expense*. They were backed by protectionist, male-dominated unions with their own agenda. Now women have to sign liability waiver forms and to accept the same standards as men in order to work. It seems that concern for foetal health has produced no corresponding improvement in work conditions. If that is not enough to show that the real issue is not really reproductive health, it should be noted that the standards of proof required for a woman to claim her foetus has been harmed by conditions at work are much higher than the standards required to send a drug- or alcohol-using woman to jail.

While cases of 'foetal protection' have largely come to an end in the United States, it seems they may only just be beginning in Britain. In January 1998 Caroline Tapp, a twenty-six-year-old police recruit, won a sex discrimination case after being forced off a training scheme by senior officers when they discovered that she was ten weeks pregnant. Despite her insistence that she was fit and able to continue, her bosses claimed they were concerned for the wellbeing of her unborn child and she was transferred to a clerical post. The tribunal which upheld her claim described the decision by the male senior officers as 'A paternalistic decision based upon the stereotypical assumption that someone who was pregnant could do no physical activity whatsoever'.

Cases of criminal prosecutions over foetal rights began to ebb in the early 1990s, perhaps because of the success of defence teams in getting verdicts overturned. In the meantime, the issue has been successfully pushed forward in civil law. Several women, including one who miscarried after contracting salmonella poison from a frozen chicken dinner, have successfully sued on the basis of wrongful death, even of foetuses which in ordinary circumstances would be considered non-viable. Decisions like that are greeted by pro-lifers with glee as the first step to a recognition of foetal rights, but they place civil liberties activists and feminists in a quandary, torn between the idea that a woman should be compensated for such a loss and the fear that foetuses are acquiring independent rights via the back door.

The lull in prosecutions against women suddenly came to an

end with a flurry of new cases in the mid-1990s. First was the extraordinary case of Tawana Ashley, a teenager who had tried to 'abort' her unborn child by shooting herself in the stomach with a .22-calibre pistol. The child lived briefly, so Tawana Ashley was charged with third-degree murder and manslaughter. The case brought to the fore the abortion issue, which underlies so much of the debate over 'foetal rights'. Outside the courtroom on 23 January 1995, when a judge ruled that she could not be charged with homicide, Catholic priests and members of the National Organization of Women screamed at each other, while Ashley herself refused to speak to the press and slipped away quietly. Her lawyer, Priscilla Smith, who has defended many women accused of violating foetal rights, says Ashley tried to raise the money for an abortion. By the time she had accumulated anything near the $1,350 necessary, she was already too far gone. Publicly-funded abortions do not exist in Florida.

Then the South Carolina Supreme Court, in a landmark decision, became the first court in the land to uphold the conviction for child abuse of a woman who smoked 'crack' during her pregnancy. Cornelia Whitner's six-year sentence, given in 1992 but overturned by a higher court, was reinstated. The tide had turned, and the timing of such decisions coincided with the renewal of the debate over welfare and the implementation in early 1997 of the Clinton administration's draconian cuts to welfare, particularly to single mothers.

In Wisconsin, a state which has received record cuts in benefits, prosecutors brought charges against a thirty-five-year-old woman, Deborah Zimmerman, who gave birth to a child with foetal alcohol syndrome after being seen in a local bar in Racine downing 'Blind Russian' cocktails just hours before the birth. Zimmerman's was a sad case. She had been raped three times and beaten up by her partner. She had a long history of chronic alcoholism and even while she was being carried to hospital shouted that she wanted to drink the baby to death.

Out of her sorry example the assistant district attorney in Racine told newspapers that they hoped to carve out new laws to prohibit pregnant women from drinking and smoking. The Director of Neonatology at St Luke's hospital in Racine went even further, telling *People* magazine that he hoped the case would make local women think twice about having a drink 'if they are planning a pregnancy'.

Public response to these cases is evidence of the growing support for the prosecution of women who are deemed 'inappropriate' as mothers. Targeting pregnant women goes ahead, while at the same time there have been absolutely no corresponding prosecutions of men. The drugs used by a pregnant Karen Henderson were supplied by her partner, the child's father. Charges were never brought against the men who had sex with their wives against the advice of the doctors, although the men knew about those instructions. In the case of Johnson's Controls, men were not barred from jobs although lead levels were known to cause them significant reproductive harm. And in Wyoming a pregnant woman was arrested for drinking when she turned up at a hospital seeking treatment for injuries inflicted by her husband's fists.[13]

That most of the women who have been prosecuted are poor and black is certainly no coincidence. These are the women who chime with the public image of irresponsible motherhood. There is a long history of denigrating black motherhood in America, from the years of slavery when black women were denied the rights of motherhood, and continued into the 1970s when the US government enforced the sterilization of thousands of African-American women. Generally, black women are portrayed as sexually licentious, slovenly and irresponsible when it comes to childbearing. The popular stereotype of black motherhood is often used as the counterpoint to the pure, white, nurturing maternal ideal. As some black feminists have observed, if black mothers didn't exist, white people would have to invent them. At least one major study, published in the *New England Journal of Medicine*, has demonstrated that although there was very little difference in drug or alcohol abuse between women of different classes and races, black women were ten times more likely to be reported to the authorities.[14]

Prosecution is by its nature a retrospective action, imposed after the harm, if there is any, has been done. At the time that Cornelia Whitner (the subject of the South Carolina Supreme Court ruling) had her six-year sentence reinstated, she had been raising her healthy son for eight years. The courts knew that to send her to prison would mean depriving the boy of a mother.

The USA has one of the highest incidences of infant mortality in the West. These prosecutions draw attention away from the real and more enduring causes of infant mortality which are, and remain, access to health care including drug-rehabilitation programmes and abortions, poor nutrition, poverty and unsafe housing. And what of the many women with AIDS? Should they be prosecuted for passing the disease on to their baby? Although a modern notion of procreative liberty has brought with it the belief that women have a 'choice' to have a baby, and can therefore be made accountable, for many women – those who are poor, drug-addicted or desperate – real choice does not exist.

The emergence of foetal rights in Britain

The notion of 'foetal rights' is being successfully exported to Britain, where the idea is gaining ground, as well as other countries such as Canada, where welfare legislation has been used to override a mother's rights in favour of those of her foetus.[15] Compared to the positive brush-fire of cases in America, fuelled by fundamentalist fervour, the push for foetal rights in the UK is a slow, steady burn which is gradually gathering momentum. In the last fifteen years parallels have begun to emerge in the social, political and legal spheres, which have produced cases of maternal–foetal conflict, and in the last two years in particular new cases have come to light.

Today, just as in America, there is growing anxiety over the future of the family, the role of fathers and concern at what appears to be the rapid decay of community spirit and values. As has happened in the past, the link is soon made between social disorder and motherhood. Today, one of the newest perceived threats to motherhood, combined with old concerns such as divorce, women's work and female independence, is the notion that motherhood has 'gone mad' and has departed too far from the ideal. A sense of ambivalence over opportunities offered by medical advances and reproductive technology has contributed to the disquiet. The worry is not so much over the science itself (although that certainly exists) but specifically about the opportunity it might offer to women. A number of stories in 1996 served to confirm these incipient fears. First Diane Blood, a woman whose husband was in a coma and likely to die, asked to be allowed to remove some of his semen so that she could be artificially inseminated and bear his child. The request, twinned with Mrs Blood's refusal to let the matter drop once the courts had refused, struck many people, even those who professed a general sympathy with her, as morbid and obsessive.

Two quite different cases were then blazed across the headlines. First a tabloid newspaper ran a front-page story, leaked by an obstetrician at Queen Charlotte's Hospital, that a single mother who was pregnant with twins planned to have one of them aborted because she could not afford to raise two children. Overnight the story was front-page news everywhere and the lead item on television and radio news. A search began for the woman in question. The SPUC (Society for the Protection of the Unborn Child) even offered her money not to go ahead with the termination. Then Queen Charlotte's announced that the operation had already taken place; indeed, it was over by the time the story first appeared in the press. Attention focused on the abortion question, whether women should be allowed to have terminations for what amounted to 'lifestyle' reasons. Jack

Scarsbrick, the longtime anti-abortion activist, was reported as being 'cock-a-hoop'.[16] 'The media are on our side as never before,' he declared.

As often happens with stories which seize the public attention in this way, the media go on a run and journalists then vie with each other to produce a new twist, dimension or similar story. Mandy Allwood came as a godsend. Here was a thirty-one-year-old divorcee, with a black lover (who already had two children by another woman), who had fertility treatment and was carrying octuplets. Allwood and her partner had engaged the services of Max Clifford, the publicist who built his reputation representing kiss-and-tell girls, to sell their story. Against the advice of her doctors who had told her she risked losing all the foetuses if she declined to undergo selective termination, Allwood was insistent on having all eight children – for the purposes of striking a better financial deal for herself with a newspaper, it was suggested. Mandy Allwood's appropriateness as a mother became the central question, with the *Daily Express* asking its readers: 'Does She Deserve Eight Babies?'[17]

Of course the stories of Diane Blood, the prospective mother of twins and Mandy Allwood are thoroughly atypical, but the interest they produced shows that they neatly touched a subconscious anxiety shared by many that the idea of reproductive rights had been taken too far. Cases are emerging of women held against their will in hospitals and forced to have caesarean sections, with the use of force sanctioned by the courts. There's evidence that fathers are starting to try to win rights over their pregnant wives' bodies. And in recent years, local authorities have tried to make unborn children wards of court. For hundreds of years the principle of bodily autonomy has been an unshakeable rule in English law. The impact these new cases could have on women's freedom and autonomy has barely been considered. In the words of Lord Reid, delivering his 1972 decision that a man could not be forced even to give blood for a paternity suit filed against him: 'English law goes to great

lengths to protect a person of full age and capacity from interference with his personal liberty. We have too often seen freedom disappear in other countries, not only by *coup d'états*, but
by gradual erosion: and it is the first step that counts. So it would
be unwise even to make minor concessions.'[18] With regards to
pregnant women, however, that first step has already been
taken.

The road to foetal rights

In the UK, the legal position is this: historically, a foetus has no
independent rights whatsoever. Under the Congenital Dis-
abilities (Civil Liability) Act of 1976, a pregnant woman can sue
for damages inflicted on her. The same Act expressly exempts
women from any liability towards the foetus, except in the
instance of car accidents, where, if the child survives, it may
claim against either the mother's or the third party's insurers
for injury in the womb. Since the inception of a system of law,
British courts have been unable to conceive of an unborn child's
rights as separate from the mother's.

More recently, the first cases which dealt with the question
of rights for foetuses were raised by men trying to establish foetal
rights as well as their own rights over a woman's pregnancy by
taking wives and girlfriends to court on the unborn child's
behalf. In 1978 a man tried to stop his wife having an abortion,
but the courts declared that neither the foetus nor the husband
had any enforceable rights.[19] Then came a very public case con-
cerning two Oxford students.[20] The story turned on three issues,
namely the right of a woman to choose abortion, the question
of foetal viability and, finally, the right to life. A young woman
who had become pregnant following a brief affair – a one-night
stand, according to some – was being taken to court by the father
of the child to prevent her from having an abortion. When the
case came to light she was already five months pregnant. As the

hearings progressed through the lower courts to the Court of Appeal and finally to the House of Lords, judges were in a race to make their decision before it was too late for her to have a legal abortion, precisely what the father and his supporters were hoping for.

A fact which received little attention at the time was that the father, an activist in Oxford University's anti-abortion society, was being backed financially by the Society for the Protection of the Unborn Child, Britain's foremost pro-life group. The case against Ms S was brought a mere two months after a failed attempt in the House of Lords by Hugh Montefiore to reduce further the time-limit for abortions. The prospective father employed almost identical arguments. He tried to take an action before the courts as 'next friend' of the child, that is on the behalf of the unborn child, claiming that abortion was a crime under the Infant Life (Preservation) Act of 1929, which protects unborn children 'capable of being born alive'. The father claimed that at eighteen weeks his child was capable of being born alive and that termination would therefore be a crime. It was a clever and lateral assault on the Abortion Act which then allowed operations to take place up to twenty-eight weeks. The potential impact of this case was phenomenal.

There was a great deal of public sympathy for the father. 'Don't kill my unborn baby!' said the *Daily Express*.[21] In the final analysis, the Lords, after hearing medical evidence, decided that the foetus, if delivered, would not be capable of surviving outside the mother's body and therefore could not bring an action to save its own life through the father. Ms S was free to have an abortion and neither the rights of the unborn foetus nor the father (on its behalf) could take precedence. The decision echoed a case a year earlier in the European Court of Human Rights when a Norwegian computer analyst took action against his girlfriend after she aborted their child.[22] If he had been successful, the case would have had serious repercussions for the reproductive liberties of millions of European women.

Although the anti-abortion lobby had lost the battle, it had gained significant ground in the war. It had successfully steered the abortion debate round to the question of viability, just as pro-lifers had done in the United States. Their long-term tactic was and is to use advances in medical knowledge to push the time-limit for terminations earlier and earlier. Shifting the debate in this way also successfully wrong-foots pro-choice supporters who find themselves in the unenviable and unsympathetic position of defending late abortions and struggling to determine at what point a foetus becomes a baby.

There is a tendency in the UK towards a certain complacency over the right to a termination, a right which most people assume is safe. Nevertheless, there have been continuous, so far unsuccessful attempts over the years to curtail a woman's right to choose, starting with the very first attempt to amend the Abortion Act in 1969, only two years after it was passed.

Around the same time as the assaults on abortion rights were taking place, social workers – prompted by the success of cases in the USA – began taking drug-addicted mothers to court on the grounds of their conduct during pregnancy. In Berkshire, a drug-addicted mother had her new-born baby taken away and given to foster parents on the grounds that she was an unfit mother, despite her protests.[23] For the first time the courts rejected the idea that the Children and Young Person's Act could only be applied to children already born. Two years later a second local authority tried to make a foetus a ward of court, arguing once again on the notion of viability – that is to say that the child, though unborn, was capable of independent existence – and that the best interests of the child took priority over the rights of the mother.[24] On this occasion the courts rejected the bid, recognizing that the local authority was trying to control the activities of the mother through the legal fiction of 'apprehending' the foetus for medical treatment. By this time the case of the Oxford students had already been well publicized and the judges recognized the implications of any decision they made on the Abortion Act. They resisted giving the foetus any rights, and for the time being efforts to give rights to foetuses in Britain came to a halt.

In a little reported case in 1992, doctors were allowed by the courts to overrule the refusal of a pregnant women, a Jehovah's Witness, who had been injured in a car crash, to have a blood transfusion even though she had signed a form declining treatment.[25] That decision then served as a precedent in another case the same year which concerned a Nigerian woman, a born-again Christian and mother-of-two, who refused to have a caesarean because of deeply-held religious convictions.[26] The only other precedent cited, astonishingly enough, was the American case of Angela Carder. In fact, anyone who has any doubts that the concept of foetal rights is indeed being exported wholesale from the USA should take a close look at how frequently American case law is cited in an effort to sway the opinion of judges in the British courts. Once again, the Nigerian woman's story came and went quietly, failing to ignite more than a spark of indignation on the part of the general public and the press who largely missed the implications of the decision. They were not lost on some members of the legal profession. In the words of Allan Levy, a family law expert and QC, the decision went 'against the weight of English tradition which has never accorded legal rights to unborn babies'.[27]

In November 1995 the Law Lords of the Court of Appeal declared that someone who injured a child 'in utero', which was subsequently born alive and later died, could be charged with murder. A man had stabbed his girlfriend, who was then twenty-six weeks pregnant, in the stomach during a drunken row.[28] The attack wounded the unborn child who was born prematurely and died four months later. Compared to the earlier cases, this one was much easier to decide. For a start there was no issue, at least immediately, of conflict between the rights of the woman and her child. Secondly, the British public would, if anything, welcome the conviction of a man who attacked a pregnant woman.

The woman's attacker was subsequently convicted of the man-slaughter of the baby in the House of Lords. Doubtless this was a correct decision, but the case contained echoes of 'feticide' legislation in the USA, which had the unforeseen consequence of opening the door to separate rights for foetuses.

Perhaps the ruling emboldened some lawyers, who read the decision as an indication that judges were finally prepared to accord more rights to the unborn. Some say events were prompted by the influence of pro-lifers in the offices of the Official Solicitor (whose brief it is to protect children) with an agenda to get foetal rights recognized in English law. Within eighteen months there was suddenly a spate of cases which turned on the question of maternal–foetal conflict. All of them involved women who had been forced into having caesareans.

The first case to come to public attention was that of a twenty-three-year-old pregnant woman who declined to have a caesarean because she had a phobia regarding needles. She was found by the courts to be legally 'incompetent', had her own wishes overruled and was made to undergo the operation. She sued for damages. Gradually, it was revealed that at least eleven other woman had been forced to undergo caesareans in the past few months.

The story of one woman, Ms S, who later sued social services for misuse of the Mental Health Act, is an indication of how women who find themselves in this position can easily be vilified as 'bad mothers', and made to look foolish and uncaring when they decide to challenge the power of local authorities and the medical establishment. The two sides in the case gave such different versions of events that even the basic facts were not agreed upon. Barbara Hewson, Ms S's lawyer, says that her client, a veterinarian's assistant, left work one day to sign up with a local GP because her present doctor's surgery was too far away to be convenient. Her blood pressure was taken and found to be high. The new GP diagnosed pre-eclampsia, a potentially extremely dangerous condition in pregnant women, and advised her to go immediately to hospital. However, the doctor also admitted that it was a long time since she had practised obstetrics and, upon hearing this, Ms S, who had experienced no problems with her pregnancy thus far, chose to ignore the advice and to proceed with her plans for a natural birth. Within a short time social services had been alerted, an application made to detain her under the Mental Health Act, and the pregnant woman was promptly transported, very much against her will, to a mental hospital and from there to a maternity ward at St George's Hospital in Tooting. Immediately a court order was made to require her to undergo a caesarean.

The local authority's account of the same story tells of a woman who was suicidal, who refused to eat or drink, who declared that she didn't care if her baby lived or died, and declared that her death would be a good punishment for her ex-boyfriend. According to them she was incapable of rational thought and the court order was made for her own good. There were discrepancies in this version of the story. The court was told that she had been in labour for twenty-four hours and could die at any moment, but her lawyer says that Ms S was only eight months pregnant and hadn't started labour. Hospital notes also suggest that her doctors seemed to think she was perfectly competent. She was a strong advocate of natural medicine and, in the course of events, she signed three statements saying that she did not want medical intervention.

Barbara Hewson, who represented a second woman, says that although judges have determined that only a woman who is declared incompetent can have her wishes overruled, virtually any decision with which a woman's doctors do not agree seems to qualify as evidence of incompetence. Plus, some judges seem to believe that just being in labour classifies a woman as incapable of knowing her own mind. Although judges in the earlier case of Re: MB, the needle-phobic woman, said that a woman could refuse a caesarean or any kind of treatment 'for religious grounds, no grounds, or any grounds at all', that thinking was clearly not applied to the Nigerian woman and her husband.

Since the 1970s the incidence of caesarean sections has tripled, and the costs to the NHS of medical negligence suits has gone from £53 million in 1990–91 to £125 million pounds in 1993–94. Doctors are increasingly being encouraged to practise 'defensive medicine', and to go against the wishes of patients if need be. After the cases of Ms MB and Ms S became public, campaigners for women's health rights queued to condemn the actions of the hospitals. Sheila Kitzinger, the childbirth guru, warned of a 'witch hunt of pregnant women whose capacity to make decisions may be attacked when they exercise their legal right to decline medical advice'.[29] There were reports of pregnant women going into hiding rather than risk similar treatment.[30]

Using the law to control the actions and behaviour of pregnant women and mothers jeopardizes a host of human rights if women are to be placed under the authority of the courts and their doctors. Foetal rights are really 'rights plus',[31] according to the American attorney Lyn Paltrow, who has defended many of the women involved in cases in the USA, including some who have been made to have a caesarean section against their will. In no other capacity does the law have the power to require one person to put themselves in danger, or to undergo an invasive surgical procedure, for another, including parents on behalf of their children; a father cannot be made to donate his bone marrow to save the life of his dying son, or a parent be forced to rescue a drowning child.

Thirty years after British women fought and won the right to control their own reproduction, they are in danger of losing that freedom. Those activists, alerted by what has already taken place in America, who can see the very real danger of the slippery slope towards state control of women's procreation, behaviour and choices, have had their warnings airily dismissed by people who think women have too many rights as it is. The mood was summed up by Rosalind Miles in the *Independent*: 'Ten years ago the right of women to control their own bodies in a brave, new world of increasing medical and technological advances barely existed. This right unpacks to reveal a whole new set of other bright and shiny "rights".'[32] There is nothing new about the right to bodily autonomy; what *is* new is the removal of that right from pregnant women.

In May 1997, following hot on the heels of the caesarean scandals, came a new assault on women's reproductive rights from a different angle. James Kelly, from Fife in Scotland, tried to challenge his wife's decision to have an abortion, using the argument that the information she had supplied to the two doctors who agreed to her request for a termination was wrong. A pivotal point in the legal debate was whether a father or any third party had the right to intervene and overturn a medical decision and, if they did, whether this conflicted with the terms of the Abortion Act. Kelly's action differed from the Oxford student's earlier attempt to prevent his girlfriend's termination in that the latter had taken the woman to court *on behalf of* the child (as though the child were asserting its own rights), whereas Kelly tried to assert his right as a father to stop the abortion. However, the issue of foetal rights was relevant to both cases, and judges in the Kelly case considered the implications of creating a conflict between the rights of the unborn child and the rights of the mother.

James Kelly succeeded in winning a temporary court order banning Lynn Kelly's termination from going ahead, and although his case was rejected by the Scottish Court of Appeal which ruled that the 1967 Abortion Act did not recognize a father's right to intervene, he was granted leave to take his case to the House of Lords. At the last moment Kelly abandoned his action, after failing to win the support of anti-abortion groups which declined to back the idea of fathers' rights. The twenty-eight-year-old roofer told the newspapers he did not want to bring a child into the world who was unloved by his or her mother. In addition, he accused his wife of putting her singing career before her husband and her role as a mother.

Historically, women have been left to make all the difficult moral and practical decisions regarding childbirth, such as whether to continue alone with an unwanted pregnancy, or to raise a severely disabled child, and they have been left alone with the consequences. Now that decisions are becoming more complicated, the fact that a few women make choices that some of us do not agree with, is being taken as sufficient reason to curtail the freedom of all women. So far, British judges have tried to make decisions so that they will not impact upon the Abortion Act, but the precedents which sanction the limiting of the autonomy of pregnant women are beginning to mount.

Pregnancy *is* a special state. There is no other physical human state quite like it. The courts are not an appropriate place to decide questions of such enormous delicacy with consequent social and human rights implications. What is morally desirable cannot be made legally culpable. To attempt to construct rights for foetuses by reinterpreting law is to use the courts to advance politically-motivated arguments.

Legally targeting mothers is simply an attack on all women. Janet Gallagher writes: 'Like the anti-abortion effort, the fetal rights drive is fueled by deep social unease over the changing roles of women and rapid changes in male–female relationships.'[33] This sense of disquiet is firmly rooted in the perception that change is achievable only at the expense of motherhood and maternal values. Cynthia Daniels has also observed: 'Forced medical treatment of women became possible only when the idea arose that women could no longer be trusted to subordinate their own interests to the interests of the fetus.'[34] It is really motherhood which is felt to be at stake, illustrated perfectly by the changes that Hollywood scriptwriters felt obliged to make to the Angela Carder story, a version of which appeared as part of the plot on *LA Law*. This time the story had a different ending. The mother died, but the baby survived, and so, too, did the romance of motherhood and maternal sacrifice. For that is what the public wanted.

When a mother kills and abuses

Women who breach, in the most extreme way, what are perceived to be the laws of nature – that is, women who kill their own children – unsettle the collective subconscious in a way that the violence of a man rarely does. Men are society's guardians of aggression, we have vested them with that particular trait, along with competitiveness, promiscuity and all the other characteristics associated with masculinity. The hand that rocks the cradle is not the hand that wields the sword. Long-held convictions about motherhood are tied to ideas about what is natural. Our lips scream 'freak', while inside each one of us an unformed thought asks the obvious question: could our own mothers have harmed us, covered our mouths and pinched our noses until we turned blue, as we ourselves lay as babies in their arms? When a man kills we exclaim that the streets are no longer safe; when a mother kills she demonstrates a far greater power and invokes a mighty fear. She can make even the strongest among us feel that nowhere is safe.

The conflict of emotions produced by the knowledge of a mother's violence towards a child, our inability to deal with the reality of maternal darkness, is immense. Typically, the public reacts in one or more of three ways. First we may refuse to accept the facts as they are stated and search for a more plausible explanation: she was deranged, her hand was forced by someone else (usually a man). If no such rationale can be found, the second reaction is rage and fury: the woman becomes a demon, a monster mother whose image resonates somewhere in the darkest part of the psyche. Finally there is the paranoia of the lynch mob which begins to see dangerous, unworthy mothers everywhere.

Celia Beckett insisted that she didn't want her children. Nobody believed her. She kept her three daughters clean, bought them new shoes and laced their food with amitriptyline, an anti-depressant given to her by her doctors to help her cope with the tasks of mothering. For more than a decade no one – not the social workers who returned the children she had told them to take away, nor her estranged husband who had his suspicions but never thought to look after the children himself, nor the police, nor the girls' doctor who saw the bruises – really believed that Celia Beckett, a mother, would actually harm her own children. 'For years, as successive disasters befell her three girls, Celia Beckett had escaped detection, cocooned by the conventional wisdom that mother knows best and that mothers *must* mother,' wrote Beatrix Campbell in the *Guardian*.[35] Even a mother whose first child had died mysteriously of brain damage ten years before, even a mother whose favourite game was to pretend to smother her children while they played dead.

In 1995 Celia Beckett was arrested for murdering one of her daughters and poisoning a second. The social workers in Nottingham who had allowed her daughter Tracy (whom she had already fed large quantities of anti-depressant tablets) back into her care had their knuckles rapped hard. Yet even the trial judge could not accept the fact of badness in a mother, only madness, the disruption of her natural functions for which she could not be held totally responsible. She was jailed for five years. The lone voice of dissent was that of her ex-husband and father of the two dead girls: 'She should have been locked up for life and the key thrown away,' he told the newspapers.[36]

Was Celia Beckett crazy? And if she was, what made her so? True, she was abused by her father, but she was also a reluctant and desperate figure as a mother. She continually told those around her she did not want her daughters; she even took an overdose on the day before her youngest daughter was to be reunited with her. In *Of Woman Born*, Adrienne Rich tells the story of a Chicago housewife, Joanne Michulski, who one summer's day butchered two of her children on the lawn in a violent expression of her frustration and anger at the demands of her role as a mother and her own inability to meet them. Her plight evoked horror and sympathy. Twelve local women wrote to a newspaper expressing their understanding of the forces which drove Joanne Michulski's behaviour. 'Instead of recognising the institutional violence of patriarchal motherhood,' wrote Rich, 'society labels those women who finally erupt in violence as psychopathological.'[37]

Did motherhood itself drive Celia Beckett mad, or was she unstable beforehand and ill-equipped to cope with the functions of motherhood? Or was she just plain wicked as Tommy Butler, the father of the children she poisoned, asserted? The truth about Celia Beckett remains a mystery even after her conviction, because we seem to find one explanation as implausible as the next. Maternal violence is not in our frame of reference. And that is wrong, says Estela Welldon, a clinical psychologist and author of *Mother, Madonna, Whore*, who has spoken out against the conspiracy of silence which blinds society to the truth: that mothers can and do harm their children. 'Irrespective of the mother's upbringing, it is always assumed that "maternal instinct" will come to the fore and will perform miracles,' she says.[38] In Welldon's view, which corresponds with the conventional psychological approach, women are less likely than men to express their anger by, say, walking into a burger joint with a machete, or getting into a street brawl. They are far more likely to direct their rage against themselves and, says Welldon, their children whom they birth, bathe and breastfeed, as an extension of themselves. Furthermore, the modern institution of motherhood, which isolates mother and child from the rest of the community and locks them into their relationship with each other, provides the perfect opportunity every single day.

Welldon maintains that it was the idealization of motherhood which delayed the acknowledgement of the reality of child battery back in the 1960s. Today, for the same reason, we are still blind to the possibility of maternal incest, the last, perhaps the ultimate, taboo. In 1984 when Michelle Elliot, a child psychologist, first approached the then Department of Health and Social Services to set up an organization to tackle sexual abuse, she was told that there were not enough cases to merit it. Seven years later, when Kidscape organized the first national conference on female sexual abuse, it faced similar scepticism. But the daytime TV programme *This Morning* agreed to run a telephone hotline and in a single day volunteers had taken more than 1,000 calls from people, 90 per cent of whom said they had not told anyone of the abuse before. In a study of 400 victims of female sexual abuse conducted by Kidscape, 70 per cent of the women and 73 per cent of the men had been abused by their own mothers.[39]

Few people who have suffered sexual abuse at the hands of their mother are believed. One man, who tried to tell his therapist about the beatings and sado-masochistic sex his mother had subjected him to, was told that he was having fantasies about his mother and needed more therapy to deal with them. Elliot has been criticized by men and women alike, and has been accused of being 'anti-women'. 'People are clinging to accepted wisdom that mothers can't hurt their children with such tenacity that you have to wonder why,' she says.[40] People have placed sexual abuse in the context of male power and to recognize that women, mothers especially, are capable of the same challenges every accepted theory from the natural capacity of women to mother, gender roles, even current research on testosterone. 'It is much easier to think that women are safe.'

The reality of sexual abuse by women is doubtless the next grenade waiting to explode in the over-heated arsenal of social disorders. Once the truth has been accepted, however, a fresh set of problems will be posed. In the 1980s the new knowledge and subsequent outcry over sexual abuse by men was transformed into hysteria which, over the years, produced accusations of mass abuse and satanic rituals, and prompted 'recovered' memories of abuse at the hands of fathers and grandfathers. Although many allegations were subsequently disproved, the collective effect has been to destroy the ability to trust men as carers. There was even a serious media debate over whether we should continue to employ male nursery workers. All this served to taint with doubt the relationship between men and children, even their own children, and to push responsibility for children even more firmly into the arms of their mothers. Now we are faced with the complicated truth that just as *some* men sexually abuse children, *some* women sexually abuse children, too.

In the same year that Celia Beckett was accused of the manslaughter of her daughter in Britain, in America Susan Smith was being tried for the murder of her two small sons. Unlike Beckett's, her trial received a flare of publicity and international attention, principally because she herself exploited the general perception of mothers as incapable of harming their children in order to cover up her crime. Just like Celia Beckett, she had no trouble finding people who would believe her. When the truth was discovered, Susan Smith faced a lynch mob calling for her to be executed.

On 25 October 1994, Susan Smith drove her two sons out to the shore of a nearby lake. She parked the car facing the water and got out, then she let off the handbrake and walked away. Her two sons, Michael, aged three and Alex who was only fourteen months, drowned, strapped into their baby seats in the back of the car. Then she ran to a nearby house weeping and shouting frantically that a black man had stolen her car and kidnapped her children, thus evoking in a single image two of the most powerful stereotypes in the modern Western imagination: the distraught mother and the dangerous black man. As Susan Smith made tearful, televised pleas to the car-jacker, the people of her town, black and white, held candlelit vigils and searched the countryside for the boys. When she confessed to her crime nearly a month later, many of the same folk stood outside the court house and bayed for her blood.

There have been few scenes as evocative of the sheer fury of the townspeople as the sight of Susan Smith running the gauntlet of abuse into the courtroom on each day of her trial. It was not so much her betrayal of their trust that galvanized them; Susan Smith, white, middle-class and apparently upstanding, had betrayed motherhood itself.

There were two Susan Smiths at her trial, one who confirmed the acceptable image of motherhood even in such horrific circumstances, and another who shattered it. The first, painted by the defence, was of a suicidal woman who meant to die together with her children, taking them with her to spare them a motherless future, a woman whose life was so closely enmeshed with those of her children that she couldn't tell where one life ended and the others began. The second Susan Smith, the prosecution's version, was a woman who murdered her children because they were in the way of her marriage to the most eligible bachelor in town, a man who had broken off his relationship with Smith on the grounds he did not want to take on a ready-made family. That was the version that the courts believed when she was convicted. She was spared the electric chair but given a long sentence. Why did she not just give them up, people asked? But, of course, Susan Smith knew that for a woman to abandon her children and hope to be forgiven was not an option. She killed her babies for sex and money. She had failed the 'sacrifice test' spectacularly.

In contrast to people's willingness to believe Susan Smith's version of events, Caroline Beale from Chingford in Essex, who was arrested at Kennedy airport in New York with her dead newborn baby in her shoulder bag, could not find anybody who would listen to her. Perhaps it was because she was a stranger in a big city while Smith was known and liked by her friends and neighbours. Or perhaps it was because, by the time her story was picked up by the British and US papers, the Susan Smith case was unfolding and Americans had, at least temporarily, lost all faith in mothers. Paranoia was setting in and people were prepared to believe any woman could kill her own infant in cold blood. Certainly the authorities were not going to be played for a fool twice and she was sent to a high security prison. The sole reason for this was the decision by the district attorney in charge of the special victims' unit. 'I represent the dead baby,' Marjorie Fisher told the newspapers.

Television footage and photographs of Caroline Beale at that time show a pale woman who looks distracted, even absent, very confused and alarmed. Unlike Susan Smith, a motive for the crime that was even half convincing was never put forward. Despite a sympathetic British public who believed she must certainly be mentally ill, she was held for eight months in a notorious New York jail. Eventually, despite the best efforts of the district attorney, Beale was granted bail and at her trial nearly a year later she entered a plea bargain of guilty to the charge of manslaughter, committed while she was suffering from a postnatal psychosis.

If Caroline Beale had killed her baby in her home country, matters might have progressed differently. In Britain, the 1938 Infanticide Act allows a woman who kills her child of under twelve months to plead what we now term post-natal depression and have a murder charge automatically reduced to manslaughter. This was the thinking behind Beale's British lawyer's decision to plead her case on the grounds that she was mentally traumatized by the birth. But the pieces of the puzzle, right up until the end, have never quite seemed to fit. Beale's behaviour was bizarre well before she gave birth, the most obvious illustration being that she hid her pregnancy in its entirety from everyone, including the baby's father. She may have been mentally ill, but whether her illness was linked to the fact of childbirth seems doubtful.

Experts nowadays point to other social causes – such as a mother's poverty and isolation, or lack of support in particular – as being more likely reasons why mothers kill their children. Certainly that was the conclusion of both the Butler Committee on mentally abnormal offenders in 1975 and the Royal College of Psychiatrists when giving evidence to the Criminal Law Revision Committee in 1966.[41] The problem, it seems, lies in external factors – the institution of motherhood and the way in which women are forced to mother – rather than in biology gone awry.

The year 1995 culminated in the trial of Rosemary West who was accused of killing and sexually abusing a series of young women including her own daughter and stepdaughters. The nation was sickened by the sheer horror of the crimes, the stories of kidnap, sexual torture and killing. At first the media speculated that the killings must have been the work of Fred West, who later hanged himself in his prison cell, insisting, as did Rosemary, that she had been unaware of what happened. For a while people were almost prepared to believe it. But during her trial, from the testimony of many, including her stepdaughter Anne-Marie, the image emerged of an obscenely depraved woman with a passion for extreme sexual sadism. Still, some found such murderousness in a woman, in particular a mother, impossible to accept. The *Observer*'s Nicci Gerrard wrote about West's actions using a theory which blends psychology and ideas about biologically-determined behaviour to explain a mother's violence as inwardly-directed rage turned on the child which she sees as an extension of herself. Rosemary West, though, did not differentiate between those girls she and her husband snatched from the streets and those she gave birth to herself.

Despite the sense of crisis engendered by the crimes of Susan Smith, Celia Beckett, Caroline Beale and Rosemary West in a period of around eighteen months, the murder of children by their mothers is not as rare as most people imagine. In Britain in the same year (1995), Ruth Neave was accused of the murder of her son Rikki; Susan Joughin was arrested and charged with murdering her daughter with an axe; and Nicola Jordan was charged with killing her eight-week-old baby. In the USA, the National Committee to Prevent Child Abuse estimates that around 700 women a year kill their children. The fact is that some mothers have always been capable of the slaughter of their own children.

When a mother kills we look for a rationale which keeps intact a generally-held set of assumptions about motherhood. Explanations for a particular crime are framed in terms of some biological or emotional malfunction. When a man kills we look for a motive that makes sense logically: ambition, rivalry, sexual jealousy. If he kills a child, even his own, we will even accept that he simply lost his temper. The cases of Rosemary West and Susan Smith are so unsettling because the facts, as they appear, do not fit the accepted paradigm. To accept that women can and do sometimes kill their own children in cold blood means altering our understanding about the meaning of motherhood and the nature of women.

Motherhood is by no means always saccharine sweet. It is capable of embracing all the darkness, violence and cruelty that is in mankind. Women are people first and mothers second. Maternal feelings may be overridden by selfishness, greed, hatred, sexual perversion or any number of other emotions and desires. The intensity and isolation of the modern mother-and-child relationship may even exacerbate that possibility, but general acceptance of such an idea, with all its ramifications for human relationships, child safety and the way in which society organizes itself, is unlikely. The public response to women who kill, abuse or neglect their children is informed by the need to defend a set of accepted truisms about motherhood. It is for the breach of that set of values, as much as for the individual crime itself, that mothers who kill or abuse their children pay the penalty.

chapter 7

Other Mothers:
Cross-cultural Motherhood

Testimony: Sonia

Sonia is married with a daughter of six. She grew up in her native Bolivia. She married an Englishman and moved to the UK when she was twenty-five.

My mother used to work part-time as an accountant. I had what you'd call a nanny, except she wasn't a paid nanny. Her mother grew up raising my grandmother. She was like my second mother, my other mother. She was there when my mother wasn't. Then there were my uncles and my aunts. There was a lot of family. My mother didn't have to worry if she wasn't there.

My parents were middle class and I grew up in a full house. I had a grandmother, I had my father, I had uncles, I had cousins. There were sixteen or more people in the same house. I was always playing in the back yard, climbing trees. I had companions, because my mother raised other children, too. When they were fifteen, sixteen, they went back to their father. But there are still bonds with the family. Early on I went to live with my aunt for three and a half years until I was five. That was while my mother was studying for her degree, and then I went back home. And for me, my aunt and uncle were like other parents. She comes over to visit me, my aunt, because I am very close to her. Her children are like my sister and brother.

When I had my own daughter, I didn't imagine it would be like this. I just thought it would be easier. My mother came over for her birth and stayed a few weeks. My husband had time off, he took holiday and so we were all there together. Once they had gone and I was alone, it was a really big change. I had to do everything. Even now, if I want to go shopping, I have to take Anna. I have to take her everywhere with me. When she was a baby I'd have to strap her in the car seat first, drive to the place, and take her out. Then afterwards I'd put her back in with all the shopping, too. I see the other women. I know it's the same for them.

I went back to work and left her with babysitters, but I wasn't comfortable. I couldn't find the right one. I was making good money, £30,000. Dolores, I told you she was like my second mother, she said she would come and take care of Anna while I was at work. But it didn't work out. I requested a visa but it was turned down. I would have been happy. It would have been ideal. In the end I said I prefer to give up my good job. So I gave up my job. Instead of working I'm going to school. I'm taking classes at night, a Masters degree. If [my husband] dies or leaves me I can work and still get a good job. But I'd go back home first.

I don't trust people here. They think I'm over-protective. But even the school is open, anybody could walk in there. I go and check. Maybe, I'm a little bit suppressing her, but I'm happy with what I'm doing. Often I say, 'I'm going back home, I'm going back home,' because this is not a society that will help children. I don't see it in the government, I don't see it in the people, even though there's a lot of education. Back home it's part of the culture. Children and old people are sacred, sacred.

In this society everybody has ideas, you know. They'll say this is child abuse, or sexual abuse – don't allow your mother or father to touch you. In this society everybody has to check each other but nobody really cares. Anna told me one day, I'm going to call the police. I said, how are you going to call the police. You're my daughter, I am trying to discipline you.

There's a lot of money in this country. They'd rather spend it on other things. Back home, we don't have so much yet we look after the population. If you see a child on the street you can say, 'What are you doing here?'. You are not trying to be mean to her, you are looking after her because you saw her in the street. But here I'm afraid to tell the daughter of my friend, don't do that or you shouldn't do that. She'd say, 'You're not supposed to talk to my child like that.' I tried once, I saw the mother was very upset. She said, 'She's a child. You're not supposed to talk to a child like that.' It was very difficult, first of all [I think that since] she's not an adult, she should respect adults. If I ask her to give me a chair, she should give me the chair. It's a very different attitude. At such times the child comes first here. But the child comes second at home.

The social contact with people for children is very different. Right now Anna is sitting in front of the computer. If she was in Bolivia she would have kids playing with her, contact with adults. Here I am the family, the grandmother, the grandfather, the uncles, the friends. I am everything and yet I am scared by the time I grow old, she'll leave me in my house here alone. She doesn't see my own mother, doesn't learn compassion. I saw my grandmother getting old and she would shout 'Bring me a glass of water,' or 'Give me the bread' or the milk, and I would do it quietly without saying anything. But my daughter, she knows her mind. She'll even tell me, 'I have my privacy.' No, I don't like that. She has less respect for me than I had for my mother. She thinks I'm wrong already. Once I said, do you want another mummy with blonde hair and blue eyes, and then she said no.

I don't want to tell you everything here is bad, because it isn't. Some things for children are better. Maybe it's good for people to respect children. But for me so much else is different and I have to get used to it.

In the spring of 1996 in Britain, the story of one small boy captured the nation's attention for a number of weeks. Sifisio Mahlangu's tale was one popularly categorized as a 'tug-of-love' case, but it was not the usual custody battle between two estranged parents. Rather, it was a fight between two women who both wanted to be the boy's mother. The first was his natural mother, a black South African houseworker. The second was a white woman called Salome Stopford, who had once been his mother's employer and who had brought Sifisio to England from South Africa and wanted formally to adopt him.

From the appearance of the first short article giving an account of Salome Stopford's battle with the Westminster local authority, the story ballooned like so many other tales from people's lives which transfix the public until the press runs out of new information to keep up the momentum. Here was a wealthy white woman fighting her former nanny for custody of a child. It appeared that Selina Mahlangu and her husband Charles had not even been aware that adoption proceedings were going ahead until they were contacted by a local black journalist. With the help of a group of radical black lawyers, they fought back for their son. Each day the papers and TV stations had a new angle – race, interracial adoption, poverty versus wealth, the politics of apartheid, political correctness – but in all the editorial posturing, none of the journalists got the real story. This was really a story about motherhood.

In her efforts to win, Salome Stopford and her lawyers depicted Selina Mahlangu as a 'bad' mother. What natural mother, her lawyers asked, could give up her child so easily to another woman and allow him to be taken halfway across the world to a country she was not even capable of locating on a map? As well as sending him to a smart, private school, the court heard, Mrs Stopford also provided the roof over his head. They lived together as a family. Plus she had formed a close relationship, a bond no less, with the boy. By her own account she, Salome Stopford, had overridden Mrs Mahlangu's biological claim and she was Sifisio's 'real' mother. The British public agreed with her. Even journalists sympathetic to the Mahlangus had trouble explaining the couple's actions. They looked for a rationale which might help their readership understand why a mother would allow herself to be separated from her child. Sifisio's case was a legacy of apartheid, the *Guardian* explained, it was impossible for a couple like the Mahlangus to challenge the whims of a white woman like Salome Stopford.

One of the few quotes from Charles Mahlangu gave an indication of the truth. 'My wife had no idea where England was,' he admitted, 'but we thought we would be closing the door for the child if we refused him this chance.' In South Africa, children are often raised by people other than their parents within a system of informal adoption or wardship that has evolved out of a community sense of responsibility for children. One of the ways people help one another out is by looking after each other's children for periods ranging from months to years. The result is that a child may have more than one family and more than one mother. One suspects that Mrs Stopford may well have been aware of all that, for she had certainly lived in South Africa long enough, but she wanted to make Sifisio legally 'hers'. Did she break the faith or was she simply a product of her own Anglo-Saxon culture in which a child can belong either to one person or the other, but not to both? Ultimately Salome Stopford failed to persuade the courts to allow her to adopt Sifisio and he returned to South Africa.

Nelson Mandela rose to prominence because his mother accepted the offer of a Xhosa chief to take the boy, raise and educate him in his own household for several years. In his autobiography, *Long Walk to Freedom*, he writes:

> I can hardly recall any occasion as a child when I was alone. In African culture, the sons and daughters of one's uncles and aunts are considered brothers and sisters, not cousins. We do not make the same distinctions among relations practised by whites. We have no half brothers or half sisters. My mother's sister is my mother; my uncle's son is my brother; my brother's child is my son.[1]

If one chose to look at it in a certain way, one could argue that far from being 'bad' mothers both Mrs Mandela and Mrs Mahlangu passed the 'sacrifice test' with flying colours. But in a country and culture in which what counts as good mothering is the creation of an exclusive maternal–child bond, Selina Mahlangu came within a whisker of having her relationship with her son effectively cancelled.

At the time, I wrote an article for one of the newspapers commenting on Sifisio's case and explaining how the African model of parenting worked. I was particularly well placed to do so, having spent most of my childhood in my family home in West Africa. The way I was 'mothered' was distinct in several ways from the experience of my British contemporaries. For a start, as a child I always had several caretakers, in addition to my parents, at any one time. Often these were cousins or the older sons and daughters of friends who lived with us while they pursued their studies and acted as minders to the children. How a woman went about her role as mother was and is not an issue in that culture. She does what she thinks is right. My African mother, who worked, did not imagine she had to be there all the time. I had other carers, other confidantes, other friends. Both men and women were my guardians and I recall an entire, hectic, Easter holiday at the age of nine spent with my uncle who was a law student in England. What is certain is that I have thrived, and I happen to believe that the home environment contributed to the uncomplicated relationship which exists between my African mother and both her adult daughters. However, the most important point to make is this: children can be mothered in a variety of ways and do perfectly well.

'There is no single style of mothering worldwide, or anything close to it,' concluded psychologists Sarah Hall Sternglanz and Alison Nash in a cross-cultural assessment of motherhood. 'In all these societies with all of these methods of raising children, *children grow up to be normal productive members of their society.*'[2] Looking at a subject like motherhood from the vantage point of other cultures does not just help us towards greater international understanding and the swifter resolution of custody disputes involving people of different nationalities; it also tells us about our own culture, and moves the debate about motherhood on from its current stalemate by helping to separate what might be 'natural' from what is culturally constructed.

Throughout the 1940s and '50s, while men like John Bowlby and Donald Winnicott were preaching the importance of a child's attachment to its mother, and long before feminists began to describe motherhood as a narrowly-constructed institution which kept women housebound in the service of their infants, anthropologists were already publishing accounts of how children were raised in other cultures. Margaret Mead wrote a popular column in the American women's magazine *Redbook*, in which she aired her scepticism about the very idea of gender and gender roles after years of working in societies in which men cared for babies, women fought and Western definitions of femininity and masculinity did not apply. Edith Clarke's account of the mothers in three Jamaican communities, *My Mother who Fathered Me*, demonstrates (as the title suggests) how the maternal role can be flexible and is influenced by external factors such as class, economics and culture.

In 1959 Selma Fraiberg, a psychoanalyst and disciple of John Bowlby, published *The Magic Years* in which she asserted that it was actually harmful for a child to be taken care of by anyone other than his or her own mother. Her work achieved national importance and her test for measuring the degree of attachment a child has to the mother is still used today. In that same year, Beatrice Whiting, one of a group of American anthropologists engaged in a long-term study of mothers in six different cultures, also published her preliminary findings. She asserted that styles of mothering were created first and foremost by environmental influences and cultural values. She and her team rejected fancy psychoanalytic theories, showing instead that every culture develops, rationalizes and justifies the way it raises children with a set of beliefs designed and developed to uphold existing practice.

Furthermore, after living and working for years with mothers from India, the Philippines, Japan, Africa and the United States, the anthropologists declared American mothers to be 'overburdened with almost exclusive responsibility for childcare',[3] the result of which was that they were (comparatively) unstable and emotionally cold. The effect on the children being beyond the scope of the study was not described. These findings barely resonated beyond academic circles, perhaps the inevitable fate of any study attempting to derail a rapidly-moving motherhood movement in the golden era of family values. Maybe it was the common tendency among people to dismiss other cultures as simply inferior to their own. Or it may have been cognitive disbelief at the possibility of any other way of raising children. An equally likely cause was the failure of anthropologists (with the exception of Margaret Mead) to find a popular audience, unlike those psychologists and psychoanalysts who published popular babycare books alongside their academic texts. One way or another, in debates about the family, cross-cultural research has largely been ignored.

The feminist movement has made the same omission in the effort to unite women under the banner of motherhood as a universal, shared experience. The failure of the mostly white, middle-class vanguard to take into account the perspectives of black women and other ethnic minority women is a central reason behind the rejection of feminism by black women. Women such as Bonnie Dill, Joyce Ladner, Patricia Hill Collins and bell hooks wrote forcefully and eloquently on the meaning of motherhood to black women. While white women demanded the right to work, black women in America, who had since the days of slavery combined work with childbearing and child-rearing, wanted the chance to spend time with their children. While white feminists fought for abortion rights, black and Native American women insisted that they wanted the freedom to reproduce which had been consistently denied to them by repressive social policies, forced sterilizations and poverty. And so it goes on. The work of today's young feminists continues to ignore the history, experience and wishes of women who are not white, even women who are not middle class, in the stubborn conviction that those women have nothing to teach them.

I set out to listen to some of those unheard voices and interviewed thirty women from different cultures and backgrounds, all of them mothers and almost all living in the West: women from West Africa, Latinas, women from the islands of the West Indies, African-Americans, Filipinas, women from the Asian sub-continent and the Far East. Their experience of coming from one culture while living in another has made them acutely aware of what even the so-called 'experts' haven't grasped: there is more than one script for motherhood. What emerges is a picture which shows different philosophies of motherhood converging and often conflicting on a public and personal level with a dominant Western ideology. Women whose own mothers had made a real economic contribution to the family resources are told they should not work or at least are given no support to enable them to do so; women who speak languages in which the word for 'mother' and 'aunt' are one and the same, are told they should not share their own child's love with anyone else; women who find themselves having to justify putting their own needs first discover the nagging self-doubt of maternal guilt. And, as Selina Mahlangu discovered, when women do not mother according to accepted mores and standards, they are quickly labelled as poor or defective mothers.

The very specific history and circumstances which created a role for the Western 'sculptress' mother, driven by social and economic realities and backed up by scientific and psychological 'proofs', which has been used to underpin existing gender roles, has simply not occurred anywhere else in the world. In a sense, it is an isolated historical incident. Hearing women from around the world talk about motherhood, what stands out above anything else is that, whatever their class and their own personal philosophy, they seem to have more in common with each other than with Western practice and ideology. In the words of bell hooks, the centre shifts, and it is Western motherhood – with its exclusive pressures on the mother – which becomes unusual.

In the early 1980s, Sara Ruddick encapsulated a concept with the phrase 'maternal thinking' and wrote: 'I speak about a mother's thought – the intellectual capacities she develops, the judgments she makes, the metaphysical attitudes she assumes and the values she affirms.' Ruddick herself admitted that she was able to draw only upon her own knowledge of 'the institutions of motherhood in middle-class, white, Protestant, capitalist, patriarchal America'.[4] So how do other cultures think about motherhood?

A mother's work

The conventional view of motherhood in Britain and America sees a mother's work outside the home as conflicting with the duties of motherhood. This is seen as true, not just in a practical sense, but ideologically too. It is asserted that mothers should be 'there' for their children, at home when they come back from school, there to put them to bed, there even when they are asleep. The very fact of a mother's presence is thought to be necessary to make a young child feel confident, happy and secure. It's not difficult to trace the roots of this way of thinking back to that old chestnut the attachment theory, and with it the attendant notion that mothers should devote themselves entirely to the every need and whim of their offspring.

Even though attachment disciples claim that this is somehow 'natural', the fact is that in much of the rest of the world mothers are hard at work. Most countries outside the West are simply not wealthy enough to allow women the luxury of staying at home to mind the children. And without an army of professionals to accuse them of damaging their children, mothers have continued to work unhindered. While work does not necessarily relieve women of the responsibilities of mothering, there is no conflict between the *idea* of a woman working and earning, as well as being a mother.

Nigerian author Buchi Emecheta's novel *The Joys of Motherhood* tells the story of the trials of Nnu Ego, a young mother struggling with the role and expectations of womanhood within the confines of tribal tradition. Though she has many problems, the ability to earn a living is not one of them – at least until she joins her husband in the expanding metropolis of colonial Lagos. Anyone who has ever read this moving novel will come across the lines: 'She might not have any money to supplement her husband's income, but were they not in a white man's world where it was the duty of the father to provide for his family? In Ibuza, women made a contribution, but in urban Lagos, men had to be the sole providers; this new setting robbed the woman of her useful role.'[5] Throughout West Africa women have historically been the ones who run the farms and who trade, often travelling great distances to neighbouring countries to buy goods. Today a visitor to Nigeria, Sierra Leone or Ghana will find few women without the means to support themselves and their children. Indeed, the women in those countries find it difficult to understand how Western women can apparently do so little, as this innocent question on the part of a Malian woman reveals: 'Is it true,' she asked me, 'that in Britain women just stay in the house all day while their husbands work?'

In Britain, women of African, Caribbean and Indian heritage with children are more likely to work full-time than white women, according to a study undertaken at Manchester University.[6] Of African-American women, Patricia Hill Collins has observed: 'the assumption that motherhood and economic dependency on men are linked and that to be a "good" mother, one must stay at home making motherhood a full-time "occupation", is similarly uncharacteristic of African-American families.'[7] A study published in 1996 by researchers at Tufts

University and the University of Michigan revealed the same finding: 'the employed mother has long been the norm for African American women.'[8]

Of course, because in Britain and America black men often have trouble finding work, particularly the kind of work that can support a stay-at-home wife and a family, black women in these two countries have historically rarely been able to afford the luxury of not working. But even among middle-class black women today, one finds the work ethic is still strong. Over time the women's circumstances have fostered a different maternal ideology, one which says a mother should work in order to be able to look after her children. Providing is *part* of the duties of motherhood. Lakesha, a young black mother, put it this way: 'Otherwise you put all your eggs in one basket. I had an aunt who gave up working, then her husband had to retire early because he was ill. She hadn't had a job for 15 years, and you just thought, why didn't she just keep on working?' Ramatu, a Sierra Leonean whose husband was an engineer, said: 'If you don't work how can you take care of them? If you have children you shouldn't be dependent on anybody.'

Denise Segura, a California-based sociologist, has demonstrated that the notion that women should mother by staying at home is not shared by Mexican women and other Latin Americans, who view going out to earn as perfectly compatible with their role as mothers. It is only the practical aspect of doing both that is considered a problem. Once immigrant women have been in the United States for some length of time, however, they begin to adopt some of the ambivalence towards work and motherhood prevalent in the wider society. Chicanas (women of Mexican descent born in the United States) particularly aspire to Western models of motherhood. Segura questions the usual assumptions that non-industrial cultures place women in narrower and more limited roles. Far from becoming more 'liberated' by Western influences, Chicanas in fact become more conservative or 'traditional'.

These Latina and African women do not question their 'right' to work and have a family. Their work is seen as valuable in its own right. Christine Oppong, a West African sociologist, says that while the archetypal white, Western family divides men's and women's responsibilities into two opposite camps – the public 'male' sphere of work and financial support for the family and the private 'female' sphere of nurturing and childrearing – most African cultures do not. Denise Segura has made the same observation regarding Latina women, even though from a Western point of view those cultures are frequently (and often mistakenly) viewed as more oppressive towards women. In none of these traditions, and a great many other besides, is mothering seen as a private, individual undertaking, reserved for biological mothers who are exclusively devoted to their own children.

One mother, other mothers

In the Western ideal a mother enjoys a one-to-one relationship with her child, at least while he or she is young. These are the moments of perfect bliss which, according to Freud, chart the course for happiness in adult life. As the child grows, he remains the individual responsibility of his mother who only gradually encourages him to venture further afield and develop other relationships. Even so, nobody, not even the child's father, comes close to re-creating the kind of bond which exists between a mother and her child. And for many women the intimacy she shares with her child is a source of great pride; indeed in our society the bonded relationship is probably the single most important measure of 'good' motherhood. Even today, many well-intentioned modern fathers find their efforts to become involved in looking after their child blocked, either psychologically by the store set on that special bond, or literally by their wives' own reluctance to share the space.

All this is not necessarily true elsewhere in the world. Among the Cheyenne of North America mother–daughter relations were supposed to be actively cool, even hostile, and a young girl was supposed to seek another female relative to act as confidante. The same is still true in modern-day Zambia. Antagonistic relationships apart, there are many more places where mother–child relationships are far more permeable and open than in the West. There are few countries where a mother is not the most central figure in her child's life, but the degree to which that is true varies quite dramatically. She is more likely than not to share her role with several other people. Although she may be a constant throughout her child's life, that does not mean she is necessarily constantly present. A child might live apart from her mother for many reasons which have their roots in culture, tradition or personal circumstances.

In Isabel Allende's novel *Eva Luna*, there is a scene in which Consuelo, the housekeeper and mother of the young Eva, argues with her colleague the cook, whom she has appointed her daughter's comrade. Allende writes: 'My mother had not believed in original sin, and had not thought it necessary to baptize me. But [Elvira] had insisted with unyielding stubbornness. All right, comadre, Consuelo had finally agreed. You do whatever you want. Just don't change the name I chose for her.'[9] The practice of appointing comadres and copadres (co-mothers and co-fathers) to help raise a child is prevalent throughout Latin America. The person who agrees to the role is expected to do a great deal in execution of the duties of the post, such as childminding and teaching as well as financial support. It is no surprise, then, that Elvira has the authority to demand that the new child be christened, not withstanding the natural mother's wishes. In the novel, Eva's mother dies shortly afterwards and Elvira, whom Eva calls *madrina* (little mother) appoints another woman as her own comadre.

There's evidence of shared parenting, particularly shared mothering, in dozens of different cultural spheres. A Pakistani woman dedicates her first book 'To my mothers', who are her father's other wives. In the book an Indian couple living in England send their five-year-old son to family and friends in Bombay for the summer. Black women writers in America have extensively covered their communities' practice of sharing child-rearing duties with 'other mothers'. These might be aunts or other female relatives, or they may be neighbours or friends. bell hooks, the New-York-based feminist writer, says of African-American society: 'Childrearing is a responsibility that can be shared with other childrearers, with people who do not live with children. This form of parenting is revolutionary in this society because it takes place in opposition to the idea that parents, especially mothers, should be the only childrearers.'[10]

When one talks about support networks among people from cultures outside the Anglo-Saxon tradition, the listener (if he or she is unfamiliar with those cultures) is wont to say, 'Ah, the extended family,' as though antiquated notions of kin and blood ties were all that explained what is, in fact, a different way of thinking about who is responsible for children. In *All Our Kin*, Carol Stack, who spent years chronicling the lives of a group of urban, African-American women, coined the term 'fictive kin' to cover people who are not blood relations but are treated by a child and her family as though they are. For example, one mother I met was helped by her two best friends, both married women who were also 'other mothers'. Letitia, a forty-year-old dance therapist had two children aged thirteen and five. Twice a week Alex, a newspaper columnist who worked to her own timetable, collected the children from school and took them to their sports club, while Letitia worked late. When the eldest girl was a baby, she often spent her afternoons after nursery playing under Alex's desk, because the newspaper office's atmosphere made it easy to babysit. In the evening, the girls would often call Daniella for help with homework. Letitia described the 'other mothers' as 'my big support systems'. Daniella had actually opted not to have children herself and to carve herself a niche as 'other mother' to as many children as possible. She grew up with a local woman who acted as second mother to a number of children, and to whom she often turned. She herself commented: 'I don't see it as a secondary role, I'm just as valuable as a resource.' She had made an early decision not to try to combine children with a strenuous career with a retail organization and freelance singing engagements. 'It's a maternal thing, but it's different,' was how she explained the arrangement.

The ability to divide duties among other people is thought to be one of the reasons why West Indian mothers in Britain have such high rates of economic participation. A 1992 Labour Force Survey showed that 59 per cent of West Indian *lone* mothers worked, a simply staggering statistic which flies in the face of the popular conception of the lazy, black single mother.[11] Researchers hazarded that this might be because they have support networks they can rely on.

In fact the central importance and value of shared parenting is now being posed as a reason for both the success and the failure of black families in parts of Britain and America. Up until recently some sociologists have blamed social problems on the disappearance of 'traditional' marriage forms, on male unemployment, and on the rise in the number of single mothers – both black and white. But another school of thought argues that it is more the breakdown of *support networks* which has made some sections of the community unable to weather the social and economic shifts of the last two decades. In some respects this fragmentation has been the direct result of the imposition of one set of values relating to motherhood. For example, where several adults might have lived under one roof two decades ago, such a household has now become several single, separate, female-headed households as a result of welfare and housing policies. At another level, young women from ethnic minority populations may aspire to a vision of motherhood which is reflected by the society around them but which does not fit their circumstances. For example, one young woman I spoke to called Anna described herself as 'barely surviving' to stay at home on state benefits. Asked why, she named a popular family TV show from the 1960's and said 'I want my family to be just like that'.

Other experts point to evidence of a regeneration of shared parenting ideals. Judith Stacey, author of *In the Name of the Family*, says: Far from dying out, co-parenting is gaining new ground in communities where people have always shared child-care to meet new demands.' Partly, families are adapting to economic necessities such as the fact that childcare can be extremely expensive, or work hours might be long or inconvenient, but the biggest impetus of all is the number of single mothers who would otherwise be coping alone.

It is possible to see how practice and ideology might interweave, especially over the issue of combining mothering and work. A white, middle-class woman with sole responsibility for her children simply doesn't have the time to work. At the same time, she will hear that, in fact, she 'shouldn't' work, because it is better for her children if she is at home – the ideology justifies the existing practice. Women who choose to hire a child-minder or send their children to daycare soon start to hear all that 'evidence' that their relationship with their child is likely to suffer; that a child *requires* her mother's presence. The ideology becomes dogma.

On the other hand, a woman who comes from a culture within which a woman's work is valued, can leave her child with someone else much more easily. Adults in communities where children grow up under the care of several people convincingly argue that such a system of mothering is in the best interests of the child. They regard the attachment to the maternal figure, which we prize so highly in the West, as impractical ('You would never get away,' Annie, Singapore) and stifling ('If a woman is with her child all the time, she'll never leave that child alone again,' Jane, Sierra Leone).

There is a Balinese custom which dictates that a child's feet should never touch the floor until past her first birthday. It's a favourite among people playing pop psychologist, who use it to illustrate how mothers in other parts of the world bond with their children. What they don't realize is that it is usually some-one other than the mother who is carrying the child at any given moment. In practice, the purpose of the custom is as much to accustom a child to other carers, as to make the child feel secure. In fact, in another Balinese tradition women play with dolls, pretending to pet and nurse them in order to arouse their children's jealousy, to detach them and start them on the path to independence and acceptance of the arrival of a new baby.

Co-parenting in communities which share responsibility is also considered healthier for the child's development ('If there are four or five people they'll have different ideas, more common sense than if it's just the mother,' Marie, Lebanon; 'More people is better. They [children] learn how to work with others. If there's only one person they don't have any experience,' Mer-cedes, Ecuador). Whereas the Western sculptress mother tries to act as an agent of control and to direct and ration her child's experiences, an Indian mother or a Chinese mother sees all experiences, positive or negative, as teaching children the realities of life, how to assess risk and take care of themselves.

The interested mother-watcher finds that in many places around the world, from Timbuktu to Tibet, from Greece to Goa, there is simply no room for the Western mantra which dictates that a child can have only one mother and one family. Children often go to live with another family for a period of months or even years. Informal adoption, or wardship, is part of life in Islamic societies, in Japan, South America, Africa, in the United States among Hawaiians and Native Americans, throughout the West Indies, India and Pakistan, to name a few places. The bonds created by raising a child are close, imperishable and exist irres-pective of genetic ties, but they exist alongside blood relation-ships and the natal family does not give up its commitment or connection to the child.

A child could move family for any number of reasons: frequently to further his or her education and experience, or to give parents time to set up a business, to get a qualification or to recover from an illness or just because it is considered more convenient or effective all round. An art historian at the Royal Academy in London who is of West Indian heritage said: 'My son lives with my mother back home. Nobody can seem to understand that this suits all of us perfectly well.' Her son went back to the West Indies while she was working hard for her PhD. Now he is happy at school and no one, including his mother, feels it necessary to disrupt his life simply in order to reunite mother and son.

The assumption that a mother is the best caretaker of her own child, and that as a mother she must *mother* her child, is notably absent from cultures where motherhood is not regarded as an exclusive undertaking. Marion explained: 'A mother might say, I don't understand this child. Maybe with some other member or family or household this child might grow to learn or have a different relationship that might work more easily.' Among immigrants to the West the practice of sending children back to live with relatives is common. Esther sent her seventeen-year-old son, whose unruliness she failed to control, back to West Africa to live with her cousin who was felt to be better equipped to deal with the boy's temper. Esther's success or failure as a mother was not seen as an issue.

A non-exclusive style of mothering opens up a wider space for men to act as parents. A 1984 study of Mexican men found that, despite the macho image of the Latin father, these men were just as emotionally nurturing and just as involved in the daily lives of their children as the mothers.[12] In many societies, even if the father himself is absent at work and less involved with his children, young men, uncles and grandfathers are often co-opted into babysitting and other duties. Carlotta, a thirty-five-year-old Mexican married to a Russian, arranges for her son to spend a day every weekend with his uncle. She describes the situation as 'ideal'. Another male cousin sometimes babysits. Evelyn also leaves her daughter Natalie in the care of her brother. In *Mothercare/Othercare*, Scarr and Dunn describe how childcare became something which British men found 'embarrassing'. This is not necessarily true in other countries. The traditional Latin male may subscribe to other kinds of behaviours to maintain his status, but being seen playing with his child does not threaten his image.

British travellers who spend time in Southern European countries, or further afield in Africa or Asia, often remark on how 'child-friendly' such societies are. People accompanied by children suddenly find that their son or daughter has no shortage of new friends to take care of him or her. It seems as though everyone loves children; even an adolescent male will buy a sweet for a child or jiggle her on his knee.

When parents from those countries come to Britain, they find their customs put them on a collision course with the authorities who subscribe to the prevailing wisdom of what constitutes good motherhood. In the 1970s and 1980s, Nigerian students who placed their children in private fostering arrangements while they studied medicine or law, found that when those families decided they wanted to keep their children, the British courts awarded the families custody. The Nigerians were seen as having 'abandoned' their children. Other misunderstandings arise all the time. Immigration authorities accuse Bangladeshi parents of trying to bring children illegally into the country by claiming that the children are theirs. Women immigrating from the West Indies are refused visas for children they have left behind in the care of relatives (while they find a home and job), on the grounds that they have abandoned them. Over-zealous social workers remove ethnic minority children from their homes on the grounds of maternal deprivation, because someone other than the mother is in charge of the child's daily needs. West Indian couples in the UK have been turned down for adoption on the basis that they are 'unsuitable' because their parenting arrangements do not fit a narrow set of criteria based on the white 'norm'.

A child of one's own

When the day-to-day care of an infant is routinely shared among different people, including parents and non-parents, the child is free to share affections, and the notion of to whom that child is seen as belonging becomes fluid. In Western maternal thinking the boundaries of ownership are fixed. The child belongs to the mother, not even the father who is rarely awarded custody of his children when a couple split up. It is hard for many people in the West to grasp how other people can live and govern their lives without clear lines of demarcation. Mother-centric Western thinking seeks to make one person morally and legally responsible for a child. Only in the last decade have we begun to enforce men's duty to their own offspring, at least as regards paying for their upkeep. By vesting everything in the mother or the natural parents in the context of the nuclear family, we have lost the general ethic of care which is there to be admired in other societies.

The accepted theory is that 'the community' became less active in childcare once people in industrialized countries moved away from the villages and towns to the big cities to live among strangers and lost their extended family networks. This is true, but only up to a point. There is also a pattern of thought that continues and maintains the cherished privacy (isolation) of the nuclear family, even among the modern 'community', the re-created networks of selected friends and contacts. This story, by a Turkish woman, illustrates the difference in thinking. In many places, including Turkey, all adults have authority over all children. The woman and an English friend, both the mothers of small children, were sitting together in the Turkish woman's home while their children played. At one point the young daughter of the Englishwoman snatched some food from the table, and the Turkish woman immediately rebuked her. Her friend was furious. 'Who gave you the right to talk to my child like that?' she demanded. The Turkish woman had unwittingly crossed a line, had entered the mother's space. It is the English-woman who will pay the price, though, because next time she calls her friend to ask her to babysit, she will find her a great deal less willing. The Turkish woman will begin to worry about trespassing on the other mother's authority and her relationship with her child.

The two women had different ways of thinking about their relationship with each other's children. A good explanation of what was going through each person's mind comes from Steph-anie Coontz, author of *The Way We Never Were*, a sceptical account of the truth behind a 1950s family idyll. She tells this story about attending a Hawaiian-Filipino friend's wedding on the island:

> I could sit and socialize and keep an eye on my toddler, and I assumed that was what all the other parents were doing. Soon, however, I noticed that I was the only person jumping up to change a diaper, pick my son up when he fell, wipe his nose, dry his eyes, or ply him with goodies. Belatedly, I real-ized why: The other parents were *not* keeping an eye on their kids. Instead, each adult kept an eye on the *floor* around his or her chair. Any child who moved into that section of the floor and needed disciplining, feeding, comforting, or chang-ing was promptly accommodated; no parent felt compelled to check that his or her *own* child was being similarly cared for.[13]

Compare that scenario to the current state of affairs where, in the average British supermarket, a stranger approaching a child might well be assumed to be bent on some ill-deed and in all probability reported by staff. Or the experience of Annette Sorenson, a Danish mother who left her baby in a stroller outside a restaurant in New York and found herself arrested on child endangerment charges. Her protest that this was standard practice in Denmark was ignored by officials until the Danish Consulate stepped in on her behalf.

The ever-widening gulf between adults and other people's children contributes to the sense of loss that people who cannot have their own children feel. Such a couple in Britain or America, with only the most restricted of relationships with the children of their friends, come to want a child of 'their own'. Adoption policies have traditionally been aimed at fulfilling this desire by placing an anonymous baby with a couple who could pass as the genetic parents. Once we even used to erase the child's entire history and start from scratch. In the last twenty years pressure to change those policies and to give adopted people the right to information about themselves, including the right to know that they are adopted, has come from the adopted individuals themselves, not from adoptive parents, many of whom would probably prefer to maintain the illusion that the children are naturally 'theirs'.

Nowadays, growing numbers of infertile couples prefer to have a child of their own by using IVF or some other form of technology. People from ethnic minority groups, on the other hand, are generally under-represented as clients seeking the services of infertility specialists. A study from the Institute for the Study of Social Change in America showed that while white women embraced the possibilities offered by science, the black women in the group showed far less interest. Diane Beeson, who conducted the study, says the central issue was control, on which the white participants placed a great emphasis. For white clients, technology is being used to do the job that adoption, now that there is only a trickle of 'adoptable' (which generally means white) children to be found, is no longer able to do. This does not mean that no other cultural or ethnic group has any use for medical technology; in fact, in 1994 at the point when a Manchester clinic was offering sex-selection techniques, Asian families wanting boy children constituted the largest group of potential clients. Nevertheless, a couple's need to produce their very own child, or the next best thing, is less urgently felt within other non-Western cultures.

One of the reasons why adoption agencies in the UK say it is hard to find adoptive couples for ethnic minority children in their care is the fact that members of Somali or Jamaican communities, say, often prefer to adopt informally through the community or through family ties. Furthermore, what is meant by 'adoption' does not necessarily correspond to the Western idea: 'We don't adopt, as such,' says Marie, talking about taking on one of her brother's children. 'They'd give her to me to raise up.' The connection between the families or the child's mother or parents would be retained. When Linda, a Jamaican, says, 'I would prefer to know who the child's family is,' she does not mean she wants to know what kind of stock the child comes from, but that she would expect the natural mother or parents to take some part in raising the child, which they could not do if they remained anonymous.

The preference for 'open' over 'closed' adoptions and informal agreements over legal ones is closely linked to inclusive mothering patterns. In such cultures, being the sole decision-maker about a child's welfare is less important than maintaining what is called the 'system of obligation'. This is the creation of networks of shared responsibility and mutual ties, which are how communities operate effectively.

One is struck over and over, in conversations about motherhood with women from ethnically diverse backgrounds, by how often they take for granted the idea that there are two (or more) ways of thinking about motherhood. In the West, although we like to think of ourselves as intellectually enlightened, we struggle to see past our own noses, and most psychologists, social scientists, politicians and policy-makers continue to bang the same 'one motherhood' drum, ignoring or choosing to ignore evidence which contradicts it. The feminist idea of single,

universal motherhood unites women in the recognition of a
shared task, but overlooks variations in style and in experience.
For, as we shall see, differences in maternal thinking can produce
an immeasurably different experience of motherhood.

Guilt

Feelings of guilt are endemic among modern mothers in the
West. The psychologist Estela Welldon of the Tavistock Portman
Clinic, author of *Mother, Madonna, Whore*, describes it as 'absolutely pervasive', among her clientele.[14] Many women confess
regularly to feeling, sometimes inexplicably, guilty. This has
given rise to the rationale that maternal guilt is somehow a
natural feeling, part of the female condition alongside other
'feminine' qualities such as nurturing ability and empathy. Estela
Welldon notes that deeper investigation reveals the cause as a
woman's sense that as a mother she 'could have done better'.

Discussions around the subject of guilt with women who do
not share an Anglo-European heritage are intensely illuminating. In fact, they turn the idea that maternal guilt is a natural
condition on its head. To some women, the concept has no
meaning. 'Guilty, like what?' was one response I received to a
question about feelings of maternal guilt. Another woman asked:
'What have I done?'

An obvious source of guilt for many women in British and
US society stems from the issue of work and, as has been
discussed, the perceived conflict between commitments outside
the home and obligations to the child. This is intensified by the
continued discussion over whether children are psychologically
damaged by being put into daycare, which focuses specifically
on the effect that daycare has on the mother–child relationship,
and whether children become 'insecurely attached' as a result.

Suzanne, a thirty-two-year-old with two children, described
herself as 'Miss Guilt'. She gave up her full-time job when her

son was two because she felt so bad about not being there. Now she says: 'I'd love to work part-time, but I'd still feel guilty if I missed something he did.' Suzanne describes the life of her sister-in-law who works full-time with two small children: 'They both work. Their son is at the sitter. She feels guilty all day long. I don't want to be like that.'

Mothering in Anglo-European culture has evolved into a demanding, full-time occupation. Visitors unaccustomed to British culture are often struck by how much British parents, mothers in particular, seem to do for their children. Even tasks which the child could adequately carry out for him or herself are often performed by the mother. One immigrant woman, a mother of five now employed as a nanny in a white household, says: 'The parents do everything for the children. At home by the time a boy is ten he can do his own laundry, but here they do everything for the girl until she is eighteen.' Anthropologists have described these two approaches, one in which the child is expected to take on tasks from an early age as 'child responsible', and the other in which the child is not expected to contribute within the adult sphere as 'child non-responsible'. Child and mother become locked in a mutually dependent, symbiotic relationship. Because she is everything to her child and sets herself high standards, the stay-at-home Western mother berates herself for her failings. 'I feel guilty because I lose my temper, then I feel I should have been more patient,' said one woman. Another, Laura, confesses she feels guilty about 'not doing something the right way'. Laura, and mothers like her, find it hard to trust anybody else to do the job as well as they do.

Before long, maternal emotions turn from care to possessiveness. There is documented evidence that mothers who are not used to sharing care of their children become jealous of other adults who form close relationships with them. An in-depth survey published in the *Journal of Comparative Family Studies* showed that white American working mothers harboured feelings of ambivalence and guilt towards their children's nannies, nursery school teachers or daycare providers, whom they are afraid might replace them in their child's affections.[15] The middle-class woman whose child runs to the au-pair instead of to her, feels dishonoured as a mother, but a woman who is used to the presence of other people as actors in her child's life is less threatened by the idea of sharing her child's affections. 'She's much better with her than I am,' says Alma of the friend who takes care of her daughter while Alma herself is at work.

All these variations, in whatever patterns they occur, serve to create different mother–child relationships from the classic Western model. Few societies demand that a mother be everything to her child in the way it is expected of Western mothers, and few are as enamoured of trying to create such an intensive, exclusive bond between the two. The guilt grows out of the fact that what Western societies expect of mothers is simply unrealistic, but this does not stop most of us from continuing to insist that mothers try to be what we want them to be. 'Idealization and blaming the mother are two sides of the same belief in the all-powerful mother,' says Nancy Chodorow in her essay 'The Fantasy of the Perfect Mother', co-authored with Susan Contratto.[16] Put the two ingredients together, stir well and the result is maternal guilt.

In some societies, a strong maternal ideology may exist side by side with non-exclusive mothering styles. For example, in parts of Catholic Latin America, in Italy, Spain and many areas of southern Europe, motherhood is practically a revered state but there is an absence of the kind of mother-baiting that has virtually become a national sport in some Western societies. A Brazilian mother, say, is likely to reap greater rewards for her role than the average Western mother. Stanlie James has described how African-American 'other mothers' achieve real community status as people from whom others seek advice, and play a pivotal role between different families or elements of the same family. She shows how such women often emerge as local community leaders, activists and organizers.

Traditional psychology takes as its working model the classic Western nuclear family, upon whose illusory qualities most theories of the family, of mothering and its influence on child development and personality development are based. Yet different mothering styles across cultures have produced, and continue to produce, balanced people everywhere. It would be interesting to witness how these theories might alter if the diversity in parenting practices which exists across the cultures were properly accounted for and incorporated. Chodorow, herself a psychoanalyst, is one of the few to recognize the limitations of psychoanalytic 'truths' which presume one style of exclusive motherhood, an assumption she has referred to as the 'false universality' of currently accepted theories. To do so would require a major rethink of the principles which underpin our theories of how women should mother. But as we move to an increasing cultural plurality, the need to do so becomes more urgent.

Conclusions

At the Beijing UN Women's Conference in 1995, Western delegates were surprised at their failure to win the backing of women from non-Western nations on the subject of abortion rights. Indeed, many women, even those from countries where abortion is illegal, appeared uninterested in the debate and even repelled by the emphasis placed by Western women on the right to a termination. On one news broadcast aired in the UK, a pair of Chinese delegates, joined by an Israeli colleague, suggested that some of the American women were unwholesomely obsessed with the topic. Here was another gap in cultural understanding. For Western women, the right not to reproduce has become fundamental to achieving equal rights, because becoming a mother within a society where neither policy nor practice caters to sharing that responsibility is a life-changing act in very many ways. For women elsewhere, motherhood itself does not pose the same threat to the ability to work, but that is a fact that Western feminism has never grasped. It is also a telling indication of the degree of cultural insensitivity at play, that the painful irony of placing abortion on the table for discussion in a country where women are denied the right to have more than one child, and where pregnant women are routinely obliged to undergo terminations against their will in the name of population control, was lost on the Western sisterhood.

In the Western nations, ignorance among the majority population towards the cultural values and ways of minority populations is rife. Two decades ago, in a famous report which still resonates today, Patrick Moynihan (then assistant secretary at the US Department of Labor) blamed the problems of black Americans on their mothers and described African-American families as matriarchies. Today in the UK and the USA, social scientists and politicians are still trying to blame family structure (mothers, again) rather than the economy, the effective disappearance of stable employment, the quality of schools or racial prejudice for the problems faced by minority communities. This line of argument is rapidly becoming a habit. If only minorities could be more like us, goes the argument, their problems (and ours) would be solved. Seeing difference as deficit when it comes to other cultures is just the flip-side of the family-values coin which also condemns gays and lesbians who become parents, lone mothers, older mothers and so on and so forth.

An emerging line of interpretation sees those family structures and styles of mothering that we see in different communities as adaptive and not deviant. Ethnic minority and immigrant populations are usually at the sharp end of change, feeling the cold winds of social shifts ahead of a generally more established, financially secure white population. It is now becoming evident that the patterns of change in the family styles of Britain's Caribbean population are rapidly becoming visible in the mainstream population in which, for example, the number of lone mothers has been rising rapidly. In fact, it can be convincingly argued that families who already make use of kin and non-kin networks, who share maternal tasks and are able to envisage flexible roles for mothers, are much better suited to respond to new social structures than those with a rigid interpretation of motherhood within the nuclear family. Unfortunately for the latter, the mystique of motherhood has served to divest other people of parenting roles. Men in particular have found that once they are no longer effective breadwinners, they have little function in the family at all. And while one is unlikely to transpose wholesale the style of mothering of a Moroccan village to Oxfordshire, there is no limit to the ideas that can be learned from looking at how other cultures mother.

The social historian Stephanie Coontz has argued that, far from being the guardian of family values, the nuclear family's emergence in the nineteenth century was actually prompted by a wish to hang on to the spoils of the Industrial Revolution and a rejection of other, wider obligations. When the First Lady of the United States, Hillary Clinton, chooses an African proverb, 'it takes a village to raise a child', as the title of a book, there is the first sign of recognition, in some quarters at least, that leaving the entire responsibility for looking after a child in the hands of one or even two people is no longer possible or desirable. The presumption that notions of community or extended family are things of the past which can never be resurrected is a mistake. A Family Policy Studies Centre briefing document, citing a 1993 study of British families, says: 'A popular myth about families is that family members have moved away from each other and have little contact.'[17] The study showed that a third of people live less than an hour away from other family members, and fewer than 10 per cent were further than five hours away. In addition, new forms of family are arising: blended families,

224 · Mother of All Myths

step-families, chosen families of friends. We really do not have to be so pessimistic about the future of the family.

The one belief standing in the way of a communitarian approach, however, is the notion of 'one motherhood', of the dedicated mother-figure who can provide everything. Exclusive mothering is *excluding* of others. For as long as we remain sentimentally attached to the idea, just as though we were indeed tied to mama's apron-strings, we are unable to see new ways of being and new ways of structuring family life.

Left Holding the Baby: How Politicians Manipulate Mothers

Half a revolution

It is currently fashionable to subscribe to the view that women have achieved equality with men and that feminism, having achieved its original objective, is now redundant. The sole reason supporting this premise is the advance of significant numbers of women into the workplace over the last twenty years, coupled with the disproportionate degree of attention given to a small number of women who hold high-profile positions. Although parity between men and women appears to be within grasp in one area (and to say even that would be to overstate the case), it is merely a veneer of equality which hides a significant fault-line. At home, precious little has actually changed for the vast majority of women who continue to do the lion's share (or rather, the lioness's share) of domestic work, in particular child-rearing. The true househusband is a mythic creature, and even fully engaged fathers and domestic partners are sighted rarely enough. An in-depth survey of 6,000 parents in their thirties conducted by the Family Policy Studies Centre in 1996 revealed that childcare was still seen as overwhelmingly a maternal re-sponsibility.[1] This was true even in apparently egalitarian, dual-income, professional households and in situations where the woman was the sole breadwinner.

It is clear that both men and women still see the mother as the central player in their children's lives and, even with 64 per cent of mothers now in the workforce,[2] it is the mother who is expected to make the necessary sacrifices to fulfil obligations which are still seen as pretty much exclusively her own, including taking time away from work. While it may be the remnants of a traditional value system that has caused the domestic workload to be so disproportionately allocated, what *perpetuates* this imbalance is the mystique of motherhood: the idea that the mother's role is unique, biological and irreplaceable. The logic, then, appears to be that if a woman is in charge of the children, she may as well do the washing, ironing and cooking as well. So, far from attaining true equality, what the average British woman has been sold instead is a form of enlightened paternalism which has extended her range of tasks to include earning money, while failing to alter substantially her old role. Fathers still merely 'help' mothers. If there has been a shift in the idea of woman in her twin capacity as 'wife and mother', it is that the 'wife' part has loosened up: women are no longer expected to greet their husbands home in the evening, fully made-up with a whisky-and-soda on standby. There has been no such relaxing of the 'mother' role, however, which demands of women alone the most exacting standards and exhaustive claims on their time and attention.

Coping with the double load means that mothers are becoming Britain's new poor. According to the economist Heather Joshi, the average British mother loses 57 per cent of her income after she turns twenty-five, when compared with a woman without children.[3] Motherhood affects women's training, promotion and retirement prospects. Women live longer than men, need more time to build up a pension and yet have less time to do it in. Mothers do the worst-paid and least desirable jobs. Half of Britain's working mothers are in the three lowest occupational categories (low paid, semi-skilled work) and only 10 per cent are in the top three, compared to France (with an established childcare system) where 22 per cent of mothers who work part-time are in the *top* three occupational categories.[4] Simply stated and without doubt, women bear an inequitable amount of the financial, emotional and practical costs of rearing the next generation, and this impacts on the status of women as a whole.

Lucy, one of many women interviewed for this book, is the mother of two small children. She has an MBA and has recently taken time away from work to care for her children. Her husband, whom she met at business school, works for a computer firm. After her first child Lucy went back to work, but found the stress of finding suitable childcare and the conflicting demands made on her time and energy simply impossible to deal with. With her second child she resigned her job and stayed at home for a period which was intended to be a year, but which was being extended indefinitely. During our conversation she seemed bright enough, chatted about her son and was even forgiving about her husband's limited contribution: 'I try not to be too hard on him.' As I was getting ready to leave she asked me a few questions about the research I was doing and, in the course of the exchange, I commented that for mothers to raise their children alone at home was historically relatively recent. She looked thoughtful and said: 'They never tell you that, do they?' She told me that even her friends with children didn't warn her of the extraordinary level of sacrifice, the stress, the sheer impossibility of the task. Over the next couple of minutes her demeanour changed significantly as she became heated. Gone was the beatific mother of half an hour before. She said their omission was tantamount to a 'conspiracy of silence' and she rounded off by asking me a question which she promptly answered herself: 'And do you know why they do that? Because misery likes company. Because they want to co-opt you into the misery of their own lives.'

That was one woman's response to the predicament of modern motherhood. The catchphrase of women's magazines in the 1980s was 'having it all' (by which they actually meant 'doing it all') and the magazines were filled with advice on how to juggle career, motherhood and marriage. Supermum is still out there somewhere as an ideal. I do not recall reading anywhere in those popular magazines the serious suggestion that men should do anything more than help out. Even today, working mothers who run themselves ragged are merely offered time-management classes, mobile phones and nappy delivery services to help them acquit themselves a little better. Now we are told that 'having it all' is a dream that died, and that many women actually prefer to stay at home rather than continue the juggling act. Yet a third option seems to be habitually overlooked, and that is the notion of 'sharing it all'.

Moulding motherhood: policy and practice

The situation of women like Lucy is not merely a twist of fate. How women function as mothers is directly influenced not just by traditional gendered divisions of labour but by current social, political, commercial and economic forces. At times, the ways in which the lives of mothers are affected may be the result of practice and social convention, at other times they are the result of policies which are constructed to change our behaviour, limit choices and control the variables of a single group of people. Policy frames motherhood.

For example, a government that sees its population declining might try to increase the number of births by taking a pro-natalist stance involving limiting access to abortion and awarding tax breaks to families. At a time of high unemployment, a government may decide it wants mothers to stay at home, so it cuts childcare subsidies and limits the number of nursery places. A sudden economic boom switches those policies into sharp reverse. Presently, governments in the industrialized nations have alighted on family policy as a favourite way to reflect the values they think appeal to the populace: by attacking lone mothers, cutting their benefits, refusing to allow gay couples to adopt and advocating the two-parent family. Motherhood is as much influenced by economic indicators and elections as is the stock market.

Policy is enacted through practice which, by design or by deficiency, pushes people towards certain patterns of behaviour. Think for a moment how much is based on the premise that children are looked after by their mothers. Child benefit, for example, is still paid directly to mothers. Even the most enlightened companies offering paternity leave still only give men an average of a few days to form a relationship with their newborn. Official documentation and paperwork regarding a newborn is aimed at mothers. Even official surveys list care by fathers under the heading 'other' care alongside hired childminders and nursery schools. The experience of ordinary parents reflects this generally-held assumption. One couple who switched roles found it was more than just a personal decision. When the health visitor stopped by to check on the baby's progress, the first question she asked the father was 'Where's the baby's mother?' Upon hearing that she wasn't at home, the health visitor said she'd be back later. Another father who collected his child from school every day received a call from his son's new school asking if everything was all right at home. They had presumed his wife must have left him. One woman commented that when her child was sick, or childcare arrangements fell apart, she was inevitably the one who asked for time off work because her boss, unlike her husband's, assumed that as a mother there would be times when that would happen.

The overall direction of family policy in the UK in the past fifteen years has been to view the family as a private unit and children as a private responsibility, and to encourage families towards self-sufficiency requiring minimal state interference. There is still a presumption that a mother will stay at home in order to care for her own children, as illustrated, for example, by the fact that school hours are not designed to fit in with the adult working day, or by the refusal by government after government to make a commitment to provide universal, affordable childcare. The trend among mothers towards returning to work has had remarkably little effect upon this underlying premise of family life and responsibility.

Recent legislative changes have increased parental obligations: the Children Act of 1989, the Child Support Act of 1991, cutting benefits to young people under the age of eighteen and changes to student funding. Gordon Brown's 1998 budget which increased Child Benefit and offered to help parents with the cost of childcare is the first time in decades that a British government has increased its financial commitment to families. As a nation we may be sentimental about children and romanticize motherhood, but we have not usually put our money where our mouths are.

Compare this approach to family with the position in other countries. According to a comparative study of family policy in European countries published in 1996,[5] there are basically three different national approaches to family matters. In the Scandinavian countries, where individual entitlements and equality for all citizens are an important part of the political ethos, policy is characterized by generous state provision in the form of benefits for parents, maternity and paternity leave and plenty of state-subsidized childcare. At the other end of the spectrum are the southern European countries such as Portugal, Spain and Italy where there isn't as much in the way of state provision (although Italy, Greece and Spain all provide more publicly-funded childcare than Britain does), but the extended family plays an important role in all kinds of matters, including looking after children. Families are expected to look after each other and those obligations are widely spread and may often be enforceable in law. Both geographically and politically, Britain lies somewhere in between. Here the emphasis is upon the nuclear family and all rights regarding children are vested in the biological parents, as well as all the responsibilities. Obligations to other relations, even of adult children to their parents, have gradually been eroded. Britain still does not have anything like the level of state support for mothers and families to be found in other nations. In fact, a growing number of observers say that Britain has no proper policy commitment towards families at all. In this, we are closer to the United States. Anne Gauthier, a social studies researcher in Oxford, describes the policies of both countries as 'implicit and reluctant' when contrasted with the 'explicit and comprehensive' approaches of countries such as France and the Nordic nations.

Despite the continuing popularity of the nuclear family (henceforth referred to as the Family) as the politically-preferred domestic unit, a growing number of other voices have begun to suggest that this attitude is the very source of our current problems. In making the point that the British family has been abandoned by policy-makers to fend for itself, an Equal Opportunities Commission (EOC) discussion paper says:

> Unless there is an extended family surrounding and supporting a young couple – even more so a lone parent – it is, indeed, unreasonable to assume that all parents will by some magic be endowed with the capacity to make the best possible job of caring for young children. Yet public policy here seems traditionally to be based on this presumption.[6]

Since, as we have already observed, mothers are the people who do most of the work in the family setting, they are the ones at the sharp end. The notions that mothers *should* cope and that children are a matter of private choice, and therefore responsibility, are often heard among the public at large. How many mothers who have raised their voices in protest, even privately, have earned the retort that it was their *choice* to have children? 'Once when I complained, I was told: "That's what being a mother is all about,"' said Marie. The message that, for the large part, help will not be forthcoming echoes public policy and practice on a daily basis. So it comes as no surprise that many mothers fail to ask for the help they need and go on trying to cope, while giving the impression that they can. In Britain and in America, parents in general and mothers in particular have never agitated as a political category because they do not see themselves, and are encouraged not to see themselves, as being owed any particular rights as a group. Doubtless, of course, most modern parents are simply too strung out to agitate about anything. Because our society sees children as an individual asset, we do not collectively value children as much as we could and should, or as much as they are valued elsewhere. That is one of many reasons why we have chosen to denigrate motherhood, because as a job it is seen as unimportant. Yet we also idealize the role because, after all, somebody's got to do it, and the new reverence for motherhood is an expression of the fear that the commitment of a mother to her child is just about all we have left of the Family.

Many of the problems of modern family life are the fault of politicians who have omitted to respond to natural and inevitable social changes. Policy-makers in Britain have allowed commitments to the extended family to lapse and disappear, while failing to replace those support systems with state systems. Instead, governments have in the past exploited the notion of 'family values' in order to shift the blame and release themselves from taking proper responsibility. This has been easily achieved by drawing on traditional notions of motherhood and making those ideas the centrepiece of the 'family values' campaign.

This is precisely why, in the USA and the UK, lone mothers have come under such heavy fire from politicians, in a way that has simply not happened in other countries. In places where there has been a similar increase in the numbers of single-parent families, governments have generally adopted a supportive stance and made extra benefits available. In Britain, the Conservatives pilloried lone mothers for years. The general attitude from the Right – that lone parents were undeserving of public support – was summed up by Tory leadership contender John Redwood's suggestion in 1995 that single mothers who couldn't afford to keep their children should give them up for adoption to couples who could. Two years before winning the general election and during the period in which the Labour Party was being restructured internally and moving to the right, Tony Blair, the architect of New Labour, publicly criticized single mothers and declared his own adherence to the Family. One of the first projects of Blair's new government in June 1997 was to shift lone parents 'from welfare to work' as soon as possible.

The irony is that payments to lone parents were originally devised to keep mothers at home with their children, where they were rightfully thought to belong, and to replace the lost male wage. As a result, Britain today has one of the lowest rates of employment for lone parents and one of the highest rates of poverty. Benefits for single parents were originally intended for divorced and widowed women, women who were once financially dependent on a man and whose style of mothering conformed to the picture of proper maternal behaviour. The sea-change in political ideology towards lone mothers has been produced by the small but growing number of never-married women who have become mothers. Even though today it would be politically unfeasible to introduce morality clauses, that is what recent policy changes are in effect.

The *volte-face* performed by politicians of every hue over the issue of whether lone mothers should work is markedly different to their approach to married mothers who work. For the latter, the decision to work has been merely tolerated but not encouraged. Compare the attitude towards British working mothers with that of the Scandinavian countries, which see providing the facilities to enable mothers to work as part and parcel of a commitment to gender equality, and you start to see the source of the gender 'fault-line' in the UK. Despite the fact that the entry of mothers into the workforce is currently being used to justify telling lone mothers to get jobs, government after government has declined to support other working mothers in any way whatsoever. Consequently, despite the large proportions of mothers who work, the conflict between work and motherhood has not ended.

Women who are mothers are routinely used as demographic canon fodder. During the war, while factories staffed by women were running twenty-four hours a day and work was seen as a patriotic duty, both Britain and America provided nursery places for every child. Nursery education was presented as being of enormous benefit to children. In the mid-1940s when men needed the jobs, the nurseries were closed. In 1945, Ministry of Health Circular 221/45 stated: 'the right policy to pursue would be to discourage mothers of young children under two from going out to work.' Right up until the end of the 1960s, both Labour and Conservative governments expressly refused to do anything that would encourage women to go out to work. In the early 1980s a brief 'demographic time-bomb' bore witness to official encouragement of working mothers who were needed to fill the skills shortage. But because the government could see that the problem would be naturally solved in the short term, no changes to social policy commitment to childcare were ever even floated. When unemployment went up in the late 1980s and early 1990s, any kind of official support for working mothers silently disappeared. The issues of demographics, employment statistics and economics are the real reasons why Britain has such underdeveloped and underfunded public childcare provision. The little that does exist is aimed at children with special needs or children whose parents cannot take care of them. So, New Labour's proposals to help pay for childcare, while still welcome, can be seen against the backdrop of projections that women will be needed to fill the bulk of new jobs created in the next decade.

Today, the question of who should look after children has become extraordinarily volatile, evoking strong feelings both on the part of lobbyists for state childcare provision and those who regard childcare as a dirty word, anti-society and anti-family. In Britain, not only is there no coherent publicly-funded system of daycare and no paternity leave, until the recent signing of the EC Social Chapter there was no statutory parental leave either. In this regard, it would be fair to say, without exaggeration, we are the worst in Europe. If New labour is committed to helping mothers they have a long way to go. Childcare services, including private facilities, are so scant that only 23 per cent of mothers use formal childcare services (meaning childminders, nurseries and so on). Meanwhile, what local-authority-funded provision exists has actually *decreased* in the last decade. In 1985, English local authorities provided 32,900 day-nursery places, but by 1995 that already small figure had been cut to 28,900.[7] In this scenario, childcare poses an enormous problem for modern mothers: finding it, retaining it, relying on it and affording it. Women travel long distances to drop their children at a child-minder, rush to collect them at the end of the day and spend most of their earnings paying for the service. It is the subject of endless discussion among new mothers. Available childcare is the single biggest determinant in the decision to stay at home or to work, and then in what jobs are available. Mothers with dependent children who wish to work but cannot because of lack of childcare are among Britain's hidden unemployed; it is a trap that renders them unable to register for benefits (and therefore be included in the statistics), because without childcare they cannot fulfil the requirement which states they must be available for work.

Back in 1995, a House of Commons Conservative-controlled Select Committee reported on the dire state of affairs in Britain and proposed European-style employment rights for mothers including childcare and paternity leave, commenting that most women were 'still forced to make difficult decisions about having and raising children or pursuing and furthering a career'.[8] Their proposals were met with a swift and negative reaction by government ministers who made known their displeasure with their own colleagues. Every single item was turned down, including the 'radical' suggestion that employers should give parents five days off to care for an ill child. Employment Minister Ann Widdecombe went on the record dismissing the report summarily, even before it had been officially published.

One of the reasons why British politicians have been able to get away with this blatant discrimination against women, whose taxes, after all, constitute a hefty part of what pours into government coffers, is the continued prevalence of Bowlby's attachment theory and the opportunity it offers to assert that care, other than maternal care, is bad for children. The theory of attachment has displayed extraordinary longevity. Back in 1966, a government paper on expanding nursery education raised concerns that this might encourage more mothers to work: 'Some mothers who are not obliged to work may work full-time regardless of their child's welfare. It is no business of the education service to encourage these women to do so.'[9] Twenty years later, child psychiatrist Barbara Tizard observed the massive and still flourishing influence of Bowlby's thesis, noting that it had become accepted wisdom among doctors, social workers and teachers to believe that mothers risked the psychological well-being of children under the age of five by leaving them to go to work, that daycare or pre-school for under-threes was wrong, and that even over the age of three it should not be full-time.[10] Ten years later, the idea that childcare is 'toxic' to children is still a favourite theme among professionals, self-styled experts, the press and broadcast media – basically, ever since large numbers of women began to enter the world of work and especially since some secured enviable positions for themselves.

Mothers who place their children in daycare are routinely castigated as 'bad mothers'. In Britain in March 1997, *Panorama*, the BBC's flagship programme under the new editorship of Steve Hewlett, produced a film entitled *Missing Mum*. The day before the programme's release the BBC issued a press statement claiming: 'Children of working mums fail to make the grade' and squarely pointing the finger at modern mothers: 'women who juggle a full-time job and motherhood may jeopardise their children's future.' The film the next day, complete with emotional scenes, expanded the point that, according to new research, children whose mothers worked full-time did less well in school exams than those whose mothers worked part-time. Informed viewers might have been puzzled if they had known that this 'evidence' was in fact from a relatively small study, as yet unpublished and subjected to peer review in the conventional academic manner. It was not at all typical of the kind of study a programme like *Panorama* might normally base an entire forty minutes on. They might also ask the question: What of the children of the stay-at-home mums? How did they do? The answer, which the programme skated over so quickly that if you blinked you missed it, was that those children did worst of all. What the survey had to say was, in fact, far more complicated than the 'good mothers stay at home/bad mothers work' claim asserted in the film, according to none other than the author of the study itself, Margaret O'Brien, a professor of family studies at the University of North London. She published a disclaimer in the quality press shortly after the programme was aired and pointed to paternal influence and environmental factors which the programme failed to expand. Instead, *Panorama* took findings based on 600 working-class, white families and applied them to a middle-class businesswoman who happened to have sacrificed her full-time career in order to be with her children. The programme was maternal correctness at its best.

In Australia, at almost exactly the same time as the *Panorama* programme was aired in Britain, a child psychiatrist, Peter Cook, published a book entitled *Early Child Care: Infants and Nations at Risk* in which he asserted that children placed in daycare would suffer attachment problems which would later emerge in the form of aggression and social deviance. His extreme views prompted protest from other experts, eventually spurring the

Australian Prime Minister to intervene with a demand to put a stop to the 'unhealthy trend' in debating the right or wrong way to raise children. Among the most vocally opposed to daycare are the highly influential popular 'gurus' like Penelope Leach, who actually compares what a child experiences in daycare to the death of a parent.

This continues despite the fact that the largest study of all time, still ongoing at the US National Institute of Child Health and Human Development, of 1,300 families over seven years has clearly indicated that, first, other factors such as economic resources are far more important influences on how a child develops and, second, that it is the quality of the care – whoever gives it – that makes the difference. The same point is made by Peter Moss, formerly co-ordinator of the European Childcare Network at the Thomas Coram Institute in London, who has reviewed international research: 'The view that non-parental care is necessarily harmful for children under the age of 3 is not supported by research in any country.'[11] There is no evidence that children in Sweden, France, Finland or any of those countries that provide pre-school services for children and parents are suffering from maternal deprivation and turning into delinquents or under-achievers. In fact, new knowledge about the way in which the brains of very young children develop, and the direction of recent research, is beginning to indicate that pre-school education and the opportunity it presents for children to interact with others and to develop socially, verbally and intellectually, may be more beneficial than being at home.

The Louise Woodward murder trial gave a new weapon to those who are opposed to the use of non-maternal care: substitute care could actually be physically perilous for children. Two months before the Woodward case was heard, the international magazine *US News & World Report* pre-empted the issues the case would raise with a cover story entitled 'Dangerous Day Care', which warned parents of the dangers to their children's safety posed by many daycare facilities. What more persuasive argument could there be for a state-supervised childcare system, one might be forgiven for thinking? After all, could what happened to Matthew Eappen happen in France, say, where a child whose mother works is given a place in the local crèche and there are fewer chances for parents to make disastrous childcare decisions? Instead, the Woodward case was used as another reason why mothers should stay at home.

The economic contribution that mothers who work make to the family well-being is vital. Most mothers need to work, not just for their 'personal growth' or their own independence (reasons airily dismissed by the maternally correct as mere selfishness); mothers work for money. The Family Policy Studies Centre's *Parenting in the 1990s* survey showed that one-third of the families with stay-at-home mothers included in the study were among those with the lowest incomes. This, said the report, 'underlines the importance of two earned incomes for a satisfactory standard of living'. Furthermore, in this day and age it is of fundamental importance for women as a whole to have the ability to earn a living for themselves and for their children and for their future dependents, though nuclear family revivalists would have us believe that if women stuck to doing their traditional duty, families would miraculously reknit and relationships last for ever.

How do women feel as a result? Do they feel like heroines? Not at all. They feel guilty as hell that they are not doing enough. A 1997 study which appeared in a US newspaper under the title 'Moms Give Selves Low Grades in Parenting', revealed that 41 per cent of American women think it is better for the family if the mother stays at home (although a full 80 per cent of American mothers work).[12] And 56 per cent thought they were less capable at mothering than their own mothers – only a tenth thought they were better. Yet the same women, when asked how they would like things to be in an *ideal* world, said they would like to work *and* be mothers. So what women say they think is right conflicts with both what they want and what they actually do.

In the UK, the EOC summed up the lives of British working mothers thus: 'a woman will quickly become familiar with the exhaustion and guilt which arises from balancing a series of conflicting demands.' Modern motherhood has become a paradox.

Compare the unhappy lot of the average British woman with that of her sisters across the channel. A typical French *maman* drops her youngest child at the nearby *'crèche familiale'*. The local authority runs the crèche, handles all the financial arrangements between the family and the childminder, and on those night-mare days every mother experiences when the childminder calls in sick and her husband is out of town, an officer at the local authority takes responsibility for finding alternative care. Her three-year-old attends the *'école maternelle'*, a free pre-school for all French children between the ages of three and five. Further north in Finland and Sweden, 80 per cent and 85 per cent of mothers work full-time, compared to Britain's 60 per cent who mostly work part-time. Sweden's childcare system is the jewel in Europe's crown: fifteen months' childbirth leave, which can be used up to the child's eighth birthday, and can be shared by or transferred between the mother and the father. In addition there are ten days of exclusive paternity leave, sixty days a year per child of compensated family leave and the right to reduce working hours. All this as well as a centrally co-ordinated, pub-licly-funded, comprehensive childcare system, for which parents are responsible for meeting only 10 per cent of costs. Finland also gives parents maternity, paternity and parental leave (up to a year which can be divided between both parents), plus a maternity allowance which is initially paid to the mother and then to whichever parent is looking after the children. Family leave (time off to cope with family emergencies) has been an entitlement since 1988; in the UK it has only just begun to be taken seriously as a suggestion. Finland is on track to provide state-run daycare for all children under school age.

Whenever British women lobby for the same kind of care for

their own children, as organizations such as the Daycare Trust, the EOC and Working for Childcare have been doing for years, they are routinely told that anything like the French, Swedish or Finnish systems would be too expensive and unacceptable to the British taxpayer. But who exactly is the British taxpayer? Half of them are women who would surely welcome this kind of initiative with open arms. In the recent past Conservative and Labour politicians hoped to make business finance childcare. Despite all the publicity given to companies such as the Seattle-based Eddie Bauer, which gives employees 'wellness days' or days off to spend time with the family, such organizations remain the exception rather than the rule with none so far reported in the UK. In fact, there are only about 600 workplace nurseries in the whole of the UK (compare that to the number of companies with executive dining rooms). If anything, the drive to leanness, efficiency and self-sufficiency in business is being seen as the way countries and not just companies should be run. The childcare debate in the UK is constrained by government's refusal to spend the sort of sums required to establish a centrally-coordinated system of reliable, quality childcare. Labour promises a national childcare strategy and more part-time education for three- and four-year-olds but it goes without saying that whatever proposals are produced, they will look nothing like the European models of family policy which provide pre-school education for all children whether or not their mothers work, and which are not linked in any way to welfare reforms.

The truth is that, in Britain, women's sense of their own responsibility plus a narrow view of what constitutes good mothering have both long been exploited to deny women the kind of support which in other nations they have been able to take for granted for the last two decades. A significant side-effect of this officially sanctioned version of parenting is that men have become sidelined as parents. Only very recently has any research been conducted on the role of fathers, or any recommendations made on men as parents. When in 1994 Michael Portillo vetoed a European draft Directive on parental leave, which would have given men the right to take time off to care for a child, there was virtually no public reporting of the matter at all, and no public debate. In fact, Britain had been consistently blocking the same directive since 1983, thus denying all European men of that benefit. In the end, under the Maastricht Agreement, the EC was able to go ahead without the UK. Among most Conservative politicians the mere idea of paternity leave prompted hoots of derision. Others quite seriously argued that the requirement to give paternity leave might cause employers to discriminate against fathers (presumably it would be all right for them to carry on discriminating against mothers). Of the few articles written at the time, one by Dominic Wells appeared in *Time Out*, a magazine whose parent company grants male employees four weeks of paternity leave. The author's account of his own experience showed that ordinary people were not much more enlightened: 'Most people, male and female, greet this revelation with frank astonishment. "But you can't breastfeed . . . Don't tell me you'll help change nappies . . . You'll be begging to come back to work after a few days."'

Fatherhood in the 1990s presents a somewhat paradoxical picture. On the one hand there is the suggestion, which has won a disproportionate share of media attention, that some 'new men' are genuinely becoming more involved as parents. On the opposite side of the coin is the 'deadbeat dad' who abandons his family and takes no financial responsibility for his offspring. The 'deadbeat dad' is the modern equivalent of the now familiar stereotype of the 'welfare queen' single mother. As an image used by politicians to promote a message of paternal responsibility, he is a good illustration of how it has only been since fathers came to be seen as reneging on their *financial* obligations that they have been subjected to public criticism. Men's official role as a father does not extend beyond paying the bills, as is clearly expressed in the Child Support Act. The Children Act came with a pledge to increase fathers' rights as well as their responsibilities, but so far most of the rights have remained paper promises. It is still highly unusual for any man to be given custody of his children in the divorce courts – only around 10 per cent of men in the USA and 7 per cent of men in the UK. In fact, the guideline introduced by the Children Act that 'the best interests of the child' should come first has frequently been used to overrule fathers' wishes and has allowed many private injustices to go unchallenged. For example, in order to have a visitation order suspended, lawyers for the mother need only convince the courts that the relationship between two parents is so bad that the father's visits and ensuing arguments upset the child.

It is apparent that this public face of fatherhood, reinforced by the endurance of traditional ideas at a personal level, must have something to do with the reason why so many fathers have been slow to adapt their behaviour. The legacy of a system of patriarchy is that many well-off fathers think their childrearing responsibilities have been met once they have written the cheque for the school fees, and low-income or unemployed fathers find themselves marginalized or even redundant because they cannot meet the one requirement demanded of them. Basically, the 'traditional' gender roles of female nurturer and male breadwinner effectively render young men who don't earn superfluous as fathers.

In contrast to the belief that working mothers are responsible for killing off family life, they have actually had a positive effect in opening up space for fathers. Two British researchers, Linda Collins and Pam Walton, surveyed men who had changed their work patterns to reduce hours spent in the office or who had taken advantage of flexible working hours, and found that nearly half had done so for childcare reasons, including a grandfather who helped care for his grandchildren while his daughter worked.[13] The overwhelming majority reported that the decision had had a beneficial effect on their home lives. The study also demonstrated that employers were likely to view with suspicion men who worked flexible hours for childcare reasons, and who thereby chose to defy commonly-held assumptions about gender roles. However, if the man was doing so for personal or career reasons, those same employers did not object.

The obsession with the function of the mother and the romance attached to notions of motherhood have played a large part in eclipsing the role of fathers. These are attitudes that are woven into the fabric of both our public policy and private lives. As stated in one report: the idea 'of mothers as uniquely qualified to take care of very young children carries with it an implication that others, in particular men, are either unfit or very much second best as caregivers.'[14]

Rethinking policy offers a solution because policy does alter people's behaviour, but it is not always straightforward. In some Scandinavian countries, legislators soon found that their brave new system of parental leave had demonstrably failed to change the way in which couples allocated responsibility. The dynamics remained the same. Often the father simply transferred his share of leave to the mother. In Norway, the decision was made to allocate four weeks of leave to be used only by the father, or not at all. Elsewhere, advertising campaigns had to be devised to persuade men to take up their entitlement. While Labour's commitment to the parental leave directive in the EC Social Chapter and the resolutions contained in it to promote men's participation in family life is certainly to be welcomed, it is unlikely to guide us to the promised land of shared parenting because we still subscribe to certain myths about motherhood. The devil will be in the detail, which must be thrashed out by 1999. At present, leave is to be taken unpaid; as men still earn considerably more than their wives, that alone might ensure that, except in extreme emergencies, it is the mother once again who takes time off. Parental leave is just one issue to be resolved among many. There is still the fundamental question to be considered: who is actually responsible for children in our society and why?

Whose job is it anyway?

It has become a popular sport to blame parents for contemporary problems related to children and families, and to see every mother who works as over-ambitious and neglectful, and every father who has lost contact with his family as a deadbeat dad. But even if parent-bashing has become commonplace, the truth could not be more different. Families are actually cracking under the pressure of modern parenting. At a time when children are young, parents are coping with maximum demands at work, the financial strain of housing costs and meeting the needs of dependent children. Fathers in the United Kingdom work longer hours than anyone else in the whole of Europe. Mothers are endlessly trying to make the pieces of a puzzle fit, without the faintest hope of doing so. Children often ruin sex lives, they virtually negate a couple's previous social life and they eat up quantities of cash. Not one of the many women I interviewed failed to mention the things that inevitably got forgotten: time for herself and time with her spouse. It is no wonder that the divorce rate is sky-rocketing.

These parents are the people whom the American professor of sociology Amitai Etzioni, whose communitarian movement has significantly influenced the thinking of the Blair leadership, has described as 'celebrating greed' and pursuing careers at the expense of time with their children.[15] The communitarian movement was established to tackle modern social problems, specifically the fragmentation of communities created by an over-individualist and consumer-driven society. The solution to the 'parenting deficit' which he describes is for one person – *aka* mum (although he is scrupulously PC in his writing, the roles nevertheless look suspiciously familiar) – to return home. However, Etzioni is right to say there's a parenting deficit. But the real problem is the disappearance of support networks for parents and of other carers in children's lives. According to the evidence, parents today actually spend *more* time engaging in activities with their children than in the past. One can only wonder at how single mothers are going to cope with full-time jobs under the coming changes, when married middle-class women with au-pairs and earning husbands can hardly balance work and family commitments. But the solution to parenting issues is not to return someone, anyone, to the home. Being at home full-time and in the long-term can become mind-numbingly boring, as desperate 'returnees' soon discover.

One of the problems of the entire debate, and this was partially a failing of the feminist movement, has been to focus too greatly on the daycare solution. Even a properly funded, public system of childcare, with a package of parental leave attached, would not go far enough in breaking down gender roles and reallocating childcare, currently purely a maternal responsibility. It merely helps women balance the roles of mother and worker, without redefining the former. Funded childcare amounts to a deal between mothers and the state, which is dependent on the state's good-will. At times of economic crisis and unemployment, childcare is one of the first things to go. Recession has threatened even Sweden's enviable system. Most state childcare is run by women for women. The present plan in the UK to use single mothers to staff after-school clubs to be used by other single mothers is an excellent example of precisely that. And in this regard there is a sobering lesson to be learned by looking at the recent experience of mothers in two countries: the former East Germany and Israel.

In the Israeli kibbutz experiments of the 1970s, children were raised communally in nurseries, separated from their parents from shortly after birth until adolescence. (Incidentally, the children raised in the kibbutz system have never displayed the kinds of emotional problems associated with 'maternal deprivation' which Bowlby described, and which opponents of childcare prophesy. In fact, they have flourished.) The dream of kibbutz life was to achieve collective goals and ideals, including equality between men and women, through community living. Typically, however, the nurseries were staffed and run by women. When in the 1980s and on, greater individual wealth began to render the kibbutz dream redundant, the communal nurseries closed down and couples kept their children at home. Despite the decades of apparent equality, not much had changed and looking after the baby became once again the mother's job. The kibbutz system had for a while freed individual mothers to work, but it left the roles of men and women regarding childcare unaffected.

In East Germany, before the fall of the Berlin Wall, the communist regime pursued a pro-natalist policy, backed up by laws which forced employers to accommodate mothers and their needs. Almost all men and women worked full-time, and women tended to have several children and to become mothers in their early twenties. When unification came it brought with it a mixed blessing for mothers who needed to work. A job market which emphasized flexibility and competitiveness placed women with children at a distinct disadvantage, and many reported being discriminated against by 'family-unfriendly' companies. In addition, large numbers of public nurseries closed – West Germany, like Britain, expects mothers to look after their own children – and the birth rate dropped rapidly, down by a massive 50 per cent immediately after unification. Stories circulated of women having themselves sterilized for fear they would not be able to get jobs. The average East German mother found herself, perhaps for the first time ever, solely in charge of her children.

In both the kibbutz system and in East Germany, when women's labour was needed, facilities were provided to relieve mothers of the tasks of childcare or to help them do those tasks more easily (in East Germany, employers were obliged to give women time off each week to do their housework!). Neither system challenged or changed the fundamental belief that childcare is women's work. When the social and economic situation changed, the responsibility for childcare immediately fell back on women.

There is a chasm between parenting and public policy, and it may be that public policy alone cannot provide the answer to all our problems. We should use the resurgent debate about childcare, welfare-to-work and other family-related policies to rethink ideas about parenting, review old assumptions and consider new possibilities. Chastising parents on the basis that they are greedy, neglectful, selfish or uninterested in their children is simply ridiculous and unfair. If parents are all those things, then we all are. Parent-bashing is a new form of mother-blaming. It assuages a collective guilt. We need to break the thought process which encourages us to regard children as private property, the sole responsibility of their parents and a personal luxury. Everyone relies on future generations to fill jobs, contribute to the social security system, fight wars and keep the trains running. We need to create support networks for mothers, fathers and children. 'Community' may have become the buzz-word of the 1990s, but what does community responsibility really mean?

All our children: social parenting

As the twentieth century, the century which celebrated the individual, freedom and choice, comes to an end, there is growing evidence that more people now want to reknit old ties and create relationships which rely on commitment. There is also a recognition that children need relationships with more people than just their parents. These changes are taking effect in old ways and in new ways.

In Britain an individual is responsible for no one but him- or herself, while a parent is responsible for a child. Nowadays it is hard for many people to accept even the idea of taking care of grandparents. In British law, there is no legal requirement for adult children to take any measure of financial responsibility for their parents. There are no incentives to do so either, for example the government will not give tax relief for pension payments made on someone else's behalf. Yet, only recently, when growing numbers of elderly people began to sell their homes in order to pay for a place in a residential home, their grown children complained about losing their inheritance. It seems that while some people do not want to owe an obligation to their parents, they do want the benefit of the relationship.

In a country like Spain, things are very different. Family members are legally responsible for providing financial support for one another to a far greater extent. Under civil law, *alimentos restringidos* (restricted support) and *alimentos amplios* (broad support) are owed (in certain circumstances) to a range of people including grandparents and siblings. The same is true elsewhere; in Portugal, for instance. As far as caring for children is concerned, other family members are expected to and do provide substitute parental care and childcare. In Britain such legally recognized responsibilities have fallen away over time. People have gradually allowed the welfare state to look after relatives who might first have been taken care of within the family setting. But now the welfare state is itself being cut back and we are likely never to see past levels of state support again. Unfortunately, in rejecting family ties in favour of personal liberty, we forgot that obligations work both ways, and that families give as well as take.

The Thatcher years in Britain epitomize for many the pinnacle of the ethos of individualism and self-reliance. Many women embraced the credo of personal success as much as men. But the legacy of the 1980s has been the realization that women, mothers more than anyone else, actually had a lot to gain from mutual support and most to lose from its disappearance. Even though the Conservatives touted themselves as the party of the Family, the 1980s marked an extraordinary low point for the family ideals of sharing, co-operation and giving. In a discussion of how women coped in the period after maternity leave, one study conducted in the early and mid-1980s reported: 'There appeared to be no clear normative expectation that relatives – as significant sources of childcare – were obliged to offer childcare assistance. It was notable that relatives were said to have "offered" rather than to have been asked for help and that women were extremely "grateful" if any help was forth-coming.'[16] The report paints a gloomy portrait of how all that cherished personal liberty panned out for mothers, who had the 'choice' to stay at home or find their own childcare solution (such as hiring an expensive nanny) and return to a job where they could expect no concessions to family responsibilities. Those who 'chose' to stay at home found themselves physically and socially isolated, and without public or personal support net-works to offer assistance in their 'choice' to have a child. Some choice! The truth is that a woman with a young child is not, and can never be, a rugged individualist.

Even for the best-equipped among us, raising children in modern society has become a daunting task. 'The dream of inde-pendence has started to wither for everyone,' according to Carol Stack, the well-known Berkeley sociologist and author of *All Our Kin*.[17] Today, after several decades of weakening ties, we are beginning to witness a small but significant resurgence in grandparents caring for children and the strengthening of that once important relationship. Presently for mothers of pre-school children, 44 per cent of women in manual jobs and 18 per cent of professional women leave their children with their own or their partner's parents during the day.[18] Often grandparents look after young children almost as much as even fathers do.[19] In fact, between 1979 and 1988 the percentage of grand-mothers who looked after their young grandchildren actually increased.[20]

Obviously, one of the reasons why women are relying on grandparents is because of the lack of an alternative system, but doubtless many still prefer to leave their children with somebody they know and trust, and who has a long-term commitment to their child. In turn it seems clear that more grandparents would like to be involved with their grandchildren. The decision and the wish to have children also involves the wish to have grand-children. As obvious as that might appear, it is worth restating. An Age Concern survey showed that most grandparents (62 per cent) saw their grandchildren once a week or more. Over half (57 per cent) said they had helped out with babysitting and childminding, and a great many (43 per cent) said they would like to see their grandchildren more often. Interestingly, only a small number (17 per cent) said that the reason they did not do so was geographical distance. Overwhelmingly, the cause was the divorce or separation of parents.[21]

As people retire increasingly early, often now by the age of fifty-five, it makes a great deal of sense for them to spend more time with their families. Life has become distinctly front-loaded. In our twenties and thirties we do it all: work, relationships, families. Then shortly after middle age, we find ourselves looking for ways to fill the days. This story of one mother's solution is an example of how inter-generational co-operation can work. Allie wanted to go back to university to read for a Masters in social work which she needed to move her career on, but couldn't afford to pay a childminder to look after her daughter. Allie's widowed mother offered to retire early and look after the girl herself. In return, Allie paid off the rest of her mother's mortgage a couple of years later. This seems like a good solution and one that might be possible for many people, but rather than seeking to encourage family care, previous governments have tried to exploit it. The Family Credit Allowance, introduced under the Conservatives, which allows mothers on low incomes a £40 tax disregard to pay for childcare, actually explicitly excludes payments to family members who do the same work. There is no point paying people who are doing the work for free, argued the government. New Labour's childcare payments introduced in 1998 can similarly only be paid to a registered childminder. This may have the unforeseen consequence of dis-couraging family care.

There is some evidence of communities recognizing the sound logic and the benefits of solving the childcare problem by drawing on one of society's most untapped resources; in parts of Britain, midwives have taken the initiative and begun to retrain grandmothers to take care of babies. At the Royal Surrey Hospital in Guildford, two midwives started babycare classes which drew many grandmothers planning to help out their adult children and their partners.

The contribution made by grandparents and other relations is proving to be a major factor which has smoothed the path of women into the workforce in countries which are currently undergoing rapid industrialization and economic and social change. India is the ninth most industrialized country in the world. In the metropolitan areas a growing number of educated, middle-class women are going out to work. Yet, 'Indian society does not appear to be experiencing the turmoil in the transition from single-earner to dual-earner families to the same extent as some other developed countries,' according to the findings of an international research project on dual-earning couples.[22] The reason for this has turned out to be the joint sense of responsibility family members feel towards the youngest generation. Young children are being taken care of by older members of the extended family. Jemima Khan, British wife of the cricketer Imran Khan, wrote in the *Daily Telegraph* of her conviction of the benefits of the Pakistani extended family: 'it is easier for a mother to work without having to send her children into a crèche.'[23]

In Britain and in the US, family and community commitments are a significant factor in helping immigrants to establish themselves in a new country. In Britain the number of West Indian *single* mothers who work matches the number of non-minority married mothers who work. Systems of pooled childcare with other mothers and help from grandparents are what makes this possible. Each of these communities recognizes the value of bonds and the reciprocal nature of commitments.

I had a conversation with a South African woman about

motherhood. She had her first child before she was married. Later I asked her a question about being a lone mother, and she said she couldn't answer me because she had never been one. Something was clearly getting lost in the translation and so I said that I had understood that she had a child before she met her husband. 'Ah, yes,' she replied, her confusion lifting, 'but I was never alone.'

Today, single mothers in the West are at the forefront of a whole new trend in parenting, that of shared parenting or what has been referred to as co-parenting or para-parenting, that is non-kin friends and contemporaries who share the parenting load, but who also act as spiritual guides, confidants or as 'uncles' and 'aunties' to children. The idea of shared parenting is an adaptation of forms of 'other mothering' or co-mothering found in ethnic minority communities (as seen in the previous chapter), but in the 1990s, as the number of single parents and even of couples who find it a strain to meet all the demands of parenting increase, co-parenting is making its way into the mainstream population.

Sheila is called 'nana' by the two young girls who spend at least every Saturday evening and often the entire weekend with her. Although they look a little alike and are dressed identically for a summer party, the children are not sisters. Each is the child of a single mother who is a close friend of Sheila. Sheila made a deliberate decision along with her friends that she would fill the empty place left by the absent male partners and their families. 'We decided it would be as though I were their paternal grandmother,' she explained. The arrangement brought Sheila, who lived alone, as about one in ten people now do, into contact with children and family life. For the mothers the relationship provided invaluable comfort, time for work, self, relationships and (often overlooked) respite from mothering twenty-four hours a day. Typically it is still mostly women who help each other out, but co-parenting fathers certainly exist, usually as someone to provide the adult-male-relative figure for a young boy in need of a role model or guidance. Such a relationship takes the pressure away from a mother's other relationships – every new boyfriend does not have to be viewed as a prospective father – and is more effective precisely because it divides parenting from romance. In that sense, and given the fractured nature of so many adults' love lives, it is far and away a more honest and stable way to parent.

These are certainly steps which should be encouraged by government in ways which are feasible. One of the success stories in the United States over the last fifteen years has been the growth of mentoring schemes, largely aimed at providing inner-city and minority youth with male and female role models. An organization such as Big Brothers & Big Sisters, which is about to open in the UK, pairs children from the age of six to sixteen with adult volunteers. Research on mentoring in Canada and the USA has shown that children involved are less likely to use drugs, skip school or get into trouble and more likely to get jobs. Thus far, only a tiny number of small-scale mentoring schemes exist in Britain and room exists for much more which might encourage people to parent, even if they don't have children.

'New extended families,' are being pioneered by people living real lives and swapping resources, labour and love. Alongside single parents are others. Gays and lesbian couples, for example, are beginning to sculpt new parenting roles. Lesbian couples in particular confound many assumptions about motherhood from the start when they become parents – most immediately the idea that a child can have only one mother. Gay men raising children will do the same and be able to show that someone other than a biological female parent can be a 'mother'. At present, in Britain, ideas about parenting which are firmly rooted in a set of beliefs about the nature of motherhood and fatherhood, and rationalized under the doctrine of the 'best interests of the child', are currently used to prevent gay people from becoming parents. In the USA, where gay couples can adopt and even plan their own families, there are bold, individual efforts underway to redefine parenthood and categories of parents and to end the assumption that only a biological parent can be a 'mother' or a 'father'.

It is surely time that these other kinds of parental relationship and familial roles should be given legal status and social recognition. 'People are inventing from the ground up. But the words don't exist to describe those relationships. Language is an important factor in recognizing their value and formalizing them,'[24] says Judith Stacey, who spent three years researching kin and non-kin ties within one Silicon Valley family. Her subjects' 'family' networks consisted of friends, ex-partners, partners of ex-partners, stepfamily, ex-stepgrandparents – you name it – as well as the more conventional family relationships. Her own son has a para-parent, a woman friend of Stacey's who is named in her will as her son's guardian, and who since his birth has played a major role in his life. People who co-parent should or could at least be given minimal guardianship status to allow them to take care of a child and, for example, deal with issues at school or consent to medical treatment. Proper legal recognition of an individual's commitment to a child would go a long way to a general recognition that people can be parents whether or not they have children, and that a man or a woman needn't have a child of 'their own' to develop a fulfilling relationship with a child or create a connection to the future.

Finally, another new development which reflects current changes in people's approach to parenting is evidenced by the growth in popularity of co-housing schemes, which began in Denmark about twenty years ago and have since spread to the United States, France, the Netherlands and Germany. On other continents, throughout Africa, Asia and South America, people have for a long time typically chosen to live in units or 'compounds' with people they are related to or are close to. In West Africa, the family compound consists of a group of buildings, individual homes for couples and their children, clustered together around a common area. These compounds are identical in principle, if not in size and architecture, to the London garden square. Young adults might leave for a few years and then find room in the family compound when they marry or have children. Even in a modern, urban context people re-create the closeness of the compound. Mamadou, a young film producer with whom I once worked in Mali, had left his home in the west of the country to work in Bamako. He and his brother rented two ground-floor apartments side by side, overlooking an open space. This was their own 'compound'. Together with their wives, children and a couple of lodgers they re-created their own community. When I asked Mamadou's wife, a biologist, what she did about childcare she smiled. 'There's always somebody here,' she replied.

Other than several thousand miles and a new city, there's no particular difference between Mamadou's living arrangements and those of Michael, a New York publisher who, together with his wife, his sister and her husband pulled down the conversion walls of a couple of flats in a large brownstone and re-created the building as a large family home, this time for four adults and five children. They made the decision to alter their lifestyles specifically so that they could share the parenting of all their children to everybody's benefit. Michael and Mamadou's do-it-yourself solution is open to anyone. Other co-housing projects in Sweden, France, Germany and the USA are more formal, and entail actually building model communities from scratch, with between fifteen and thirty-five self-contained households sharing some common play areas, rooms and dining facilities. The primary reason people are motivated into building their own home in conjunction with a group of other people is more often than not the parenting issue. In fact, the one thing which makes these communities seem a little artificial is the preponderance of young couples with children. Most are entirely composed of fairly young families. An article on co-housing in *Single Mother's Newsletter* talked about the benefits to single parents of this style of living, the attractions of which include a ready-made group of surrogate siblings, on-site daycare and informal babysitting between adults, and an end to the isolation from adult company for parents (single or otherwise) who are at home looking after a young child.

In a way, these housing communities are a reminder of the communal living experiments of the 1970s but with one vital and illuminating difference: these are intentional communities in which the people share no particular set of beliefs or philosophies except the desire to live and to raise their children in a more social and human environment.

Some people are intensely sceptical about the possibility of re-creating community, or of redefining roles. They are the gloomy pessimists who think that some forms of social change are inevitable, always negative, and that certain aspects of human behaviour can never be changed (such as persuading people to be co-operative instead of competitive or to give something without getting something tangible in return). Strangely enough, these people are often the same ones who hold on to the 'traditional' Family and motherhood as an ideal, without seeming to realize that people, by their own volition, are already restructuring their lives.

People become attracted to something else at the point when they realize that what they have doesn't work. The style of family of the 1950s would not meet the needs of the same group of people in the 1990s, which is why it is all but defunct. Now, a critical mass of ordinary people is emerging which says that the imploding family of this decade isn't so much independent as isolated and unworkable. They are looking for solutions and their intention to do so overcomes a host of so-called obstacles including, for example, geographical location. Sheila, who helped parent her friends' daughters, lived an hour away from them both. The old street community may have effectively disappeared, but the people who belong to other kinds of new 'communities' are bound together only by the willingness to be so. We can all create ties and new extended families, but this time in a different political and social context. The future direction of policy should be to capitalize on these emerging sensibilities and to encourage the sharing of old parenting roles and the creation of new ones altogether.

To do this effectively means countering the conviction that mothers in particular, and women in general, are the only people who can parent competently. Adaptable parenting means learning to ignore the politically-inspired rhetoric about motherhood which pervades modern debates about family responsibilities and gender roles. Change has not been slow in coming because people don't want or need it; it has been slow in coming because beliefs about mothering are so deeply entrenched that they are woven into the policies and practices of the entire country, and in turn limit the choices we as individuals make every single day. Only with the clearest vision can we disentangle and dispel the myths to complete the circle of change.

chapter 9

Conclusion:
Relinquishing the Myth

*The great enemy of truth is very often not the lie –
deliberate, contrived and dishonest – but the myth –
persistent, persuasive and unrealistic.*

JOHN F. KENNEDY, 1962

The institution of motherhood, that is to say the cultural and
social construction of how women should mother, is the framework which promotes and sustains the myth of the Perfect
Mother to whom all must aspire. At a certain level, Motherhood
(with a capital letter) is an abstract idea, not a reality. It does
not describe how most women do mother, or necessarily wish
to mother, or even could mother. Everywhere, but particularly
in contemporary, Western society, motherhood is a product of
time, place and circumstance. Yet today, here and now, the
Motherhood Myth is being presented as timeless, universal and
natural. Like the nuclear or 'traditional' Family, the mother-
figure echoes a distant, disappearing world. Even though the
reality for most of us was and is different, the false memories
of the Perfect Mother resound more powerfully than those that
are authentic.

The invention of 'tradition' is the most common malaise
of contemporary Western society. Applied to the idea of

Motherhood, the authority of 'tradition' is interwoven with ideas about what is natural and apparently God-given. Women hear that they are biologically impelled to have children, a calling they resist at the expense of their own happiness and fulfilment. Then they are corralled by every social, economic and political force into mothering in a particular style which ensures that an individual woman is left with total responsibility for her child. Voices of dissent and dissatisfaction are increasingly met with dismissal and a response which has a particularly modern twist: that it was their own choice to have a child. The heavy artillery of the myth-brokers is, of course, the child itself. Conformity to the boundaries of Motherhood is elicited finally and effectively by pointing to the potential for harm, and the alleged betrayal of her own child by the woman who resists that conformity.

Motherhood is the largest single remaining obstacle to women achieving equality in contemporary, post-modern society. The problem is not children, having children or the love and care of children, but the framing of Motherhood and the endurance of the myths that surround it. For all the promises of a decade ago, for all the talk of a new post-feminist generation, women once they have children are every bit as constrained as their own mothers were. The only difference is in precisely how. Today lip-service is paid to a host of rights for women, while the reality is that women with children are not free to exercise some of the most limited of those freedoms, or else are free to drive themselves to an early grave in the very effort to do so. Our mothers may have been prisoners in their own homes; mothers today are tangled in a web of responsibilities and conflicting, competing demands and roles. Today's 'problem with no name' is the myth about Motherhood. The myth denies that the problems of hundreds of thousands of women are real or valid and instead insists that they are natural and inevitable. And in so doing it negates efforts at analysis, even the creation of a rhetoric or framework which would allow women to discuss the source of their problems.

At a personal level, women clearly recognize what is happening and respond by making specific attempts at damage control, such as waiting until their thirties, until their career is established (or so the thinking goes), in order to have children. But, in a society where work has become fluid and unreliable, increasingly we have discovered that all that makes very little difference. The woman who chooses to start her family after the age of thirty-five finds that she has merely deferred the sentence and may even have compounded her problems with a host of unforeseen difficulties: declining fertility, the possibility of bearing a baby with a disability, and grandparents too old to be able to help where once they might have. All these new, additional hazards are presented to women as more evidence of Nature's way, and the impossibility of defying Her.

For the individual woman, Motherhood curtails life choices and personal liberty; forces her into financial dependence upon her partner; has the potential to make her vulnerable to manipulation and regulation by hospitals, and to control by the law and the courts. For all women, Motherhood limits access to resources and will go on ensuring that women as a group will never really compete with men. Sociologists talk about the feminization of the family, and the feminization of poverty as growing facts of life: two trends which are firmly rooted in a belief system which places the family within the realm of female responsibility, constructs Motherhood in a certain way by artificially dividing the realms of the public and the private, and consequently severely limits the ability of a mother even to earn an income. Instead of recognizing that it is the very fact of our adherence to a rigid set of beliefs about Motherhood which is creating and compounding emerging social problems, the existence of those difficulties is taken instead as validation of conservative attitudes.

So, far from diminishing, the Motherhood myth is growing more powerful and is enjoying a popular resurgence, propelled by the insistence on linking ideas about Motherhood to every social ailment from crime statistics to personal happiness. But for everyone, the child, the mother and society, the myth of the Perfect Mother, like a false lover, is alluring, elusive and deceptive. It offers hope, promises so much and ultimately delivers only betrayal.

The challenge for women

The greatest single myth of all is the belief in exclusive mothering, with the attendant notion that everything a child needs is contained in that mother/child dyad. This is central to the myth of the Perfect Mother. The relationship between mothers and their children is special because of the work put into it, and not because of a mystical biological impetus. The insistence that a wonderful relationship is not only possible but necessary, even a birthright – and the consequent and frequent failure of such an unrealistic expectation – is the reason why so often relationships between adult children and their parents are as fraught as they are. The biggest con is that this is a fundamental and unavoidable aspect of mothering, but despite the best hopes of the average Freudian analyst, that is simply not the case. The truth comes only with the realization that it is society itself that creates the expectation of perfection, which binds women and their children into a flawed dyad. Women need to be profoundly aware of the double-edged nature of the sword of idealism.

The apparent reverence for mothers which the myth promotes makes it especially seductive and especially hard to discard. Motherhood offers women a role which is additional and distinct from men, a source of unimpeachable authority and, for a while at least, absolute power. This is something that some women guard jealously because, frankly, they don't entirely want to share their child's love even with their partner. Being the sole object of a child's unconditional love has undeniable attractions. And, if women are to be left with virtually the entire responsibility for rearing a child, it might surely be considered justifiable reward. But women should be clear and careful in separating these elements from each other, for the success of the myth is its ability to be transformed into a self-fulfilling prophecy. A child who is nurtured primarily by her mother will obviously turn to that parent for succour at other times, which when repeated thousands of times over in a thousand, myriad families feeds the deep-seated belief that children need their mothers, and only their mothers.

The religion we have built up around Motherhood, buttressed by notions about biologically-determined roles and relationships, means that for a woman to be the Perfect Mother, she must be a child's natural mother. This belittles the efforts, the real love and commitment which exists between adoptive parents or step-parents and their children, and condemns that relationship to be for ever regarded as something less than the real thing, second best.

Most of this book has been devoted to illustrating how, for women, the myth is a poisoned chalice and we drink from it at our own peril. There will always be women, however, who want to discard the 'bad' bits of the myth, while retaining the 'good' bits – that is, the bits that apparently benefit them. It is as well to remember that you can't play the 'good' mother game without invoking the spectre of the 'bad' mother too. It is impossible to exploit an idea as powerful as that of the Perfect Mother and hope to control it. Mothers have to learn to share, for their own sakes, for the sakes of their children and their partners, too.

The challenge for men

The problem for men is that a mother-centric philosophy of childrearing has rendered fathers biologically essential but socially superfluous. Many men respond by effectively shutting themselves out of their children's lives or by exploiting the state of affairs to carry on with their own activities, leaving most of the day-to-day responsibilities to their partners. A lot of men can make a pretty good case out of appearing to be happy with the status quo, until you look a little more closely.

Fran, a young mother talking about the intense possessiveness of some mothers, suddenly stopped and asked the question: 'Do men suspect? Do they know?' She meant, do they realize that they're being excluded. Then she remembered her own partner accusing her of precisely the same behaviour. Of course men know. That's why some men are currently making strenuous efforts to revitalize notions of fatherhood and to find a role for fathers at a time when they have become virtually sidelined by the obsession with mothers.

A part of the incipient men's movement, in a desperate attempt to find some kind of distinct function for male parents, has decided to concentrate on resurrecting the hunter-father. This is the type of approach which places an emphasis on male bonding, specifically on father–son relationships, and is simply a new slant on the old male breadwinner, head-of-the-family role. They try to look for ways in which fathers are *different* from mothers, but finding new approaches to fathering is an uphill struggle for both men and women. So much is vested in the idea of Motherhood that there simply isn't enough left for anyone else. The truth is that we cannot redefine fatherhood until we have redefined motherhood and ended the primacy of mothers over fathers.

Existing studies on parental influences have shown that sons learn empathy and other emotional skills from paternal involvement when they are young. A boy who sees his father care, nurture and provide in a similar way to his mother, goes on to become that kind of father himself. The reproduction of fathering is as much a fact as the reproduction of mothering and this is a challenge for both men and women.

The myths about Motherhood have helped to create the present dire state of fatherhood in so many communities. Men, once they are divorced from their wives, almost invariably lose contact with their children. Young men father children, but don't see what purpose might be served in spending time with them or helping take care of them. Those same young men who are effectively cast out of family life, are unsocialized, have nothing invested in the future. We need to create space for men in the family emotionally, socially, psychologically and politically and stop simply talking about it.

The challenge for everyone

It is time we stopped looking at children as the individual responsibility of their parents. As a society, we have spectacularly failed our children. The hypocrisy of the myth-makers is that they declare that they are pro-family and pro-children but they are among the many who would continue to deny children basic standards in education, fail to protect their human rights, and care little about levels of child poverty in Britain and America which are simply unacceptable in such wealthy nations. Parents' employment, access to education, health care and housing, safety from crime and violence – these are the things that make a difference to the development and lifetime opportunities of vast numbers of children. Whether a pregnant woman drinks a martini, or smokes a cigarette, or goes jogging, or leaves her two-year-old with a childminder is frankly largely irrelevant. Society places responsibility for children on to mothers. We pretend that some maternal, nurturing force will overcome or perhaps compensate for all these social inequities and injustices and we hold culpable women who falter or who don't measure up in other ways. Whatever instinct women might have, as parts of this book have demonstrated, may be vulnerable, fragile and variable and does not necessarily transcend individual circumstances and external burdens. The Motherhood myth is sold under the strapline 'All You Need is Love', when of course mothers and children need a great deal more.

Motherhood has become a moral touchstone for a myriad malaises. Blaming mothers prevents us, or perhaps protects us, from getting to grips with the kind of self-examination which might produce real answers. When a woman has a child she enters the institution of Motherhood, which binds her to her children with cords woven from her own compassion, and makes her a target for the incompetence, selfishness, neglect and posturing of others. The way we treat mothers has become the index of our self-disgust.

Notes

1. INTRODUCTION: THE MOTHERHOOD MYTH

1. On a daytime chat show: Sally Jessy Raphael, 30 January 1997.

2. 'The price of delaying pregnancy is high': Article entitled, 'I Forgot You, Babe', *Observer*, 17 March 1996.

3. 'The brood instinct is a biological time-bomb': *Guardian*, 23 February 1994.

4. 'What time is it by your biological clock?' *You* Magazine, 27 August 1995.

5. In 1995, researchers ascertained: 'The Content of Mother Stereotypes,' *Sex Roles: A Journal of Research*, Vol. 32, nos. 7–8 (April 1995): 495.

6. 'When I finally got home, John was waiting': Kinko's office products advertisement, 1996.

7. In 1997 the BBC programme *Panorama*: 'Missing Mum', *Panorama*, BBC TV, January 1997.

8. In England and Wales alone in 1994: *Marriage and Divorce Statistics, 1994*, Office for National Statistics.

9. A 1993 survey published: Gina Johnson, 'Childless Women Revisited', *British Medical Journal*, Vol. 307 (30 October 1993).

10. An OPCS survey: Central Statistical Office, *Social Trends* (London: HMSO, 1993).

11. Women are primarily responsible for children in 96 per cent of families: *General Household Survey, 1991* (London: HMSO, 1993).

2. A BRIEF HISTORY OF MOTHERHOOD

1. 'The little band of scholars': Edward Shorter, *The Making of the Modern Family* (New York: Basic Books, 1977): 169.
2. 'once the baby was left': Elizabeth Badinter, *The Myth of Motherhood* (London: Souvenir Press, 1981): 98.
3. 'Do they know, these gentle mothers': Jean Jacques Rousseau, *Émile*, Book I (New York: Basic Books, 1979): 44.
4. Olwen Hufton in her account: Olwen Hufton, *The Prospect Before Her* (London: Fontana, 1997).
5. 'At the very least': Badinter, *The Myth of Motherhood*: xxi,
6. 'The history of childhood': Lloyd de Mause (ed.), *The History of Childhood* (New York: Psychohistory Press, 1974): 1.
7. 'I lost two or three children': Michael de Montaigne, *Essays*, Book II, ch. 8, in Philippe Aries, *Centuries of Childhood* (New York: Vintage Books, 1982): 39.
8. 'She is very much upset': Madame de Sévigné, letter, 19 August 1671, in Badinter, *The Myth of Motherhood*: 63.
9. 'Now by the late 18th century': Shorter, *The Making of the Modern Family*: 204.
10. 'Lady Abergavenny whipped her daughter': Christopher Hibbert, *The English* (London: Grafton Books, 1987): 393.
11. In colonial America: Diane Eyer, *Motherguilt* (New York: Times Books, 1996).
12. 'revolution in sentiment': Shorter, *The Making of the Modern Family*: 6.
13. 'Not satisfied': Rousseau, *Émile*, Book I: 44.
14. 'But let mothers deign': Rousseau, *Émile*, Book I: 46.
15. 'It put women in a particularly difficult bind': Elinor, Accampo, *Industrialization, Family Life and Class Relations* (Los Angeles: University of California Press, 1989): 63
16. 'There was a young man': J. Echergray, quoted by Jessie Bernard, *The Future of Motherhood* (New York: Dial, 1974): 4.
17. a growing awareness of economics: Rousseau, *The Social Contract*, 1762 (London: Penguin Books, 1968).
18. Alongside these new ideas: Christina Hardyment, *Perfect Parents* (Oxford: Oxford University Press, 1995).
19. an observation later rubbished: Mary Wollstonecraft, *A Vindication of the Rights of Woman* (1762) (London: Penguin Books, 1983): 128.

20. In it he warned women: William Buchan, *Domestic Medicine* (Edinburgh: Balfour, Auld & Smellie, 1769).
21. Andrew Combe's *Treatise*: Andrew Combe, *Treatise on the Physiological and Moral Management of Infancy*, 1847 (Edinburgh: Maclachlan, 1940).
22. Beeton's *Housewife's Treasury*: quoted in *New Scientist* (25 December 1993/1 January 1994).
23. 'Mother love has been discussed': Badinter, *The Myth of Motherhood*: xx.

3. PYGMALION MOTHER: THE MAKING OF THE MODERN MYTH

1. wrote of their 'sense of inferiority' . . . 'insufficiently equipped': Michael Jacobs, *Sigmund Freud* (London: Sage Publications, 1992).
2. American investigative journalist: Richard Pollack, *The Creation of Doctor B, A Biography of Bruno Bettelheim* (New York: Simon and Schuster, 1996).
3. 'much wastage of infant life': Mary King, *Truby King, the Man* (London: George Allen & Unwin): 208.
4. 'changes of mother-figure: John Bowlby, *Child Care and the Growth of Love* (London: Penguin Books, 1953): 38.
5. 'a warm, intimate, and continuous relationship': Bowlby, *Child Care and the Growth of Love*: 11.
6. 'we must recognise that leaving': Bowlby, *Child Care and the Growth of Love*: 16.
7. 'The mother needs to feel an expansion' . . . 'The provision of mothering' . . . 'The provision of constant attention day and night': Bowlby, *Child Care and the Growth of Love*: 75.
8. 'cause permanent damage': WHO Expert Committee on Mental Health, *Report on the Second Session, 1951* (Geneva: World Health Organization, 1951).
9. 'mothers who play with their child': Michael Rutter, *Maternal Deprivation Reassessed* (London: Penguin Books, 1981): 20.
10. 'there is no scientific evidence to justify': Ann Dally, *Inventing Motherhood: Consequences of an Ideal* (London: Burnett Books, 1982): 10.
11. A study carried out in the late 1970s: T. S. Weisner and R. Gallimore, 'My Brother's Keeper: Child and Sibling Caretaking', *Current Anthropology*, Vol. 18 (1977): 169–90.
12. 'Over the last forty years we': Dally, *Inventing Motherhood*: 279.

13. 'I am trying to draw attention': D. W. Winnicott, *Home is Where We Start From* (New York: W. W. Norton, 1986): 124.

14. 'you do not even have to be clever': D. W. Winnicott, *The Child and the Family: First Relationships* (London: Tavistock Press, 1957): 4.

15. 'hard and strict and unrelenting': Winnicott, *Home is Where We Start From*: 131.

16. 'There are very subtle things here': Winnicott, *Home is Where We Start From*: 145.

17. 'If a mother knew': Shari L. Thurer, *The Myths of Motherhood* (Boston: Houghton Mifflin, 1994).

18. 'Of course, I don't mean that the father': Dr Benjamin Spock, *The Common Sense Book of Baby and Childcare* (New York: Duell, Sloan and Pearce, 1958): 18.

19. 'If a mother realizes clearly how vital': Spock, *The Common Sense Book of Baby and Childcare*: 570.

20. 'Strange new problems': Betty Friedan, *The Feminine Mystique* (New York: W. W. Norton, 1963): 29.

21. 'the chaining of women': Adrienne Rich, *Of Woman Born* (London: Virago, 1977): 276.

22. 'I only knew that I had lived': Rich, *Of Woman Born*: 15.

23. 'The responsibility falls on to mothers': Harriette Marshall: *The Social Construction of Motherhood: An Analysis of Childcare and Parenting Manuals*, in: Ann Phoenix, Anne Woollett and Eva Lloyd (eds), *Motherhood* (London: Sage, 1991).

24. 'You have to be a maternal': Hugh Jolly, *Book of Childcare* (London: Unwin, 1986).

25. 'For a woman having a baby': Penelope Leach, *Children First* (New York: Knopf, 1994): 45.

26. 'any personal indifference is damaging': Leach, *Children First*: 84.

27. 'Every mother wants her baby': Leach, *Children First*: 66.

28. 'The story of babies' fragility': Sandra Scarr and Judy Dunn, *Mothercare/Othercare* (London: Penguin Books, 1987): 71.

29. 'aberration of the normal maternal behaviour': Marshall H. Klaus and John H. Kennell, *Bonding: The Beginnings of Parent–Infant Attachment* (London: Mosby, 1983): 4.

30. 'more supportive and affectionate': Klaus and Kennell, *Bonding*: 43.

31. 'The newborn infant, when held horizontally' . . . 'Studies based on video-tapes': Vera Fahlberg, *A Child's Journey through Placement* (British Agency for Adoption and Fostering, 1994): 21.

32. 'The research on bonding': Diane Eyer, *Motherguilt* (New York: Times Books and Random House, 1996): 85.

33. a Swedish study: S. G. Carlsson, H. Fagenberg, G. Horneman, C. P. Hwang, K. Larsson, M. Rodholm, J. Schaller, B. Danielsson and C. Gundewall, 'Effects of Various Amounts of Contact between Mother and Child on the Mother's Nursing Behaviour: a Follow-up Study', *Infant Behaviour and Development*, Vol. 2 (1979): 209–14.

34. rigorous 1980 study: M. J. Svejda, J. J. Campos and R. N. Emde, 'Mother–Infant "Bonding": Failure to Generalize', *Child Development*, Vol. 51 (1980): 775–9.

35. 'it is surely unprecedented': Wladyslaw Sluckin, Martin Herbert and Alice Sluckin, *Maternal Bonding* (Oxford: Basil Blackwell, 1983): 20.

36. by 1973 mothers: Commission on Social Justice, *Work and Welfare: Tackling the Jobs Deficit* (Institute for Public Policy Research, 1993).

37. 'a socially and historically': Nancy Chodorow, *The Reproduction of Mothering: Psychoanalysis and the Sociology of Gender* (Berkeley: University of California Press, 1978): 76.

4. MOTHERHOOD IN POPULAR CULTURE

1. In 1995, an advert appeared: Advertisement for the NSPCC.

2. 'A mother's diet during pregnancy': 'Diet Clue to Heart Disease', *Daily Express*, 5 July 1994.

3. 'Pregnant women drinking three cups': *Independent*, 23 December 1993.

4. 'Women who smoke during pregnancy': *Independent*, 2 February 1994.

5. 'Smoker mums kill babies': *Daily Express*, 12 March 1998.

6. 'red tape puts babies at risk': 'Failing the Acid test', *Daily Mirror*, 8 March 1995.

7. 'When winter's chill is too much for baby': *Independent*, 23 November 1993.

8. 'men have been spared': Cynthia Daniels, 'Between Fathers and Fetuses: The Social Construction of Male Reproduction and the Politics of Fetal Harm', *Signs*, Vol. 22, no. 3 (Spring 1997): 579–616.

9. Recent stories: *The Times*, 16 February 1996.

10. Once her super-baby is born: *Independent on Sunday*, 3 April 1994.

11. it was the findings of two researchers: K. L. Jones, D. W. Smith, C. N. Ulleland and A. P. Streissguth, 'Pattern of Malformation in Offspring of Chronic Alcoholic Mothers', *Lancet*, Vol. 1 (1973): 1267–71.

12. The fact is that foetal alcohol syndrome is: S. K. Clarren and D. W. Smith, 'The Foetal Alcohol Syndrome', *New England Journal of Medicine*, Vol. 298 (1978): 1063–7.

13. Another study by Robert Sokol: R. J. Sokol, S. I. Miller and G. Reed, 'Alcohol Abuse During Pregnancy: An Epidemiological Study', *Alcoholism: Clinical and Experimental Research*, Vol. 4 (1980): 135–45.

14. So how did such findings: *Today*, 3 December 1990 and *Daily Telegraph*, 19 June 1993.

15. Popular baby books: Belinda Barnes and Suzanne Gail Bradley, together with the Association for the Promotion of Preconceptual Care, *Planning for a Healthy Baby – Essential Preparation for Pregnancy* (London: Vermillion, 1994): 102–4. Wendy Rose-Neil, *The Complete Handbook of Pregnancy* (London: Marshall Editions, 1984, 1991): 22.

16. A typical advice leaflet for pregnant women: published by MLCCA, Liverpool.

17. In a paper for the World Health Organization: Moira L. Plant, 'Women and Alcohol. A Review of International Literature on the Use of Alcohol by Females, WHO, Regional Office for Europe (1990).

18. Kenneth Jones, whose original research brought FAS: J. M. Aase, K. L. Jones and S. K. Clarren, 'Do we need the term "FAE"?' *Paediatrics*, Vol. 95 (September 1994).

19. In Toronto as the state debated: Addictions Research Foundation, *The Journal*, Toronto, Canada, October 1993.

20. Doctors Henry Rosett and Lynn Weiner: *Alcohol and the Fetus* (Oxford: Oxford University Press, 1984).

21. Although Dr Rosett has since died: *Guardian*, 27 May 1991.

22. It is now also thought that: E. Abel and R. Sokol, 'A Revised Conservative Estimate of the Incidence of FAS and its Economic Impact', *Alcoholism: Clinical and Experimental Research*, Vol. 15, no. 3 (1991): 514–24.

23. One carefully controlled study: Nesrin Binglo et al., 'The Influence of Socioeconomic Factors on the Occurrence of Fetal Alcohol Syndrome', *Advances in Alcohol and Substance Abuse*, Vol. 6, no. 4 (1987): 105–18.

24. The 'Scandal of mothers who risk starving': *Mail on Sunday*, 21 August 1994.

25. 'Could it ever happen here?': *Daily Mail*, 19 July 1994.

26. 'Defying nature to become a mother': *Daily Express*, 18 August 1994.

27. One Sunday paper headlined its piece: *Mail on Sunday*, 31 July 1994.

28. 'Whose life, hers or her baby's?': *Today*, 17 July 1995.

29. A *Sunday Times* piece: *Sunday Times*, 14 May 1995.

30. In *The Times* an article: *The Times*, 19 January 1996.

31. 'Esther finds a cause at home': *Daily Telegraph*, 23 April 1996.

32. In the *Daily Telegraph* Lesley Garner: *Daily Telegraph*, 19 February 1993.

33. 'Yet while we live in a society': *Guardian*, 19 February 1993.

34. The programme's findings were quoted in Parliament: Hansard, 26 January 1994, col. 309.

35. even in a briefing issued by Central Office: 'The Reform of the Homeless Legislation', July 1994.

36. 'Today we've made the lone parent': Sue Slipman, personal interview, 23 January 1996.

37. 'A hideously orchestrated campaign': Reuters, 22 February 1996.

5. FUTURE PERFECT

1. In 1993 a report published by: *US Contraceptive & Fertility Product Markets* (Frost & Sullivan Market Intelligence, 1993).

2. Today in England and Wales: British Agency for Adoption and Fostering, 'Changing Trends in Substitute Care', drawn from figures published by OPCS, 1991.

3. 'The increased use of infertility services': National Center for Health Statistics, 'Fecundity & Infertility in the United States, 1965–88', Advance Data, no. 192 (4 December 1990).

4. According to United Nations figures: UNICEF Speakers' Notes/8/Adopt.1 (1 November 1994).

5. Figures of up to $50,000: United Nations Economic and Social Council, 'Rights of the Child: Sale of Children' (12 January 1993): 10.

6. $1.3 billion: Reuters Texline, *Business Wire*, 29 February 1996.

7. 'the intense competition for patients': Bernard Lo, speaking at 3rd World Congress of Bioethics, San Francisco, 22 November 1996.

8. 'women will be placed': Robyn Rowland, *Living Laboratories* (London: Reed, 1993): 4.

9. In the words of: George Annas in 'Techno-babies', *Vancouver Sun*, 27 November 1995.

10. 'We used to think': Techno-babies', *Vancouver Sun*, 27 November 1995.

11. The average live birth rate for IVF: Human Fertilization and Embryology Authority, *The Patient's Guide to DI and IVF Clinics*.

12. 'Still poor results': Anthony Dyson, *The Ethics of IVF* (London: Mowbray, 1995): 42.

13. 'a divine throw': Robert Winston, *Making Babies: A Personal View of IVF Treatment* (London: BBC Books, 1996).

14. 'most couples overestimated': Lorraine Dennerstein and Carol Morse, 'A Review of Psychological and Social Aspects of in Vitro Fertilization', *Journal of Psychosomatic Obstetrics and Gynaecology*, Vol. 9 (1988): 159–70.

15. 'Patients viewed probabilities': J. Modell, 'Last Chance Babies', *Medical Anthropology Quarterly* (1989): 125–38.

16. Recently at least one member: Dr Robert Edwards speaking on the *Today* programme, 5 March 1998.

17. In 1991 a study: C. Newton, M. Hearn, A. Yuzpe, M. Houle, 'Motives for Parenthood and Response to Failed In-Vitro Fertilization: Implications for Counseling', *Journal of Assisted Reproduction and Genetics*, Vol. 9, no. 1 (1992).

18. In one chapter: James H. Monach, *Childless: No Choice. The Experience of Involuntary Childlessness* (London: Routledge, 1993).

19. In an Australian study: V. J. Callan, John F. Hennessey, 'Psychological Adjustment to Infertility: A Unique Comparison of Two Groups of Infertile Women, Mothers and Women Childless by Choice', *Journal of Reproductive and Infant Psychology*, Vol. 7 (1989): 105–12.

20. 'For the woman with a strong': Dennerstein and Morse, 'A Review of Psychological and Social Aspects of In-Vitro Fertilization'.

21. Snowden, Mitchell and Snowden's: R. Snowden, G. D. Mitchell and E. M. Snowden, *Artificial Reproduction: A Social Investigation* (London: Allen and Unwin, 1983).

22. A fact sheet available: Bay Area Fertility Medical Group, 1995.

23. Judith Modell: J. Modell, 'Last Chance Babies'.

24. In its policy document: BMA, *Changing Conceptions of Motherhood* (1996).

25. Anna L. Johnson: Johnson v. Calvert, 93 CDOS 3739, 20 May 1993.

26. 'That genes will be on tap': Paul Billings, CALBAC conference, San Francisco, August 1996.

27. back to 1942: Skinner v. Oklahoma, 316 US 535, 541 (1942).

28. Carey v. Population Services International 1977: Carey v. Population Services International, 431 US 678; 97 S Ct 2010; 52 L Ed 2d 675 (1977).

29. Casey v. Planned Parenthood: Casey, 112 S Ct 2791 (1992).

6. PERSECUTING MOTHERS: MOTHERHOOD AND THE LAW

1. A pregnant cancer patient: Re: AC 533 A.2d 611 (DC Ct of App., 1987).
2. Another woman is charged: State v. Pfannenstiel, No. 1-90-8CR (Wyo Cty Ct Albany Cty, 5 January 1990).
3. A court rules in favour of a husband: Reported in the *Boston Globe*, 2 May 1989.
4. A thirty-year-old crack addict: The case of Rosena Tolliver, reported in the *Washington Times*, 13 August 1992.
5. 'symbol of hope and fear': Janet Gallagher, 'Fetus as Patient', reprinted in Sherrill Cohen and Nadine Taub (eds), *Reproductive Laws for the 1990s* (Clifton, New Jersey: Humana Press, 1991).
6. A woman whose newborn: State v. Inzar, Nos 90 CRS 6960, 90 CRS 6961 (NC Super Ct Robeson Cty, 9 April 1991).
7. another was prosecuted: People v. Stewart, No. M508197, Reporter's Transcript, at 4 (Cal Mun Ct San Diego Cty, 26 February 1987).
8. a woman in Charleston: Cynthia Daniels, *At Women's Expense: State Power and the Politics of Fetal Rights* (Cambridge, Ma: Harvard University Press, 1993): 104.
9. a woman in California: Daniels, *At Women's Expense*: 105.
10. The case of Angela Carder: Re: AC 533 A.2d 611 (DC Ct of App., 1987).
11. until 1994 when the courts: AC 1990 Mother Doe vs. Baby Doe, 1994.
12. the case of an African couple: Gallagher, 'Fetus as Patient'.
13. And in Wyoming: *The Nation*, 26 March 1990.
14. At least one major study: I. J. Chasnoff, H. J. Landress and M. E. Barrett, 'The Prevalence of Illicit-drug or Alcohol Use during Pregnancy and Discrepancies in Mandatory Reporting in Pinellas County, Florida', *New England Journal of Medicine*, Vol. 322 (1990): 1202–6.
15. countries such as Canada: Yukon territorial legislation gives special powers to state authorities in instances where a pregnant woman puts her child at risk of foetal alcohol syndrome. The law was tested and overruled in Joe v. Director of Family and Children's Services (1986) 1 YR 169. In Re Baby R (1988) 15 RFL (3d) 225, welfare officers 'apprehended' an unborn child whose mother had refused a caesarean. The mother later consented and the healthy child was immediately removed from her care as soon as it was born.

16. 'cock-a-hoop': *Independent on Sunday*, 11 August 1996.

17. with the *Daily Express*: *Daily Express*, 12 August 1996.

18. 'English law goes to great lengths': Wv. W [1972] AC 24.

19. In 1978 a man: Paton v. Trustees of BPAS [1978] 2 All ER 987 [1979] QB 276.

20. Then came a very public case: C v. S [1987] 1 All ER 1230, [1988] QB 135.

21. 'Don't kill my unborn baby': *Daily Express*, 24 February 1987.

22. a Norwegian computer analyst: Reported in the *Independent*, 24 February 1987.

23. In Berkshire: Re D [1986] 3 WLR 1080 HL.

24. Two years later: Re F (in Utero) [1988] 2 All ER 193 (CA).

25. In a little reported case: Re T. (Adult: Refusal to Consent to Treatment) [1992] 3 WLR 782, CA.

26. a Nigerian woman: Re S (Adult Refusal of Treatment) (Fam Div) 3 WLR (6 November 1992), and [1992] 4 All ER 167,

27. 'against the weight': *Guardian*, 14 October 1992.

28. A man had stabbed his girlfriend: Attorney-General's Reference (No. 3 of 1994); House of Lords, 24 July 1997.

29. Sheila Kitzinger: *Daily Mail*, 27 March 1997.

30. There were reports: Contained in a letter from the Maternity Alliance, published in the *Guardian*, 28 March 1997, and in a letter to the *Glasgow Herald*, 15 March 1997 from the Association for Improvements in Maternity Services.

31. 'rights plus': Personal interview, 14 February 1997.

32. 'Ten years ago': *Independent*, 20 February 1997.

33. 'Like the anti-abortion effort': Gallagher, 'Fetus as Patient'.

34. 'Forced medical treatment': Daniels, *At Women's Expense*: 35.

35. 'For years, as successive disasters': *Guardian*, 11 November 1995.

36. 'She should have been locked': *Guardian*, 9 May 1996.

37. 'Instead of recognising': Adrienne Rich, *Of Woman Born* (London: Virago, 1995): 263.

38. 'Irrespective of the mother's': Estela Welldon, *Mother, Madonna, Whore* (London: Guilford Press, 1992).

39. In a study: Kidscape Conference, Female Sexual Abuse of Children: What We Know, 8 May 1997.

40. 'People are clinging': Personal interview, 11 April 1997.

41. Royal College of Psychiatrists: Reported in *The Times*, 19 March 1996.

7. OTHER MOTHERS: CROSS-CULTURAL MOTHERHOOD

1. 'I can hardly recall': Nelson Mandela, *Long Walk to Freedom* (London: Little Brown, 1994): 8.

2. 'There is no single style': Sarah Hall Sternglanz and Alison Nash, 'Ethological Contributions to the Study of Human Motherhood', in Beverly Birns and Dale Hay (eds), *The Different Faces of Motherhood* (New York: Plenum Press, 1988): 32.

3. 'overburdened with almost': Leigh Minturn and William Lambert (eds), *Mothers of Six Cultures, Antecedents of Child Rearing* (New York: Wiley, 1964): 282.

4. 'I speak about a mother's thought': Sara Ruddick, 'Maternal Thinking', in Barrie Thorne and Marilyn Yalom (eds), *Rethinking the Family* (New York: Longman, 1982): 77.

5. 'She might not have any money': Buchi Emecheta, *The Joys of Motherhood* (New York: George Braziller, 1979): 81.

6. In Britain, women of African: Ethnic Minority Families, Fact Sheet 6, Family Policy Studies Centre, 1994.

7. 'the assumption that motherhood': Patricia Hill Collins, 'The Meaning of Motherhood in Black Culture', *A Scholarly Journal on Black Women*, Vol. 4 (Fall 1987): 3–10.

8. 'the employed mother': Linda M. Blum and Theresa Deussen, 'Negotiating Independent Motherhood', *Gender and Society*, Vol. 10, no. 2 (April 1996): 199–211.

9. 'My mother had not believed': Isabel Allende, *Eva Luna* (New York: Bantam, 1989): 46.

10. 'Childrearing is a responsibility that can be shared': bell hooks, *Feminist Theory from Margin to Center* (Boston: South End Press, 1984): 144.

11. A 1992 Labour Force Survey: R. Bartholemew et al., 'Lone Parents and the Labour Market: Evidence from the Labour Force Survey', *Employment Gazette*, 1992.

12. A 1984 study of Mexican men: P. Bronstein, 'Differences in Mothers' and Fathers' Behaviors Toward Children: A Cross-cultural Comparison', *Developmental Psychology*, Vol. 20 (1984): 995–1003.

13. 'I could sit': Stephanie Coontz, *The Way We Never Were* (Basic Books, 1992): 210.

14. 'absolutely pervasive': Personal interview, May 1997.

15. An in-depth survey: Rosanna Hertz and Faith Fergusen, 'Child Care

Choices and Constraints in the United States', *Journal of Comparative Family Studies*, Vol. 25.

16. 'Idealization and blaming': Nancy Chodorow and Susan Contratto, 'The Fantasy of the Perfect Mother', in Thorne and Yalom (eds), *Rethinking the Family*: 65.

17. A Family Policy Studies Centre briefing document: J. Finch and J. Mason, 'Negotiating Family Responsibilities', *Putting Families on the Map*, Factsheet 1, Family Policy Studies Centre (London: Routledge, 1994).

8. LEFT HOLDING THE BABY: HOW POLITICIANS MANIPULATE MOTHERS

1. An in-depth survey: Elsa Ferro and Kate Smith, *Parenting in the 1990s*, Family Policy Studies Centre, London (November 1996).

2. 64 per cent of mothers: Employment Committee, *Mothers in Employment*, HMSO (15 February 1995).

3. According to the economist Heather Joshi: 'Leave of Absence from Work for Family Reasons', Equal Opportunities Commission Briefing Paper, no. 6 EMPSWORK.927.

4. Half of Britain's working mothers: A. Mouriki, Flexible Working: Towards Further Degradation of Work, or Escaping the Stereotypes', Warwick Paper in Industrial Relations (1994).

5. According to a comparative study: Jane Miller and Andrea Barman, *Family Obligations in Europe*, Family Policy Studies Centre, London (November 1996).

6. an Equal Opportunities Commission discussion paper: 'The Key to Real Choice', Equal Opportunities Commission (October 1990).

7. only 23 per cent of mothers ... In 1985, English local authorities: 'The Childcare Gap', Daycare Trust, 1997.

8. 'still forced to make difficult decisions': *Mothers in Employment*.

9. 'Some mothers': Central Advisory Council for Education, *Children and Their Primary Schools*, Vol. 1 (London: HMSO, 1966).

10. child psychiatrist Barbara Tizard: B. Tizard, *The Care of Young Children: Implications Recent Research* (London: University of London Institute of Education, 1986).

11. 'The view that non-parental care': 'The Key to Real Choice', Equal Opportunities Commission (October 1990).

12. A 1997 study: Pew Research Centre for People and the Press (May 1997).

13. Two British researchers: Linda Collins and Pam Walton, 'Balanced Lives: Changing Work Patterns for Men', New Ways to Work (1995).

14. 'of mothers as uniquely qualified': 'The Key to Real Choice'.

15. 'celebrating greed': *Independent*, 15 October 1993.

16. 'There appeared to be': Julie Brazen and Peter Moss, 'British Households after Maternity Leave', in Susan Lewis, Daphnia N. Israeli and Helen Hootsmans (eds), *Dual-Earner Families* (London: Sage, 1992).

17. 'The dream of independence': Carol Stack, personal interview, March 1997.

18. Presently for mothers of pre-school children: 'Daycare Services for Children: A 1990 Survey for the Department of Health', Seltzer (1994).

19. Often grandparents: Ferro and Smith, *Parenting in the 1990s*.

20. In fact, between 1979 and 1988: Susan Marcie and W. O. W. Daniel, *Maternity Rights, the Experience of Women and Employers* (London: Policy Studies Institute, 1991).

21. An Age Concern survey: For Age Concern by the British Market Research Bureau Limited, reference: BMRB/ECM/1181-680.

22. 'Indian society does not': Lewis et al. (eds), *Dual-Earner Families*.

23. Jemima Khan: *Daily Telegraph*, 24 November 1997.

24. 'People are inventing from the ground up': personal interview, 25 April 1997.

Index